Urban Tidepool

© 2013

Foreword

Urban Tidepool is a book about virgin birth. The author may well not see it that way but she'll probably indulge me in an explanation.

Virgin birth stories aren't unique to the Christian Gospels; they appear across many cultures and traditions. One role they serve is to confirm deity -- that's not what I have in mind. Another function is to acknowledge the amazing mystery of barren land bearing fruit, of good things coming from bad beginnings, of flowering where there is no evidence of roots. Even before the Enlightenment and the dawn of the Scientific Age, people have known to expect, and look for, cause and effect. Virgin birth stories are one of the ways they have accounted for effects for which no cause can be identified. *Urban Tidepool* is that kind of virgin birth story.

Baby Boomers like me tend to be well acquainted with the Dorothy Law Nolte poem *Children Learn What They Live:*
"If a child lives with criticism,
he learns to condemn....
If I child lives with acceptance,
he learns to love...."

I'd quote more but then we'd encounter copyright issues and, besides, surely you get the point. There is no reason, no discernable cause and effect, for the abused and abandoned child whose story this book tells to have turned into the loving, self-giving adult she is today. Good fruit from barren land, rootless blossoming, very good things from bad beginnings -- virgin birth.

Not, I hasten to add, because Nancy remained untouched by the life she lived. Quite the contrary; as an older friend at her side through the deaths of her oldest brother, her sister-in-law, a beloved dog, I had a close-up view of the childhood wounds she still carried. Just inches under the surface of the grieving adult hovered a heartbroken, terrified, and resolutely defended child. Desperately needing, and craving, support, reassurance, and affection yet afraid to open up to receive it, that abused child and the scars she bore were evident. That is the true grace and glory of this story. Not that the child somehow lived through it all unscathed -- that would be more pathological than miraculous -- but that she came through it, bleeding wounds, tender scars, and all, as a strong, brave, and compassionate adult, nonetheless. That she opens herself to love and care for her friends and for the hurting teens to whom she has devoted her life not because her experience has rendered her invulnerable to suffering but in the very face of the wounds that still lurk close to the surface, that is the miracle in this story.

Read this book. Read it because it's a page-turner, a powerful story well told. And when the tragedy of the story threatens to overwhelm you with sadness or rage, keep reading. It's still a good story; you're going to want to know what happens next. But more than all of that, this is a story of hope. Amazing things happen -- not just in this book, but all around us, all the time. This story reminds us, against all reason, that cause and effect are not the only dynamics of this life. There's also virgin birth.

The Very Rev. Dr. Katherine Hancock Ragsdale
Washington D.C.
September 2020

Introduction

2011

I didn't start out wanting to write this book. **Some** book, yes, **someday**, but not **this** book. When the idea first occurred to me, I dismissed it as self-indulgent. Everyone has a story and I didn't view mine as more interesting than anyone else's, at least not until the night we said goodbye to Max.

My staff person Max left for Tahoe at the end of July to finish his bachelor's degree, accepted into an outdoor recreational program about which he was very excited. The rest of the staff and I were all very excited for him as well, except for the little part about him having to leave to go to Tahoe. Max had been part of our work for six years, first as a youth in our drop-in centers, then as a youth leader, then as a volunteer and then as an employee. He was and is a wonderful community educator, engaging, funny, and insightful. He made the agency look good, even in those times when he made us laugh so hard we couldn't speak, or maybe especially in those times.

Max spoke openly and frequently about his story, about coming to the agency that I run as a seventeen year old, direct from an inpatient unit. When he talked at one of our galas about sitting through his intake with stitches still in his wrist and knowing with everything in him that he had found a place where he could truly be himself, there was not a dry eye in the room. Max brought us honesty and openness and good humor at seventeen and at twenty two. When he was seventeen, the drop-in centers definitely lacked something when Max took a night off. When he was twenty two, our community education work definitely lacked something when Max took a night off. He was an integral part of what we were doing.

I hated to see him leave. It's always hard when the kids who grow up to become the staff eventually move on. I always wish them well and hope they'll remember what they learned in group: Play nice. Be respectful. Be loving. Get tested. Most of all, remember that you mattered to us for a long time and you will still matter to us after you leave. We're cheering for you.

We took him out for pizza before he left, gathering at a local restaurant where we had held numerous staff social nights just to spend some adult time together. The evening would not have been complete without the Spiderman cake that Lorrie from the Tuesday night drop-in center had gotten for him. As our night ended and I had to leave, Max came from the other side of the long table. I wondered fleetingly if it would be awkward, having never had a reason to hug him before.

It wasn't. He hugged me and I hugged him back and the words rushed out before I could stop them. "I'm gonna miss you, my friend. You grew up good."

He squeezed me a little harder around the neck. "Thanks, Nancy," he whispered. "You helped."

How the hell did that happen?

Part 1

Setting the Stage, 1973

We never said the "C" word.

As far as I know, no one ever told her what the problem was, beyond the fact that it was the late 1960's and she was married to the father. He didn't want her told so the doctors didn't tell her. I was four, so no one told me either.

The clearest memories I have of her relate to her illness. I shared a bed with her when she could no longer sleep with the father. He slept like a windmill, she said. She covered her side of the bed with a sheepskin mat to cushion her skin because she'd lost so much weight. I brought medication to her as she rested on the couch in the afternoons, guided by directions to bring two of **this** color pill and one of **that** color. I went to doctor appointments with her when she received chemo treatments, where nothing important ever seemed to be said. So unimportant were the conversations that it wasn't until I began asking questions related to this telling that I found out those were her chemo treatments. For forty years, I believed them to be other kinds of appointments, blood draws, checkups maybe, but in the early 1970s, her chemo treatments were delivered at the office of our family doctor. There I sat, playing with cars or reading books, while she tolerated the injections.

For as long as I can remember, she was physically fragile. I have no memory of her as a healthy person. She had scoliosis, which we occasionally referenced as "mommy's back problem". By the time I went to first grade, she was bent forward and sideways with a hump on her back. "Mommy's back problem" masked the real problem for some time. When the spine warps and internal organs compress, one would expect discomfort, then gradually pain. Now we know that warping and compression can hide the growth of a tumor because one just expects to live in pain every day. Eventually the time comes when that tumor creates problems bigger than the twisting of the spine and smashing of organs. It wasn't until then that they even knew to look for another problem. By then, it was too late.

I speculate now that the tumor developed not too long after I was born. Maybe when I was two. Certainly no later than when I was three. There's no way to know. She was diagnosed when I was between four and five.

A few memories escape direct connection to her illness. Once in first grade, I came home for lunch and she wasn't home. I checked the basement and the bathroom. Where would she have gone at that hour? I looked out our front door and there she was, just three houses away, returning from the store where she'd gone to pick up my lunch. I launched myself at her, my nervousness melting away. She wrapped me in her old shaggy brown coat, buttoned me in and walked back to the house with me laughing, tucked inside, just my eyes showing above her middle button, matching her footsteps.

Conversely, there are other memories that don't involve her but relate to her illness, such as my Uncle Bill teaching me to ride a two-wheeler. That job fell to Uncle Bill, the mother's younger brother, during the summer of one her surgeries. The visit to his house lasted three weeks, maybe four, and produced highlights such as taking off my training wheels, eating powdered sugar donuts while kneeling backwards on a kitchen chair so I could rabbit watch (we didn't have rabbits at home), and catching lightning bugs at dusk. We didn't have lightning bugs either. It also produced one confusing morning when I woke up with the sensation of choking on something. My repeated swallows didn't help and with no warning, the lump dissolved into sobs that I didn't understand. I had just woken up—how could I be sad? I hid my head under the pillow to muffle the sounds. Three weeks is endless when you're five. It's plenty of time to get homesick. It's also plenty of time to get really worried that things aren't okay and you can feel that but no one's talking about it.

***

I made my first Communion on May 6th. I dreaded the white dress that every girl was expected to wear. I would have felt much more myself in one of the white suits that the boys wore. For some reason, both parents continued to labor under the idea that I was irrefutably female.

I refuted. I refuted plenty, let me tell you.

I still got stuck wearing the dreaded white dress. It was bad enough that I'd have to wear it for the mass during which I would commune for the very first time with the priest with the big red nose, Monsignor Waldron. But tradition dictated that people wore the little white suits and dresses most of the day, long after standing in line for the Holy Styrofoam. Some families had parties. We would be having dinner out. It was a parade of the newly communed little Catholic kids. What a nightmare! But what did I know? Just days after the sentence of the white Communion dress, the real nightmare began.

It was late evening, mid-week. I had already gone to bed. The mother was in the bathroom for the longest time. That was saying something, because since her surgery, every visit to the bathroom took her a long time. Something was wrong. The urgent speaking from downstairs made the little hairs on the back of my neck stand up. Who was talking? My sister Pat, who was nineteen years older than I, had lived with us over this past year but she and her son Bobby had moved into their own place just a couple of weeks before and the father was downstairs alone. His voice was not quite loud enough to be completely understood, but clear enough that I could pick out a word here or there. "Hemorrhage." She was hemorrhaging. What was a hemorrhage? What did it have to do with what was taking the mother so long in the bathroom?

A short explanation was offered: the mother needed to go back to the hospital. She would be fine. Everyone could go to bed now. We went through the following days not speaking about it. The father visited the hospital in the evening. Kids weren't permitted to visit, so the only contact that I had with the mother was by phone when she was feeling up to it.

My brother Chick and his family came from Virginia, where he was stationed. Chick was sort of a mystery to me. He was twenty one and stationed in Germany when I was born. I couldn't say that I knew him well; I barely knew him at all. He was big and loud and very gruff, and he scared me just a little. He and his first wife had a son a year after I was born. Upon returning to the US, he was stationed in Arizona so we rarely saw him. He had just married his second wife, who also had a child. I had met his new wife, Jedda, and her daughter once before when they arrived for this stay. It's always been a point of curiosity for people hearing about our family: given the age range between us, I had siblings old enough to be my parents. Their children were more like siblings to me than they were. My brother Chick and my sister Pat and I would learn how to be siblings to each other in adulthood. In 1973, they both lumped me into the category of "one of the kids".

    Chick, Pat and the father alternated visits to the mother's hospital room. Chick and his family had been with us a few days when I overheard a lunch time phone call between him and the mother. I don't remember what I heard; I just remember feeling sick to my stomach as I listened. He asked pressured, urgent questions, gripping the handset tightly. When he hung up, he turned to me and tried to play it down as if all was right with the world, and it was time for me to go back to school for the afternoon. I knew something was terribly wrong and they weren't telling me. I refused. I was sick. I was scared. I wanted to see the mother right now. Right now right now right now. Jedda stood off to the side with an arm folded across her stomach and the other hand clamped over her mouth, her fingertips digging bloodless ovals along her jaw. His voice broke mid-sentence and he picked me up, holding me tight. Chick was 6'2". It was a long way up. I didn't care what he said because I knew everything was all wrong and now I was in mid-air.

    He paced the living room with me hanging onto him like a baby Rhesus monkey separated from its mother in Harry Harlow's psychological experiment. It breaks my heart now to think of him holding me then, walking slowly up the steps to the bedrooms with me suspended from his shoulders and torso, just a sad, frightened monkey. He was twenty eight. I was seven.

    He sat down on the bed, parking me next to him, and talked about how our mother would want me to go back to school, that it would all be fine. I should try not to be so scared, even if it was hard. And it was hard. I kept refusing. He kept talking and hugging me. When he pressed my face to his shoulder, he smelled like strong coffee and smoke, a combination I associated with him long into adulthood. Maybe he just needed me out from underfoot. Maybe he really thought keeping to routine was helpful. I did eventually agree to go back to school that day but it felt disconnected and surreal.

They stayed with us more than a week but less than two. In the second half of their stay, the father told us that my brother Michael and I could go and see the mother in her room. He had gotten special permission but we would have to be very quiet and very careful and we couldn't stay long.

Somehow the detail that I'd need to wear a dress was overlooked until we were getting ready to leave. Chick asked me to wear a lilac dress, one that I particularly detested. If this was the price for getting to see the mother, though, I would wear the hated dress, wondering the entire time what harm it would do if I wore a shirt and pants like Michael was wearing. Nerves had started to fray between the constant running back and forth between home and hospital and the close quarters of South Philadelphia row homes. In the parking lot, Chick yelled at me for walking too close to a car. I might get the hated dress dirty before we got upstairs to see the mother.

"But I didn't touch it!"

"I couldn't put a goddamn coat of paint between you and that car!"

It brought tears to my eyes that he would yell at me at such an important time. I blinked them away hard and made a show of inspecting myself for dirt, embarrassed that I had made such a stupid mistake and equally embarrassed that I had tears in my eyes.

The floor where they kept the mother was very quiet. A blur of white uniforms moved continually in the background but they gave us space. I wanted so badly to hug her, to curl up next to her as I had done for so long at home. Bars along the bedside prevented me from getting close. I could just see over the top rail. *So what's the point of wearing a dress when all she can see is the top of my head and my eyes?* Poking one hand through the bars, I had to avoid the tubes extending from the IV so I could pet her hand gently.

She was awake, even lucid, which I later found out had not been the case when Chick and Pat visited. They stayed with her while she hallucinated and cried out for her own mother, begging for the pain to end. Now she sat up, drawn and bony, but alert. She looked at me with an expression I didn't understand. "Do you want a Lifesaver? They're in the drawer there."

I found tangerine Lifesavers in the nightstand drawer and unstuck one from its litter mates. It hadn't even fully dissolved and suddenly it was time to go. I wanted to hug her, wanted her to hug me. There were bars in the way, and beyond the bars, tubes and wires connected to big, beeping machines.

My "Bye, Mommy," was soft, carried on a wave of tangerine Lifesaver.

"Bye, baby. I love you," again with the expression I didn't understand.

We returned to the routine of news over the phone or what the father brought home after a visit. Chick and his family left for Virginia. I missed the mother so much there weren't words for it. I could probably count on one hand the number of nights I hadn't slept with her in the past couple years. The bed was big and there was no one on the sheepskin mat to call me Grasshopper at the end of Kung Fu or hold my hand while we watched Twilight Zone.

My cousin David and I scraped up enough coins, literally overturning couch cushions to find them, to buy a packet of flower seeds at the corner store. We scratched at the compacted dirt in what passed for a garden in front of our house—an ugly dirt square surrounded by an even uglier hedge—gouging out the shape of the letters in her name. When she finally came home, there would be flowers blooming in the shape of her name. Anne. It was my formal name too, but everyone called me Nancy. We dumped hundreds of tiny seeds into tracks we made with a tablespoon and pushed spoonfuls of dirt on top of them. We didn't know to water them.

Good news came on the afternoon of the 26th. The father reported that the mother wanted to sit up by the window and she felt more energetic. That night, so hopeful that it would help, I wedged myself between the wall and the fridge and I prayed. I didn't want dinner. I sat, rocking, and I prayed for her to come home, for this good streak to continue, because I missed her and the bed was too big. I didn't know if God would realize the bed was too big unless I informed Him so we had a chat. I fell asleep against the fridge, still praying, and the father eventually carried me to bed.

I attended mass on the 27th with my class, as I did every Sunday. The nuns took attendance and expected a note from your parents if you missed, so there was no way around it. I had just slid into the pew and knelt down to pray a little more and Sister Vincent Ann slid in beside me.

Propping her elbows on the pew in front of us, she whispered, "How's your mother?"

"She's getting better! Last night, she even got up and sat in the chair in her room!" I whispered back. I wasn't sure why I should whisper, since I'd explained to God the whole bed being too big dilemma just last night and He already knew I was worried.

She looked relieved and happy for me. That was noticeable because most of the time she just looked angry. My second grade classroom had a door that adjoined her classroom. At least once a day she'd storm in and yell at us for being too loud, but now she smiled at me. How odd.

After church, the father went to the hospital for a visit and I went to my aunt's house. My cousin David and I ran back and forth between Aunt Connie's and my oldest cousin's home across the street, giving new meaning to the rhetorical, "Do we have a revolving door on this house?" which was yelled at us several times in various forms.

A little after noon, as I was pinning a kitchen towel around my little cousin's neck to make him into Underdog, my aunt called me from her porch. The father had phoned and asked that she bring me home. I didn't think anything of the request but it should have been the first clue. I'd been walking the city block between our house and Aunt Connie's since I was old enough to cross streets alone. Aunt Connie avoided the father. Now she had an invitation to come to our house and she was going.

The father sat on the edge of the bed in the small back bedroom, waiting for me. Aunt Connie stood in the doorway behind me. He touched my forearms gently, guiding me with his fingertips to stand between his feet. His eyes, level with mine, were bloodshot.

"Do you remember last week when we talked about Mommy going to heaven?"

I nodded. It was suddenly very cold.

"Well...she went. Mommy went to heaven today."

Some words are so big, they suck all the air out of a room and leave you unable to breathe.

"It'll be okay. Just don't cry. Just don't cry." One tear slid from his bloodshot eye and he patted my forearms with his blunt fingertips. Behind me, Aunt Connie made a sound as if someone had just punched her in the stomach. "It'll be okay, just don't cry," he repeated.

I tried hard. I didn't completely succeed. Aunt Connie muffled a noise. She tried hard too.

***

Irish Catholic funerals lasted two days; the wake on the first afternoon and evening, followed by coffee and donuts at some relative's house and then the funeral mass on the second morning or afternoon, followed by a gathering intended to celebrate the loved one's life. As if anyone really feels up to a party?

I don't remember the father being present at the mother's wake. Later, I heard it was because Chick needed to go get him from Dean's corner bar every so often. We stood alongside the casket, speaking to neighbors who brought condolences. Most of these same neighbors had sent get well cards. I have wondered how many of them thought she really might get well, but I've never seen a line of cards with the greeting, "Please die peacefully," or "Now that you've accepted your mortality…" Although I'm not sure the mother had accepted mortality, she had to know she was seriously sick. But we never said the "C" word. How much could she know? Was she also expecting that she'd get well? We didn't talk about it. So the father kept sneaking out to drink and I kept fidgeting with yet another detested dress.

The gathering after the wake came together at Aunt Connie's house. No one knew where the father was and lacking a key to get into our house for other clothes, I borrowed a Mickey Mouse tee shirt and a pair of shorts from David. We played outside even after it grew dark. There were cousins, and cousins of cousins from the other side of their family, and neighbors, and Aunt Connie's house was very crowded. I think it was a Thursday.

South Philly has certain smells that I have never noticed anywhere else. In the middle of summer, it's hot tar as the streets get soft enough under the beating sun that bottle caps can be pushed into the surface and steam on heated iron when it rains. On warm spring evenings, it's concrete and metal on one street, rubber and motor oil the next street down and the green of hedges and small front lawns just the street beyond that. There's an air of expectancy in a neighborhood full of kids who have known each other since birth, known everyone's whole family, when school has just ten more days to it. In that neighborhood, we spent a lot of time playing literally in the street, breathing those smells, all of it as familiar to us as our own skins. It was one of those nights in all other regards. School would end in two weeks and summer with its hot tar and gushing fire hydrants outside un-air conditioned row homes would stretch out forever in front of us, with handball and halfies, buck-buck, Mr. Softee and the water ice truck.

It's unclear how it was decided it was time to go home or where the father was. I suppose the people who didn't live on the street piled into their cars and the group of kids dwindled as each one was called to come inside. No one called for me, but at some point, carrying my dress under my arm and wearing David's Mickey Mouse tee shirt and shorts, I went back to our house.

The father showed up for the funeral, pasty and hungover. He didn't speak much. I lost track of Pat about halfway through the morning and found her sitting in the back room alone, crying, the sound stifled by the surrounding heavy velvet drapes and cushions. Not sure of what else to do, I climbed into her lap and hugged her head.

At the end of the allotted time, we gathered in front of her casket to say our goodbyes, first the extended family and then we were the only ones left. Laid out in a blue dress, the mother's crystal rosary beads intertwined her fingers. Even I could tell they put too much make-up on her. What about her favorite Hush Puppy shoes? They were the only ones she ever wore.

"Do you want to kiss her goodbye?" Pat asked.

I nodded, stepped on the kneeler in front of the casket and leaned down to kiss her forehead. Oh. Oh. Oh.

No one had said she'd be cold. The jolt shot through me as if someone jabbed me with an ice pick and I recoiled, horrified, one hand flying up and scrubbing at my lips. (Mommy?!) Pat took my other hand and stepped back from the casket, pulling me in tow. I don't think she noticed. My eyes bugged and there was a catch in my throat that I kept trying to swallow.

"You have to wait outside now."

I didn't see who spoke but it was directed at Michael, my sister's son Bobby, and me. We all were the "you" who had to wait outside. Ushered out the door and directed to stand right there, we waited, clueless about the practices unfolding inside as the funeral director and the father (I assume) unwound the rosary beads from her hands, covered her with a sheet and closed the casket lid.

Slowly, we assembled outside the funeral home. Even more slowly, they brought the casket out and we followed it across the street to the church with stiff movements like puppets jerked along on strings. The bright warmth gave way to dim lighting, cool marble and smell of old incense. My second grade class was there, as was Michael's sixth grade class. Pat held my hand as we walked up the aisle. My classmates stared at me.

Who knows what was said for the service? I huddled against Pat and focused on not crying. (Just don't cry. Just don't cry.) *Bye, Mommy.* ("Do you want a Lifesaver? They're in that drawer.") I stared at the casket, set in the center aisle, covered with flowers and the singularly absurd thought struck me that I'd never see her again. We had said goodbye.

A few rogue tears escaped. Nauseated and fighting tunnel vision, I followed the casket back out of the church when it was over, Pat holding my hand again. On the periphery, my classmates stood like fun-house mirror shapes, still staring. (Just don't cry. Just don't cry.) I couldn't look back. How could they not stare? How could they comprehend this? How could any of us? ("Bye, baby. I love you.")

Bye, Mommy.

We rode in the limousine the half hour drive to the cemetery. The funeral procession seemed endless and no one spoke for a long time. When I finally did, it was the only normal thing about this day so far.

"Pat?"

"Yeah, babe?"

"I gotta pee." That whole line of cars? They waited for me.

Those flower seeds never germinated. A week later, the father sent me away.

***

I don't remember how the news was broken or who said it. That seems unimportant compared to the fact that it was said. The father was going to send me away. Not away as in with strangers, but away as in being shipped off to stay with Chick for the summer following the funeral, which equaled away with strangers. I couldn't even finish the last week of school. Chick needed to get back to his base. In the middle of that week, I was to empty my desk and we would all pile into

Chick's tiny Toyota hatchback and drive to Hampton. Where I had never been. With people I hardly knew.

Apprehension edged with hopelessness ached in my stomach. I packed my pencils and crayons and notebooks and gave all of my books back to my second grade teacher. I didn't say goodbye to anyone. Since no one knew, no one said goodbye to me either. As I knelt on the floor beside my desk, wondering why I couldn't just stay in our house with the father, my teacher knelt down next to me.

She didn't say anything at first, but I thought that she might. She looked really sad and it crossed my mind that perhaps I had caused that but I didn't know how. She reached out to me.

I cringed in the opposite direction.

She startled backwards. "What's wrong? Are you okay?"

I nodded, looking at her outstretched hand.

"I was going to hug you. Can I hug you goodbye?" she asked.

I didn't want a hug, didn't want to be touched. I wanted the mother and I wanted not to have to be sent away. I wanted to stay home with the father and our dog, Rusty, and go to Aunt Connie's every day to play with David, just like normal. But nothing was normal.

"No."

She nodded and her hand lowered. I finished jamming things into my school bag and stood up. She didn't move right away, kneeling there with her head bowed as if she were praying. When she tipped her head back, I saw she was crying and I stood still. What should I say? Two or three seconds passed, each stretching into a lifetime, and I scrounged for the right words to make her feel better. The silence between us echoed with everything neither one of us was saying.

"Okay," she said finally. "Try to have a good summer then. And be good."

On the walk home, alone because clearing out my desk had given everyone a head start, I noticed the breeze had picked up and the sky had clouded over. I passed Aunt Connie's house as I did every day and looked at her front door, wishing that I could just go home and put on play clothes and come back. As I did every day. If it rained this afternoon, David and I (and maybe Ricky and Doreen too) could sit cross-legged in front of the TV to watch cartoons until we could go outside. But not today. Not for a long time.

Someone had packed my clothes, maybe the father, but more likely Jedda. The father wouldn't be bothered with such a job. Chick was already loading the car. We were leaving this afternoon. It felt creepy that Jedda would touch my clothes. The mother did that when we went on vacation. How would Jedda know what to take? How would she know what I liked? Those were my clothes and I barely knew her and this was **not** like going on vacation.

I hung up my uniform out of habit. Not that it mattered, since I'd wake up tomorrow in Virginia and by the time I came home I would probably need a new one anyway. *What if the new one doesn't fit? Daddy doesn't know anything about that unless it's for football—gotta ask Aunt Connie.* But it was part of being home, that blue plaid uniform hanging on the front of a closet door with its red tie attached to the front panel at the waist so I always knew where it was.

I detoured to our back yard, a concrete pad enclosed by a high cinderblock wall with five steps leading down to the cellar and five more leading up, where our dog Rusty sat peeking in the kitchen door. I rested my cheek against her head, poking fingers into her brown and white fur and breathing in her dogginess.

"Nance, let's go!" Chick bellowed from out front.

I rubbed Rusty's flappy ears and whispered into one that I would come back as fast as I could and did she know I would miss her? I kissed her snout.

The father came outside to say goodbye and wave us down the street. He squashed my head against his side with one rough hand and ruffled my hair. "Bye, Boo. I'll call on the weekends and I'll come see you in July."

July was the month of our birthdays. The father's birthday fell a few days before mine and every year we went on vacation for the birthday week, usually to the New Jersey shore.

A couple summers ago before the mother's stomach was turned into a bag taped to her belly making it almost impossible to hug her (*why would anyone ever want their insides taped to their outside?*), we had taken a big trip and had gone to visit Chick in Georgia, before he and Jedda had met. From his house, we towed a pop-up trailer to a campground near Disney World and we camped for the birthday week. Killer whales, dolphin shows, and theme park rides outweighed the father getting pickpocketed in the Philadelphia bus terminal, at least from my perspective. The father drank until he passed out just about every night we were there, which I assumed made sleeping on the floor of the pop-up trailer more comfortable, since Michael, Chick's son and I had to step on him to get out. He would appear late morning, sick and pale, but with no sign of our footprints on his chest. It was that summer, without access to a kitchen and not wanting to bother anyone, that on the morning of my birthday I went to the side of the road near our campsite, made a birthday cake out of dirt and sand, stuck sticks in it and sang happy birthday to myself. The father snored harmoniously in the background. The mother came over halfway through, bent down beside me and finished the song with me. I think it was six sticks but it may have been five.

    Would Chick remember my birthday was during the summer? Would he know that the father and I always had our birthdays together? Should I remind him? Now wouldn't be a good time. Maybe it would be better if I just stuck sticks in a mud pie again and sang to myself.

    The father prompted me along with his hand still on the back of my head, disengaging my arms from around his waist, propelling me toward the car. Chick had lowered the back seat and we crowded into the flat space wherever we could fit, Jedda, her daughter, Chick's son and I in the back, with Chick in the driver's seat and Michael up front with him. We pulled out, the father waving from in front of our house and me gazing out the rear window.

    Bye, Daddy. Who's gonna take care of you?

    My breathing hitched.

Chick turned off of our street and the next hitch in my breathing came as I looked down the neighboring street for my cousins. ("It'll be okay. Just don't cry.") I swallowed hard over and over. A grey wall formed in my chest, filling up all the places where my heart was supposed to be and where I was supposed to breathe. Like our backyard fence, it climbed cinderblock on cinderblock into my shoulders and then into my throat until all I had left were the thoughts circling in the top of my head: *I won't be any trouble. Don't send me away.*

The mother would not have sent me away for a whole summer. Chick turned another corner and our neighborhood was gone.

***

Hampton was a strange world, filled with weird bugs and odd sounds and odd sounds that came from weird bugs. There weren't many bees in my neighborhood because the only common splash of floral color came from the dandelions in the vacant lots where buildings had been demolished. It was the rare neighbor who managed to cultivate flowers in that ugly dirt square in front of their house, which is why those flower seeds that my cousin David and I planted would have made such an impression on the mother upon her return home. Minimal flowers meant minimal bees. But in Hampton, bees were everywhere, along with cicadas that made it sound like the trees were about to take off, crickets the size of my palm, biting horseflies and a bunch of other things I didn't want to get too cozy with.

One evening, I stepped on a giant slug in the car port, reaching for something on a shelf that Jedda had sent me outside to retrieve. I wasn't wearing shoes. I had never *seen* a giant slug, let alone had one squish up between all five of my toes. I yipped like someone poked me with a pushpin. I don't think I took my shoes off for the rest of the summer.

I shared a room with Jedda's daughter, whom I liked but didn't know very well. It was akin to suddenly moving into the bedroom of a neighbor that you've talked to a few times—

superficial and occasionally awkward, with a sense of an expectation placed on you to interact with this person like a sibling while your real sibling was too removed and too angry to interact. I didn't tell her I thought Hampton was strange. I didn't tell her I had a hard time understanding her accent sometimes. Well, hers **and** Jedda's and most of the people around us. I didn't talk to her about anything important. As if by unwritten rule, we never spoke about the mother. I missed David. I could have told him any of those things. Except maybe about yipping like a girl when I stepped on the slug. No, probably not that.

While I was busy not speaking to the pseudo-sibling about the mother, I learned to multi-task and simultaneously not to speak to anyone else about it either. It was as if we had simply not just had those experiences. There was no lengthy hospitalization, no running back and forth from Hampton to Philadelphia on Chick's part, no morning I was called home from Aunt Connie's house, no mother-in-a-box, no cold skin and jab with an ice pick, no having to pee in the middle of the funeral procession. Perhaps in the privacy of their room, Chick talked about those things with Jedda. Or maybe he called our sister on nights after 11 pm when phone rates went down. If he did, he didn't mention it to me. Nor did Jedda. But I knew those things had happened, if for no other reason than tangerine Lifesavers made me sick to my stomach.

Chick went to a lot of meetings that summer. For a while, I thought him a very important person to have to go to so many meetings. It wasn't until a couple of summers later that I realized the meetings had more to do with him recently getting sober than the fact that he was important. Regardless, it was obvious that he was very unhappy and he angered easily. He tended to be loud when he wasn't angry. When he got angry, it frightened me to be in the same room with him, and I learned quickly to give him a lot of space when he came home from work, when he mowed the grass or did other unpleasant chores, or simply when he was just breathing in and out. Even if I wanted to talk to him about the mother, the opportunity did not present itself.

I worried about where the mother was now. Not the part we buried—I got that. That was at the cemetery. The other part, that made her **her**. Both the nun who had taught me in first grade and the teacher I had just had this year had told us that Catholics who did not go to church go to hell. Sister Vincent Ann, she of the Storm the Classroom and Demand Quiet Routine that was practiced almost daily, had told us the same thing in religion class. The mother was, at least during my years with her, a Christmas and Easter Catholic.

Still believing in a parochial school God, I bargained on her behalf. She was sick, I told Him in the same patient tone I had used to explain that the bed was too big. Didn't He see me bring her those pills every afternoon? Didn't that mean that she could be in Purgatory and if we all prayed hard enough, that she would go to heaven?

I thought a lot about how sick she had been. There had been days when she could barely stand up when I came home and found her resting on the couch. But she did stand up—not straight, and not always for very long, but she **did** stand up. Wasn't it an awful lot to expect of her to make it to church every week? Wasn't there some allowance for being that sick for that long?

I wrapped my thoughts around her being in Purgatory and I prayed for her from the middle of that cinderblock wall that had taken up residence in my chest. I doubted that God was paying attention, since I had prayed with the same desperation the night before she died and she died anyway. As growly as Chick was, there was no point in asking him questions and Jedda wasn't Catholic. The first few weeks in Hampton were endless and I wrestled with terrifying questions about the mother's afterlife and terrifying questions about life after Hampton and prayed to a God I knew wasn't listening to get the mother into heaven faster because the alternative--which I had been told for two years-- was unthinkable.

***

She wasn't **just** the mother. She was the balance, the protection, the sanity. It wasn't that things went wild unexpectedly after she died. Things had always been a little wild but she stood in the way of them, lessening the impact on me. The father didn't start drinking when she died; he had a drinking problem long before I was born. Michael didn't suddenly go off the deep end when she died; he had never been okay to start with, despite the father's insistence that he was fine.

The mother managed Michael, trying to bring some amount of control to our lives. Michael was the kid on our street who was constantly in fights, in trouble in school and at home. He was the kid whose eyes lit up when he pulled the wings off flies. He sneaked away with matches to burn ants and other bugs alive. The mother chased him and took the matches back. The father never said a word. I was also fair game, especially if the mother wasn't looking. Hurting me made him laugh, more so if he made me cry.

My eyelids drooped a little and I struggled to keep them up so no one would notice and suggest I call it a night. I drifted, our black and white Zenith a soothing buzz in the background.

Michael started to walk past me, an inconvenient blur of motion between myself and the TV. He paused, placed a hand on the side of my head and dug his thumb into my temple, leaning into it. I came to, yowling, my head about to explode. He straightened and backed off a step, laughing.

"Michael!" the mother yelled. "Leave her alone!"

Before she could get to her feet, he ran for the stairs. He was halfway up by the time she limped to the bottom step so she winged her shoe at him, catching him with a solid *whomp*before he made it to the top. He squawked. She sat down and squeezed me, sighing.

"You okay? Yeah, you're okay!" She brushed my hair out of my eyes.

Two lessons: One...Don't mess with the mother. Two...Don't close your eyes.

She was the only one who stood in his way. When he came to get a bat to go after another boy, she posted herself in his path and would not be moved, telling him he'd have to go over her to get out. When he came in to get a hockey stick for the same reason, she picked up the other hockey stick and stationed herself in the doorway so he couldn't get by, the skinniest goalie I had ever seen. But she stopped him. She was the only one who **could**.

When Michael was eight years old, the mother convinced the father that something really was wrong –little boys didn't do the things Michael did. Reluctantly, the father agreed that they should have some tests done and our doctor admitted Michael to a hospital. The particulars of the tests weren't shared with me as I didn't have a degree in social work when I was four, so I don't know what they were looking for. I do remember, though, that the house felt different with him gone. And I remember that I didn't miss him.

They didn't keep him long—three days, maybe four. Then the doctor called and demanded that we come get him because they couldn't handle him. He must have been in a medical wing rather than on a psychiatric wing where they might have been able to deal with his disruptive behavior. The father could be convinced to beat Michael all over the house on bad days and would sometimes even do it of his own initiative, but he could not be convinced that Michael needed a psychiatric evaluation.

That summer in Hampton set the stage. The mother was gone. Control was out the window.

***

I doubt that my sister-in-law, Jedda, would have signed up for two extra kids in the first two years of being married to Chick, especially one that was significantly disturbed. They had enough of their own bumps and bruises to deal with, and within weeks of the mother's death, Jedda confirmed that she was pregnant. She often joked about having "his and her" kids, which grew into "his, hers and ours" when my third nephew was born and morphed further still into "his, hers, ours and theirs" when I was around.

She and Chick already had their hands full with "his" and "hers," with Chick's short temper and surliness and their own grieving of the mother when Michael and I ended up in Hampton. Jedda saw the portents in Michael's behavior first and years later told me how the conversations between Chick and her went.

"Chick?! Chick, come over here and look at this!" She held the curtain aside and gestured him to the window overlooking the backyard.

He stepped up to the window, glanced out and grunted, then walked away.

"Chick!" she said insistently. "He's on top of your sister! Don't you see that?"

"He's fine."

"I'm not worried about **him!** Go out there and get him off her!"

He ignored her.

"Chick, honey, that's not normal. Look how he's holding her down. You need to do something!"

"He's fine."

I was unaware that we were being observed. Michael had knocked me down and gotten on top of me, straddling my chest and pinning my arms under his knees. He pinched my nose closed with one hand and put his other hand over my mouth so I couldn't breathe. I pitched upward then sideways, trying to throw him off. He clamped tight with his legs. The harder I struggled, the tighter he held on. I kicked, pulling my knees upward and thumping against his back. He rocked with each kick, laughing.

My lungs burned. Panicked screams created a log jam in my throat. I could hear the muffled "aaaaggghhhh," but his hand smashed my lips against my teeth, so I heard it inside my head. I bucked and he ground against me. I wanted to scream for the mother, for the father, for anyone who would pull him off. My vision started to blur at the periphery and my next kick was not as demanding as the first few had been.

("Mommy?")

He rubbed against me a couple more times, then released my nose and removed his hand from over my mouth. Air whooshed into my aching lungs, and he stood up laughing as I rolled onto my side, clawing the grass. The greyish fog at the edges of my vision receded. I gagged. He spit on me.

He walked slowly toward the carport. I cowered on the ground, crying into the dirt as my thinking cleared. With my back to the house, I never noticed when the curtain closed.

("Bye, Mommy.")

Downward Spiral

      School ended for the holiday on Friday, four days before Christmas. Aunt Connie's house was busier than usual with relatives and friends from Uncle Dick's job popping in, drinking eggnog, and dropping off celebratory bottles. All of the cousins would be at Aunt Connie's for Christmas, as they had been for Thanksgiving. I had spent Thanksgiving with the father and Michael and the father's new girlfriend, who had gone to great lengths to cook traditional Italian dishes that my traditional Irish taste buds found revolting. The only things familiar about Thanksgiving were the canned biscuits, burned until they resembled Michael's hockey pucks, and the fact that the father was drunk most of the weekend. As soon as dinner ended, I ran to Aunt Connie's house and tried to describe the fiasco of something that looked like seaweed soup. The whole charade ranked up there with the year the father, again inebriated, picked up the turkey by its legs to move it to a serving platter and dropped our dinner on the kitchen floor. He stood there, befuddled, with two drumsticks in his hands. The mother cried.

      I couldn't tell what to expect for this holiday. Plainly, the father wasn't going to get this cooking thing. We didn't have Christmas cookies in our house like at Aunt Connie's, no friends or other relatives stopping by to wish us well and toast the holidays. It didn't occur to me that the father had no friends. The father and Aunt Connie had had a big fight, and she had stopped speaking to him after we came back from Hampton. I didn't know what it was about. All I knew was that Aunt Connie didn't even want to hear his name, especially now that he had a new girlfriend. So Aunt Connie and Uncle Dick were definitely not dropping by to raise a glass and drink eggnog with the father.

      The mother had complained the past couple of Christmases about the father insisting on a real Christmas tree. She said the needles were too hard to get out of the carpet. The father ignored that and kept getting real trees, under which he usually passed out on Christmas Eve afternoon. The mother wasn't going to be here to pick up the stubborn pine needles this year, so the father bought an artificial tree for the first time.

    On a dreary mid-December afternoon, Michael and I cleaned the living and dining room and dragged the Christmas decorations out of the old storage trunk in the cellar. The nativity scene with the clay figures that the mother had painted and glued into place was stationed at its post on top of the TV that I polished with lemon Pledge. (There's a good chance I also polished the TV screen while I was at it.) We tried to hang the hanging things where the mother would have put them. We went through a mountain of tape sticking other things to the front windows, now streaked with half-circles precisely the length of my arms, like the mother would have done. Well, maybe she wouldn't have left so many streaks, but I was quite proud of the way I hung backwards out the window ten feet above the ground to get the outside clean. Across the street in Mr. Aubrey's cellar window, his annual miniature train scene whirred on tiny tracks through a festive tiny village, weaving from one pane to the next, then back again. Almost every house on the street blinked shades of red and green. Some things were the same. But nothing was the same.

    We planned to put the tree up on Christmas Eve, as always. We had the whole weekend and then one more day before it would be Christmas, once school let out. The father decided that the new tree needed its own platform so it came exactly to the ceiling once the tree topper went on. When we had real trees, sometimes he used the sheet of plywood set up for Michael's Lionel train set as the stand for the tree. More often than not, the tree leaned too much or fell over completely, wrecking the effect. Then again, I'm not sure what effect we should have been looking for with the father passed out under the tree and on top of the plywood, with the tree propped up on him.

    The father cut the wood for the platform over that weekend and I watched, pretty sure he was a smart guy to be able to figure out how to stand our new tree up. He used two-by-fours as the feet, leaving just enough room to run a strip of chimney paper around the platform, and covered it with textured green paper. Once the platform was built, we set it aside until Christmas Eve, which was Monday, and we would build the new tree and decorate it when he came home from work.

Too bouncy to stay in bed Monday morning, I got up before he left for work. It was show time! We could assemble the tree and then put all the stuff on it and then it would be Christmas! The father thought he might come home a little early, too, because there was going to be a party at his work.

"I'll try to get home by three," he said, picking up his bagged lunch and tousling my hair. He locked the front door on his way out.

Like the cleaning day, Michael was nice to me on Christmas Eve. Maybe the father had told him he'd get better presents if he didn't hit me. Bribery worked sometimes, on that front. That afternoon, we set the platform in place and Michael dragged the pieces of the tree up from the cellar two at a time, piling them on the living room floor. I carried up boxes of lights and balls and tinsel. Rusty slept under the dining room table or nosed through the pile of tree pieces until we shooed her away.

Three o'clock came and went. I waited.

Four o'clock came and went. The street got dark. Windows lit up and blinked.

Around five o'clock, we decided to build the tree. If the father was stuck at work, he wouldn't want to be slowed down when he finally got home by having to put the tree together. It was simple. We could figure it out. Somebody had to do it, so we did it.

We had the tree up by six o'clock, and we were getting hungry. We made sandwiches—our Christmas Eve tradition, because doing tree stuff **and** cooking had been too much for the mother. We fed Rusty and waited a little while longer.

Guessing now that the father was very busy at work, we decorated the tree. We decorated the front the most, reasoning that's what everyone would see. I thought it was beautiful and knew the father would be very proud when he got home. We even put the tree skirt on. I wondered if the tree might prefer pants, like I did, but I had just been through all of our decorations and I knew we didn't own any tree pants.

We hung up our stockings, tying them to the white wrought iron railing at the fourth step up with Michael's higher than mine. The stuffed elves, curled up on the blue carpeted stair edge with their skinny red and green felt arms around their even skinnier, tucked-up felt legs, approved. We hung up a stocking for Rusty that had rawhides and a squeaky pork chop in it. From under the dining room table, Rusty approved.

Nine o'clock rolled around, and we had not heard from the father. Neither one of us could imagine where he might be. He couldn't still be at work. Maybe he'd had an accident. Should we call the police? What if he had gotten hurt while we weren't with him to help? We couldn't call Aunt Connie. That would only make a bad situation worse. We had to wait this out.

Eventually, Michael turned to me and said, "You could probably go to bed. I'll wait up. I'll wake you up when he comes home."

I was tired. This made sense. I went to bed.

***

Michael didn't wake me. In the morning, I woke on my own in grey daylight and ran to the top of the steps. Stretching out on my belly, I could see between the stair tread and the living room ceiling to find out what was going on downstairs. In the half light, I saw packages lining the bottom steps and landing. I could also hear the father snoring.

I jumped up. Michael's room was directly behind me.

"Mike! Mike! Christmas happened and Daddy's home from work! Wake up!"

He rolled over, barely acknowledging me. I shook him.

"Mike, wake up! Daddy's home and Christmas came!"

His eyes opened. "Daddy's home?"

I nodded.

He threw back his blanket. Before his feet touched the floor, I was heading down the steps.

"Dad! Dad! Dad!"

The father snored loudly on the couch, one arm over his face, the other hanging off the edge of the cushion. He wore the clothes he'd left for work in yesterday morning and he reeked of old beer. No matter. I grabbed the arm hanging off the side of the couch and pulled. He didn't respond.

I put my hands on his chest and bounced him up and down.

No response.

Michael appeared behind me. He, too, put his hands on the father's chest and bounced, yelling, "Dad, wake up!"

Nothing.

Brushing his arm aside, I took the father's head in my hands and shook it back and forth like a cantaloupe.

Nothing.

I looked at Michael. He looked back at me and shrugged, then his expression brightened.

"Wait! Like Mommy would!" He got a glass of water from the kitchen and dumped it on the father's head.

The snoring continued undisturbed.

I sat down on the steps amid the presents. Some of them were marked with Michael's name or mine, set out neatly but in the wrong places. Christmas gifts went on the couch, with Michael's stuff on one end and mine on the other. We never put presents on the steps. The two bottom steps were for sitting when you opened your stocking. Everyone knew that. So who put these presents out?

"He's not getting up," I observed.

"Nope," Michael agreed.

"What should we do?"

"I don't know."

I considered this. If calling Aunt Connie last night was unwise, today it was likely to be dangerous. Chick and Jedda had been transferred to West Virginia in September. I didn't know how far away that was. They'd been in Virginia. That had been about an eight hour drive. Now they were...west. Slowly, Michael made his way across the room and around the dining room table. He picked up the phone and I watched him dial.

"Pat? Can you come get us? Daddy's drunk."

***

After asking a few questions, Pat stormed the house within the hour. She swept me up in a hug, holding my head tight to her shoulder.

"Let's get some clothes together—you're both coming with me."

I nodded. "I got some new toys. Can I bring 'em?"

She looked at the pile of presents that Michael and I had sorted and assigned to their proper locations, and then unwrapped while waiting for her to arrive. The father slept through our Christmas morning. "Bring just one or two things, okay? There won't be a lot of room."

"What about Rusty?"

"Rusty will be okay."

"What about Daddy?"

She said nothing. She rallied us, got us packed and herded us out the door to drive back to her apartment where her son and their Christmas morning were on hold.

Up and down the street, windows blinked and lit-up Christmas trees could be seen from the pavement in virtually every house. I climbed into Pat's car, battling guilt. The father was going to wake up alone on Christmas day. Shouldn't we be there for him? Who would take care of him? Who would make his dinner? Who would feed Rusty and let her out and play with the squeaky pork chop with her?

I glanced at Pat. I didn't think she cared too much right now who would keep the father company. I buttoned my lip and swallowed the guilt whole.

***

Michael stayed with us only a day before he asked to go home. Pat tried numerous times to get the father on the phone to no avail. This meant either the father was still passed out or he had gotten up and continued drinking. From calls to Aunt Connie, details began to emerge about the couple of days prior to Pat having to swoop in and grab us up, filling in some of the gaps about Christmas Eve night.

We assumed that the father started drinking at his work party. We didn't know where he went afterward, but it was obviously someplace he could continue drinking while Michael and I waited and decorated our tree without him. I was able to hear only Pat's side of the conversations, but it gave me enough to clear up the picture.

The father had bought our Christmas gifts in the weeks leading up to the holiday. Not trusting that Michael wouldn't ransack the house to find them, he had left everything at our cousin Maureen's with the understanding that he'd come get them on Christmas Eve after Michael and I went to bed. Maureen and her new husband Joe waited up half the night. By early morning, they figured that he was not coming, so they wrapped the presents, bagged them and carried everything to our house. They set up the presents on the stairs and locked the door behind them when they left. Maureen was furious that the father never showed up. So was Aunt Connie.

It wasn't clear if the father wasn't home when they came over, or if he had already returned and passed out, but it didn't matter. Either way, Maureen and Joe did what they could to make a passable holiday for us and now swore they'd never help the father with anything else ever again. Not that anyone could blame them!

Pat was reluctant to take Michael back to the father's house but after he asked several times, she agreed. I don't remember if I chose to stay or if it wasn't an option to go home, but I spent the remainder of the school break at Pat's, wondering why the father wouldn't call me, missing the mother horribly in the new upside down world, and wondering if Michael remembered to feed Rusty every day. I don't remember wondering if anyone was feeding Michael.

I didn't tell Pat that I missed the mother or that I wished the father would call me. I missed him too. She didn't have to say out loud how angry she was; I could see it in her expression and hear it in her voice whenever any reference was made to the father. Pat was so angry, she didn't want to see the father when she took me home. She certainly didn't want to speak to him.

School was about to start. The father missed his first day back to work after the New Year holiday, stretched out on the couch, groaning.

"Nance, I'm sick. Call work and tell 'em I'm not coming in."

"You're not sick, Dad. You have a hangover," I said brightly, hoping that my clarification would be helpful.

"No, no, I've got something. The flu maybe," he insisted. "Call me in."

I dialed the phone, resentful that he asked me to lie. He'd been drunk for days. Did he really think those ladies in the office would believe me when I told them he was sick? What if they fired him because I wasn't a good liar? It would be all my fault. Hands a little sweaty, I lied to the woman who answered the phone. She didn't say much other than thank you. Did she believe me?

The father groaned again and put an arm over his eyes to block the light.

I picked up my school bag and left. When I stopped in to Aunt Connie's house to join David, Ricky, and Doreen to walk the rest of the way, I offered nothing about how the holiday week had gone and especially nothing about the father missing work and asking me to lie and call him in sick. That would only make Aunt Connie **and** the father angrier at each other. Nobody needed that. Aunt Connie reminded me to stand up straight before we headed out the door.

***

I hoped that Easter would be an improvement over Christmas. We didn't have to get far into the spring to realize it had the potential to be as big a mess as Christmas had been. Maybe the father was just trying to hold onto how we used to have holidays, when we had the mother. Maybe he just couldn't read the clues, subtle at first but increasingly blunt over several weeks, that the whole "new Easter dress" idea made me really uncomfortable. Maybe he didn't care. Whatever it was, we ended up fighting over where to spend Easter (*at the new girlfriend's? WHY?*) and what he thought I should wear (*a dress that makes me look like I'm five? WHY?*).

I tried to explain my discomfort. All I asked for was a pair of pants. They could be dress up pants. But being forced to wear a dress —and not just to church, but the entire day—was torture. I could no more feel at home in a dress than I could walk down the street on my hands, juggling bowling pins with my toes. I felt like an imposter, stuck in someone else's clothes. I never knew how to sit right, or stand right, or where to put my arms and legs. More importantly, I didn't care. I didn't want to know. Pants, I knew how to operate.

It was useless to disagree with the father when he was drinking, which amounted to every weekend at the time. He didn't pay attention or he didn't make any sense, or both. When he was sober again, he didn't remember what we had talked about. If I persisted, it wasn't unheard of for him to pass out in the middle of trying to talk to him. It was equally useless to talk with him when he wasn't drinking because it seemed to anger him, or at least inconvenience him and make him irritable if I had an opinion about something that didn't match his.

I resigned myself to Easter being a lost weekend. The father drank his way through it. When he'd drunk enough that I knew he wouldn't notice or care what I was wearing any longer, I changed. He passed out.

The following weekend, however, had potential to be great.

"Hey, Boo, want to take a ride this weekend?" he asked, mid-week.

"Where we going?"

"Let's go down the shore!"

"Yeah!" I said. "Let's go down the shore!"

Wildwood, where we spent our vacation week, was about a two-hour drive. Atlantic City was only about an hour and people from our neighborhood took day trips to Atlantic City regularly.

I was disappointed that he asked the girlfriend to come along. Michael refused, and the father didn't argue with him. If the father had been paying closer attention, he would have noticed that over the counter medications were disappearing fast out of our medicine cabinet and Michael had gotten even weirder. I preferred that he not come with us, even if the girlfriend was coming along. She drank too much and the father drank too much when they were together, but at least she wasn't likely to knock me down or punch me in the head.

The weekend after Easter was hot. Summer was going to come early. Maybe I could walk on the beach for a little while if there was time. I wouldn't swim. I hated to get wet and sandy and not have dry clothes to change into for the ride home. It was like riding home sitting on sandpaper.

The day started out with the sun shining on us as we walked along the boardwalk. Atlantic City hadn't yet gone casino crazy, so the boardwalk and the beachfront were the attractions. Boardwalk history shouted from the storefronts, advertising Steel Pier fudge, water taffy, *American Bandstand*, and the Miss America Pageant. Old billboards for suntan lotion towered above the buildings, featuring a little cartoon girl and a puppy pulling at her bathing suit, two years before Jodie Foster became a household name with the movie *Taxi Driver*. The air smelled of salt, seaweed, sunburn and tanning lotion.

I don't know when or where the father had his first drink, but I knew with that sinking feeling in my stomach as soon as I saw him that he wouldn't stop. He couldn't.

"I hafta stop at da tap room," he said, his words starting to slur. He did have to stop, but it wasn't to use the restroom. It was to get another drink.

By early evening when we should have been on the way back to Philadelphia, he staggered to the car, mumbling about dinner. My stomach dropped even further. Dinner with him in this condition could go on for hours as he put down drink after drink until he passed out, and then how were we going to get home? The new girlfriend didn't drive. Even if she did, he wouldn't let her. He always insisted that he was fine no matter how much he was slurring and stumbling. I don't remember where we stopped, but I remember that he was no longer ordering beer. He was on to Seagram's 7 and Seven-Up now, one after the other. The girlfriend joined him.

"Dad, can we go now? Can we go home?"

"Mmmm..wai...yeah. We'll go soooooonnn."

I thought he said we would go soon, if I had understood that correctly. His dark eyes were glazed, and he wobbled when he reached for his glass. Setting the glass down became a routine of set and slide, as he'd clunk the glass on the table and push it forward. Maybe he couldn't tell it was already down. His head swung unevenly and sometimes tipped forward unexpectedly. On the opposite side of the table, the girlfriend was doing the same thing.

Another drink. Getting angry and starting to get scared, I asked again if we could go. He could do this drive—it was just an hour. We had to get home!

It was dark when we finally left and he lurched toward the car. It took several tries for him to seat the key in the ignition. He fidgeted with the rearview mirror, but each move seemed to make the angle worse. He swore at it. At least I think that's what that was.

He got the Torino in drive and hiccupped out of the parking lot. When I offered the map, he snarled, "Wassamoofenou? Shuddahellup!"

I thought he was telling me to shut up. I shut up and looked around. I had no idea where we were. I didn't see any signs for the highway, and I didn't recognize the name of the next town as we crossed over its boundary line. He pulled into a parking lot and said, "Haftausedataproom," and he fell out the door.

The girlfriend said nothing. I sat there quietly for several minutes. I knew he had gone in for another drink. We did this weekly but usually in Philadelphia. Some days, he stopped at almost every corner bar on the drive home from his girlfriend's house or the grocery store. He could leave a location perfectly sober and be drunk by the time we got home, a few miles away. This was different. We weren't close to home. I didn't know where we were and I couldn't walk home from here. He wasn't going to stop drinking until he passed out. I couldn't call Chick to help. Pat and Maureen had driven us to West Virginia in February for the christening of Chick and Jedda's new son, and I knew how far away they were now. I scanned the front of the building but I couldn't find a pay phone. Even if I wanted to, I couldn't call Aunt Connie or Pat, and what difference would it make if I did? I couldn't ask them to come get me. I didn't know where I was.

The father weaved his way back to the car and flopped down. He fumbled clumsily with the rearview mirror again.

"Dad, maybe you shouldn't be driving..."

His bloodshot eyes met mine in the mirror. "D'laskyou? Sh'up."

"Dad—

"Hey!" he yelled. He pointed at me unsteadily and drew his hand back toward his shoulder, knuckles out in my direction. "Shuddahellup! Immasmackyouinnamouff!"

I doubted he could keep his balance long enough to smack anybody, but how far could I push this? Cold sweat collected on my neck and forehead. He could barely walk and he was insisting that he try to drive us—at high speed, on a major interstate and then over the Delaware River—back to the city. **If** he could figure out where the highway was!

He turned with determination in the opposite direction when we exited the lot. He ran the stop sign at the end of the road and hugged the white line, still mumbling to himself. I suspected that was about me. When he cruised through a red light a few streets down, an oncoming car narrowly missed us, horn blasting and the driver flipping us off as he blew by, a silhouette in our headlights.

The girlfriend made some incoherent sound.

"Immafine!" the father yelled.

Good. Let him smack her.

He eased off the brake and accelerated to the next intersection, where he promptly turned the wrong way into a one-way street.

The girlfriend squawked again and I stiffened. No other cars were coming, but still...

Slowly registering his mistake, he stopped and backed out into the intersection, blind to any oncoming cars. I held my breath, head whipping from side to side, making sure we had passage. Still no other cars. He set the gearshift in drive and pulled back onto the street he'd been trying to turn away from.

My heart hammered. If he couldn't manage small roads and streets, how was he going to manage the expressway? We crisscrossed the double yellow lines repeatedly. I didn't know what the lines meant, except that he wasn't driving on our side of the road, and it was entirely possible that cars on the other side might want to use their road.

"Immastopanusedataproom," he announced, gesturing at a building about half a block ahead of us on the other side of the road.

"Dad, please," I started.

"DintItellyushuddup?"

I didn't have time to answer before he jerked the wheel and tried to turn left, cutting across all four lanes. He aimed for the sloped curb at the entrance, missing it by several feet, ramming the Torino's front end up over the regular curb. He braked. We neatly intersected the sidewalk, with the back end of the car blocking a lane. I dove onto the floor.

"Oohhhshiddd."

He started to back up. The front end had just dropped back onto the blacktop when flashing red lights pulled alongside us, which I saw reflected on the glass from my position on the floor.

The girlfriend stirred.
"OohhCholley...whaddahelljoudo?"

The cop rapped against the driver's window.

Go ahead, I thought. *Tell HIM to shut the hell up!* I poked my head above the edge of seat.

The father grappled with the window crank, losing his grip several times and punching himself in the leg or thumping against the steering wheel.

"License and registration, sir!" the cop demanded.

"Wassssaaprobum?"

The cop shined a flashlight in the father's face. "Sir, have you been drinking?"

"Me? Noooo...."

"Step out of the car, sir."

"Out?"

"Step out of the car, sir. Now."

He groped for the door handle. The cop stepped back to let him open it and he half-fell, half-rolled out the door. I watched as the cop gave him some directions and pointed at the ground. The father put his heel in front of his other foot and tried to walk on the white line. The cop spoke to him again. The father raised a hand and almost jabbed his finger in his own eye.

The cop's partner appeared from behind us and asked the girlfriend to step out of the car. Then he saw me. "Okay. You too, honey. Come on out of there."

I levered the seat forward and climbed out as the first cop was saying, "Sir, I'm placing you under arrest..." I started around to the driver's side but before I could reach the father, the second cop put a hand on my shoulder.

"Just stand here for a minute," he said.

The first cop directed the father to place his hands on the hood of our car. When the father didn't move right away, probably still grappling for the meaning of the words, the cop grabbed him and shoved him roughly toward the front end.

"Oooooofff!!" The father sprawled face-first on the hood and in the glare of the headlights from the police cruiser, I caught the surprise that momentarily focused him.

"DAD!" I tried to take a step forward and the grip on my shoulder tightened a little. I stopped again.

The first cop pinned the father's hands behind him and snapped handcuffs around his wrists. The father yelped.

"Thasstootight—hurts!"

"Don't hurt him!" I yelled, pulling against the hand on my shoulder.

The cops paid no attention to the father's objections or mine. One grabbed his elbow and pulled him upright, pushing him into the back seat. The other one finally let go of my shoulder and waved me toward the open door. "Go ahead. You have to get in too."

Get in? I was being arrested too?

The road around us was very dark. We had not seen a single car since we'd jumped the curb. They could leave me here, but we were in the middle of nowhere, or I could be arrested too and get in the back seat. Or I could run, like on TV. But then I'd be the only fugitive in third grade. I got in.

The father squirmed and complained nonsensical syllables. Maybe the cops heard those a lot, because they seemed to understand.

"Yeah, well, you're not supposed to be comfortable so shut the fuck up," the second one said.

"C'mon," the father groaned. "Notinfronnamykid."

"The kid you been driving around drunk all night?"

The father groaned a little more and tried to move his arms.

At the police station, they opened a door to a room with a bench in it, just off the main room where their desks were. One nodded at me. "Wait in here."

I walked in.

Before he turned away, he asked, "How old are you?"

"Eight," I replied. His lips pressed together and thinned. I perched on the edge of the bench in the otherwise empty space. The windows in and next to the door were reinforced with mesh or wire. It dawned on me that this was probably where they kept people locked up. He left the door ajar so I could see where they told the father to sit down. The girlfriend sat across the room by another desk. They ignored her. On the bright white clock under the glaring fluorescent ceiling lights, the hands read just after midnight.

His handcuffs removed, the father scrabbled through his pockets and took out a cigarette, poking the wrong end into his mouth. When he lifted his lighter, one cop leaned over and slapped him in the face. The cigarette flew sideways, landing soundlessly on a desk several feet away.

Without thinking, I was on my feet and at the doorway. "Dad!"

The first cop's head snapped around and he glared at me. I shrank back from the doorway, but I didn't sit down. I heard him snarl, "You don't need to smoke in here!"

I wondered if the father would have been any less surprised if the cop had warned him first, "Immasmackyouinnamouff!"

***

They processed his paperwork and told us we were leaving. I didn't see who made the arrangements, and I didn't know if this was normal for drunken driving arrests or if they bent the rules because I was there. Maybe the rules were different in 1974. Groups like Mothers Against Drunk Driving wouldn't form for another six years, and New Jersey wouldn't pass laws mandating ignition interlock devices for another thirty-six years. When they finished, they simply took us somewhere for him to sleep it off.

We spent the rest of the night, or more accurately the early part of the morning, at a motel where the cops left us. They told me that morning shift cops would come by to pick us up and take us back to our car. The father collapsed on one bed as soon as we got inside. I pulled his shoes off and covered him with half of the bedspread, rolling him up into a Dad burrito. The girlfriend fell asleep beside him.

I didn't sleep well, afraid we'd miss the cops' return and we wouldn't be able to get home. In the morning, I woke the father and called the number the cops had given us to let them know we could be picked up at any time.

When they dropped us off in the parking lot where we had abandoned the Torino, I was tired and hungry and afraid to say anything to the father that would put him in a worse mood. I drank part of the warm black cherry soda in the cup holder since yesterday when we'd left for New Jersey. The father glanced at me with heavy lidded, red eyes, his eyebrows down.

"Keep your mouth shut. You don't need to tell anybody what happened here."

That was code for "Kindly refrain from sharing this experience with anyone else in the family."

It was certainly clearer than "Immasmackyouinnamouff!"

The Pigeon

Some days, Michael's rage was directed somewhere other than at me. I was never sure, though, that it was easier to tolerate when it was directed against some helpless furry or feathered critter. I found the pigeon on the pavement right outside our house on a blinding bright morning after school had let out for summer. We lived across the street from a Presbyterian church that took up half a city block. Pigeons roosted in its eaves. People on the street fed them bread scraps so they hung around, as city pigeons do, making themselves at home on your pavement. But this pigeon was sick. Or injured, maybe. I couldn't tell.

Regardless of the diagnosis, I wanted to help the pigeon, but rumors about pigeons and their diseases were abundant. Don't touch them; you don't know what they're carrying. This particular pigeon listed to one side on the warm concrete, talons bunched up underneath him. Or her. He or she clearly wasn't carrying anything. Still, I wasn't going to touch him and tempt fate.

I went back inside to retrieve a piece of newspaper to wrap him in. The initial plan was to wrap him up and take him across the street to the steps of the Presbyterian Church. His bird buddies would be able to care for him. If not, at least he wouldn't be alone. It was a beautifully simple plan. The old newspapers were in the basement, less than a minute away.

When I returned, I came to a standstill at the screen door. My stomach dropped. Michael's sneakers framed the pigeon. He turned toward the house, with his back to the street, smiling and holding a blue and bright yellow can of Ronsonol lighter fluid. Breaking eye contact with me only long enough to glance downward to ensure he hit his target, he squirted lighter fluid onto the pigeon.

"NO!" I shouted, charging out the door. "NO!"

He shoved me off to one side and I fell, smacking the concrete and knocking the breath out of me. Still smiling and looking at me, (*to make sure I'm watching?*), he lit a match casually and dropped it on the pigeon.

Whooomph!

The next shriek may have been me. It may have been the injured pigeon. It may have been both of us. I lurched up and dove toward the bird, flailing at the flames, now ignoring all the precautions we'd ever heard about not touching pigeons because you couldn't possibly know what they could give you. I flailed some more, screaming, burning my hands, but I couldn't let this poor pigeon burn alive.

Michael stood above me and laughed.

The flames beaten out, I picked up the pigeon, tears running from my eyes. The feathers on one side were gone and in the interior of the black ring I saw charred skin, some of it glistening, blood seeping from too many places to count. I touched only the unburned parts of my bird acquaintance, sickened by the smell and the oozing, blistery chicken look. "I'm sorry, I'm sorry, I'm sorry, bird. I'm so sorry." How could I let this happen? Why had I waited? Gone for newspaper? "Oh, bird, I'm so sorry."

As I lifted him up to eye level, he turned his head toward me. His small beak opened and bloody white foam bubbled out. His eyes glazed over as he died in my hands. "Oh bird, I am so sorry." I could barely whisper.

Michael found this hilarious. "Hey, now you can tell people what you did this morning—you can tell 'em you put the bird out!"

I couldn't respond. I couldn't even look up from the blackened mass with foam welling out of his throat. I suppose that wasn't much fun for Michael. Maybe he'd been looking for more of a reaction. After a few minutes of laughing at me for being upset about the burned avian mess in my hands, he went back in the house. I sat on the pavement a while longer. When I could stand up again without my knees threatening to give out, I took the bird into the garden, tucked his body under the hedges and covered him with dirt and the newspaper originally intended to help him.

It was a blue and grey pigeon. And it was a blue and yellow can of lighter fluid. The father never asked about the burns on my hands.

***

I turned nine that summer and we had dinner at Pat's apartment. There are photos of it. The father gave me a tiny television for my room but mostly I remember that he was half drunk before we went and continued to drink while we were there. Pat asked me sometime after that birthday dinner if I wanted to come and stay with her.

Could I? Should I? The father would be alone if I left. Who would make his coffee in the morning? Who would keep him company? How could I tell him I wanted to live somewhere else? Wouldn't that hurt his feelings?

On the other hand, being in the father's house meant being with Michael, who was almost twice my size. Every day with Michael meant being hurt. It meant being choked until I started to pass out, or my fingers twisted, or my arms wrenched. He had a new approach that had started over the last few months. When he'd catch me in my room, he knocked me down and climbed on top of me, rocking and rubbing, my arms pinned to the bed or the floor with his legs like he had done in Chick's yard. Then he'd put a pillow over my face.

I always fought. I always lost.

First, it got hot under the pillow and I twisted my head from side to side as best I could. Then I noticed that I was breathing the hotness because nothing cool was available. Breathing the hotness was okay the first couple times if I remembered not to breathe too deeply. Breathing deeply was a bit challenging anyway with Michael sitting on my chest. After a few breaths, the hotness turned grey and my lungs burned and I needed to scream.

The pillow trapped the screams inside with the hotness and the greyness and I writhed under him, desperate, panicking. If he pulled the pillow off and I saw him, he was laughing and would have this weird light in his eyes. Other than the panic, I didn't know why I screamed. No one was coming to pull him off. No one was home to hear the screaming. When I tried to explain this practice to the father, he interrupted impatiently and pointed out that if I would just leave Michael alone, he wouldn't bother me. And for Chrissake, don't go telling people. Nobody needed to know what was going on in our house.

I wasn't sure what qualified as bothering Michael, since this occurred when I was playing or reading alone in my room. Michael would come upstairs to use the bathroom or to get something from his room and detour, uninvited, by my room. Sometimes he came in slowly, calling me names, and I had warning that it was about to start. Other times, he'd run from the hallway and jump on top of me. My book would go flying, and he'd yank the pillow off the bed or from under my head and crush it over my face.

A few years before the mother died, we did some renovations to our house. In an effort to modernize, the father removed the solid oak doors that locked with skeleton keys from three of the four bedrooms with the intention of installing some lighter weight doors with updated knobs and locks. He never replaced those doors. I had no option to close my door and lock myself in because I didn't have a door. If I wanted privacy, I dressed in the bathroom. I could not lock myself in, nor could I ever lock Michael out. When he wanted to get to me, he had very few obstacles to overcome.

So I always fought. And I always lost.

I sat with Pat's offer for many days, debating. She said she couldn't tell me what to pick, that it was my choice. How do I choose? My home and my dad and my dog? My sister and not being mauled on a regular basis? Pat didn't need me. The father needed me. He told me that a lot, especially when he was being really honest, just before he stopped making sense, when The Emotive Father would make a brief appearance through a haze of Piel's beer. Had she talked to him? Did he even know I was thinking about this choice?

I tried to envision what expression might come over his face if I told him I wanted to live with Pat. How mad would he be? What if I went and something happened to him? What if he didn't want me to come back—ever? But what if he didn't ever understand that Michael was hurting me? What if he never did anything to stop that? Did it matter then that I wouldn't be able to come back? Plus, I would be very far away from Aunt Connie and David. Too far. No, I couldn't go.

It was a blue and grey pigeon. And it was a blue and bright yellow can of Ronsonol lighter fluid. The bird and I screamed together. The father never noticed.

Could Michael hurt me like that? Would he? Would that make him laugh? Was he telling the truth about that stray cat and the firecracker he said he stuck in its...uhhh...back end and how its guts started to come out when the firecracker exploded? My stomach flip-flopped. Pat couldn't tell me what to choose. (And for Chrissake...) I couldn't tell Pat the things I had seen or what he was doing to me.

I told the father at dinner one night when it was just the two of us. "Dad, Pat asked if I wanted to stay with her."

His eyebrows gathered and he stopped chewing. "Whadd'jou say?"

Whadd'jou say, coming from the father, meant *how did you answer that?* It didn't mean that he hadn't heard me or hadn't understood. If he meant either of those things, he simply would have looked at me and irritably barked, "Haanh?" He had a hearing loss in his right ear from serving in World War II. I was accustomed to "Haaanh?" It was a common question in our house, even though I always thought it was a sound a constipated penguin might make.

I couldn't look at him, so I stared at my plate of something fried to the point of being inedible. I poked it with my fork. Charred filet of Johnny Jumper, maybe. "I didn't say anything to her yet." I didn't know how to ask him if he would be okay alone if I went or how to ask him if he could put a leash on Michael so it would be safe for me to stay.

"You wanna go?" he asked.

No, I thought. *This is home and you're my dad and that's my dog.*

My skin prickled as I recalled the *whomph* of ignited pigeon.

"Yeah," I said softly. "I'm gonna go."

***

I traded one plaid uniform for a different plaid uniform to start the school year. The father dropped me off every Sunday night at Pat's, and I spent the week there, then he'd pick me up Friday to go home for the weekend. There were advantages: weekends being less structured, Michael was out of the house more, which translated into fewer bruises for me. There were disadvantages: weekends being less structured, the father drank through many, if not most, of them.

Saturday night was reserved for the father to go out with his girlfriend, the one we had gotten arrested with. Michael left after dinner and stayed gone until midnight. It didn't occur to me that most parents didn't want their thirteen year olds out until after midnight. I didn't care where he was, as long as he wasn't in the house. With our heavy oak front door locked and Rusty sleeping just inside it, I would fall asleep watching the Carol Burnett show on the tiny television that I'd gotten for my birthday. The father and the girlfriend would come in after I was asleep. Sometimes I heard them return, and I woke up long enough to turn off the TV. Sometimes, if the father was still cognizant enough, he turned it off. And sometimes I woke up early the next morning to a grey test pattern because neither one of us had turned it off.

On a good weekend, the father sported hangover face and spent part of Sunday sleeping. I left him alone, getting up and going to church without waking him. On a really good weekend, he was awake when I got home, pale and grouchy and complaining his head hurt. On a bad weekend, he'd be awake and start drinking again mid-morning and be drunk long before it was time for me to go back to Pat's. It amounted to thirty five weeks of unpredictable, quick slides from a really good weekend to a really bad one, punctuated by falling asleep while Harvey Korman tried to keep a straight face on-screen with Tim Conway or Eunice argued with Mama.

Regardless of the father's condition, I had to get back to Pat's every Sunday night. I tackled the half hour drive between one home and my other home with The Emotive Father, The Amusing Father, The Angry Father, and the I've Drunk Myself

Stupid Father. On some trips, I could get in the car with The Emotive Father and reach our destination with the I've Drunk Myself Stupid Father after he stopped for several drinks on the way. To keep me guessing, different versions of the father offered different reactions to me and the circumstances, including my efforts to make sure I arrived at Pat's in one piece.

A plea for the father to keep both hands on the steering wheel could net a range of responses, from The Emotive Father's sloppy, sentimental "I lub you, how come you donwanna lib wit' me?", to The Amusing Father's "'n' mebbe a foot?", to The Angry Father's "Shuddahellup", to an unfocused glance and something unintelligible from The I've Drunk Myself Stupid Father. I didn't know how to predict how long each appearance might last before another sort of father stumbled along.

The girlfriend's presence only made things worse. Pat hated her. Michael hated her. I tolerated her because it seemed like the father really liked her. I didn't risk forming an actual allegiance with her because everyone else hated her so much and was so vocal about it. I didn't want to get caught in that. Not again.

One afternoon in the early spring, I had come home after school not feeling well. While I still had my tonsils, I caught whatever bug came down the pike and ended up with tonsillitis that took me off my feet for a week. On that day, pretty sure that's what I was getting, feeling achy and feverish, I arrived home wondering if anybody was around who I could call to check my temperature and sit with me when I climbed into bed and drifted off, which was all I wanted to do. I touched my forehead and the back of my neck. Hot. I didn't think I should call Aunt Connie—she would be home making dinner for her kids. Pat was working. So was the father. He'd be home in a couple of hours, but a couple of hours might as well be three weeks. I decided to call the father's girlfriend.

I knew she couldn't do anything. She couldn't take me to our family doctor. She **might** know how to read a thermometer. I didn't even know that for sure. But I thought maybe she could sit with me and I would put on my pajamas and try to sleep.

I didn't think it was asking a lot. When I called her, she was happy to grab the next bus and come sit with me. Problem solved. Sometimes you have to be creative when the person who normally takes care of you is gone.

Michael arrived home from school as I was hanging up the phone and demanded to know who I was talking to. I felt too sick to argue with him, so I told him.

It was like an episode from *The Flintstones*. Smoke practically billowed out of his ears and he shouted at me that I should NEVER ask her to come to our house, that she only caused trouble when she came, that he HATED her, and he NEVER wanted to be around her. He grabbed the phone receiver in one hand and my hair in the other, yelling in my ear, "Call her back! Call her back right now!"

I couldn't yell back at him. That hurt too much. But then so did the fact that he was ripping my hair out. He whacked my upper arm with the phone receiver and forced it into my hand.

"Call her! Tell her not to come here!"

Tears leaked out of the outer corners of my eyes as he twisted my hair and yanked my head backwards.

"DIAL!"

When I didn't move, he tore the receiver out of my hand and dialed Pat's work number himself.

"Pat! She just called HER and asked her to come here! Make her call her back and tell her not to come." He shoved the phone at me again.

Pat's voice was level, but calling her in the middle of her work day was hardly ideal. "Babe, did you call her?"

"Yeah," I croaked. "I'm sick."

"Call her back and tell her not to come. It's only going to cause problems."

"But I'm sick..."

I don't remember what she said in response to that but it's doubtful that she knew I was being forced into this phone call by having my hair torn out. I agreed I would call the girlfriend back and tell her not to come. When Pat hung up, I hesitated.

I must have hesitated a little too long. Michael slapped me.

The first cry escaped, rasping against my raw throat, as I gave in and dialed her phone number a second time. One ring. Two. Five. Six.

She had already left for the bus stop. I pushed the receiver back at him.

"She's gone," I choked. "I can't stop her."

He slammed the receiver down and picked up the base of the phone, holding it above my head as if to clobber me with it. I couldn't get away with him holding me by the hair. I put my arms up to protect my face and head. He flung the base away, the receiver sailing separately on its own trajectory at the end of its whirly cord. I didn't see it land because he flung me next.

He dropped on top of me, pinning me partly on my side and partly on my back, his weight pressing into me on his one leg, the other leg stretched out behind him for balance. He grabbed my hair again and cracked my head against the floor.

The bedroom carpeting had minimal padding under it, if any. The carpet pile didn't absorb much of the blow. I saw stars.

He jerked away from me. "I won't be here if she's gonna be here!" he shouted, yanking his plaid uniform tie off. "I won't!" He ripped at the buttons of his uniform shirt and ran to his own room. By the time I got off the floor, he had changed into street clothes and pounded down the steps, slamming the front door behind him.

Given that, I wasn't surprised when Pat asked that the father not bring the girlfriend to her apartment. After the blow up on the afternoon I got sick, I hesitated to mention anything about her—not to Pat, and never to Aunt Connie. Between not being able to tell Pat anything about the girlfriend, and the father directing me not to tell Pat anything about his drinking, telling her anything about my weekend visits at all got pretty tricky.

"Dad, please put both your hands on the wheel!" I said loudly from the back seat.

The I've Drunk Myself Stupid Father smiled at me vacantly in the rearview.

In that heartbeat of a moment when he took his eyes off the road and raised them to the rearview, the VW Bug ahead of us braked for a red light. The father plowed right into the back end of the Bug. I jolted forward and bounced off the back of the front seat.

"Uuuhhhohhh," the father breathed, jerkily reaching up and setting the gear shift in park.

The Bug's driver door popped open and a young guy with long hair and dirty jeans emerged. He leaned back in, gesturing to his passenger. With his interior light on, I could see it, a "take it easy" patting gesture. He approached our door quickly.

The father fumbled around and unlatched the door. As he stood up, the young guy said, "Man, are you drunk? You been drinking? Are you shittin' me?"

The father started to answer but the young guy drew back a fist and punched the father in the face, a solid, head-rocking blow.

"Dad!" I bellowed, helpless, from the back of the Torino. I reached for the lever on the driver's seat to get out. I probably felt that punch more than he did, since he had essentially anesthetized his brain and was hovering in the version of father just before The Passed Out Father.

The guy grabbed the father by the shirt and jacked him up against the car, closing the driver's door with the ever-handy father and cutting off my exit route. "You're drunk?!" he yelled. "Man, my wife is pregnant! If you hurt her, I swear to Christ, I will KILL you!"

I couldn't hear a word the father said. Ahead of us, a very pregnant young woman emerged awkwardly from the Bug and waddled in our direction. She, too, spoke to the guy holding the father up on his toes, his behind against the driver's window. Eventually, the guy released his hold on the father's shirt, and they exchanged some kind of paper. Was it cash? Was it insurance information? Both? I couldn't be sure. Then the guy and his very pregnant wife returned to their Bug and drove away.

When we got to Pat's a while later, I censored myself all that night and the entire week. I didn't want to mention that the girlfriend had been with us. I couldn't tell her, upon pain of death as threatened by the father, about the accident or the father getting his lights punched out in front of me. As it turned out, watching him get his lights punched out that time ended up being practice anyway.

One weekend, Pat sent me home with a request to the father to take me shopping for new school shoes. I could have predicted that this would not go well, but no one asked. It was a slippery slope weekend, and I started out shopping with The Amusing Father but ended up at the shoe store with The Angry Father.

I wondered regularly if The Angry Father was actually angry **at** me, or if he was angry because he had to spend money on things I needed rather than on alcohol. He told me frequently that he didn't have money to buy me new clothes or the kind of sneakers I really wanted. But he always had money to drink and since we had had the run-in with Bug Guy, I suspected some money was also shelled out to cover up his under-the-influence fender benders.

Once inside the store, The Angry Father picked out a pair of shoes that were about the ugliest things I'd ever seen. They were also the least expensive shoes in the store. I told him I didn't like them.

"Tough shit. Ya think I'm made o'money?" He gestured at the salesman. "Get dose out here."

The clerk scurried away.

"Don' run yermouth," he said. "Siddown."

I sat.

The clerk returned with the box. According to the size on the side of the box, they should have fit fine, but they didn't. They were too small. The clerk had to shoehorn and push to get my foot in. They pinched and rubbed against my little toes.

Relieved because I didn't like them to start with, I said, "Dad, they don't fit."

"Bullshit! Don' lie t'me!"

I looked up as the clerk glanced away and refused to make eye contact with me.

"I'm not lying! They don't fit. Ask him!"

The clerk looked supremely uncomfortable. Blood crept up his neck and colored his face.

The father snatched up the box. "You don' like 'em—that's the problem!" He shoved the box at the clerk. "Ring 'em up!"

"Dad—"

"Keep it up! Imma smack you right indamouff!"

Where to go with this? I looked from The Angry Father to the clerk. I was not imagining this—the shoes didn't fit. The clerk all but ran for the cash register to ring us up and get us out of the store.

I put those shoes on and walked to school every day. They slowly wore the toenails right off the ends of my little toes, making them look like two bald little old men. I contemplated putting tiny dots on them to resemble eyes but decided Magic Marker on bloody skin probably wasn't my smartest move. The father had told Pat I didn't like them and that was why I was complaining about them. I didn't bother to complain.

***

It was a Friday in spring during the window of time between coming home from school and the father arriving to pick me up. Bobby's dad had come to get him for their weekend visit already, so I waited alone. The phone rang. Surprised, I picked it up, thinking it might be Pat with last minute requests about the weekend. I was even more surprised to realize it was Michael.

"Daddy's not there yet, right?" He sounded wired.

"No."

Why would he call me? I didn't want to talk to him in person when there were no alternatives.

"I have to tell you something."

"What?"

"Rusty died."

My stomach flipped just for a second until it occurred to me that Michael would say something like that just to get a reaction from me. "No, she didn't!"

"Yes, she did! She died yesterday."

I couldn't decipher the tone of his voice. Was he...happy? It sure wasn't the voice of someone who was sad or upset. This was a bad joke.

"I don't believe you. Leave me alone." I hung up on him. But doubts nagged. Could Rusty really be gone? She was fine when I left on Sunday. No, this was a joke; just Michael's awful sense of humor. But still...could it be?

When the father arrived, he came into the kitchen where I sat at the table underneath the wall phone. I didn't turn around to face him, didn't look up.

"Did it happen?" I asked. "Is Rusty dead?"

He stopped in his tracks. "Yeah," he said just as quietly. "She's dead."

"She was okay last weekend. What happened?"

"She got a cold, and it went to her brain."

What the hell did that mean? She was only five. And who got a cold in their brain?

And then...the image of oozing blistered pigeon invaded. *WHOMPH!*

My throat constricted. I traced a pointless pattern on the table surface. Did Michael...? The father patted the back of my shoulder with one clumsy hand. I didn't move.

What did he do to her? The flipping sensation in my stomach resumed. Why had he called me an hour before the father arrived to tell me what –in anyone else's family—would be terrible news? And why did he sound happy about it? Cold in her brain? No! What really happened? I tried to shut down the image of Rusty's smooth brown and white fur suit scorched and smoldering.

Did she scream? Did anyone try to help?

Why wasn't I there for her?

***

I knew I had to go home. The combination of not knowing what really happened to Rusty, plus the weekly conversations with The Emotive Father in which I repeatedly had to explain to him why I wasn't living at home were troubling. On top of that, as it had been that first Christmas morning when Pat took us to her apartment and I wondered who would make his dinner, the guilt was huge that I was making him so sad.

He gazed at me over half a beer with big, brown, dejected puppy dog eyes, propping his chin in his hand. "Huccomb you don' wanna lib at home wi'me?"

The first question was always the easy one. "'Cause of Michael," I told him, every time.

"You could come home. If youjus' leab him alone, he'll leab you alone."

"I DO leave him alone. I hate him."

"He's yerbrudder. You don' really hate 'im."

I knew I did so I usually didn't reply to that. After running this course a few times, I could script the conversation from memory.

"Will you come home soon? I needjou der."

Mostly the best answer was that I'd be coming home again the very next weekend, but I knew that wasn't what he meant. He signaled the server to bring him another beer and me another Coke. My teeth were already floating but I didn't object.

"Der's nobody to take care ob da house."

"I can help when I'm there."

That wasn't the answer he wanted either.

He reached across the scarred wooden table and put his hand over mine. "Don' you lub me anymore?"

I hated this question. It didn't matter what I said—it wouldn't be right. It wasn't even fathomable that I might tell him I didn't love him. He was my dad. But if I told him I loved him, he went right back to the question about why I wasn't living with him and taking care of the house. When my silence stretched on, he approached it from his other favorite angle. Going in for the kill? Wait for it. Wait for it!

"If you lub me, you'll come home."

There it was. If we were having this exchange in our dining room, I could try to change topics. I could get up and bring him another beer myself or tell him I had to do something and then disappear. It was harder here in one of his favorite bars. I had no escape, so I just had to sit there and watch him cry, literally, into his new beer.

At my other home, Pat kept assuring me that she wouldn't make me stay if I didn't want to. She insisted it was up to me, that I could make the choice to stay with her or go back to the father's. The father wouldn't force me to come home. He said he wouldn't force me to do anything I didn't want to do.

I didn't feel forced. Exactly. I didn't actually have a word for how I felt, sitting across a tavern table from him in gloomy lighting and watching him cry. Even before Rusty died, I had already been leaning in the direction of going back to his house. Once the specter of what Michael might be capable of glided out of the shadows, I couldn't waver. I had to go home. What if something happened to the father and I wasn't there? The thought terrified me. I had to be there, if for no other reason than I had to watch out for him. I couldn't defend him. I couldn't even defend myself when Michael came at me, but I could watch out. That had to be better than being half an hour away.

One Sunday over the winter, the father dropped me off at Pat's according to the normal schedule, hugging me goodbye outside as was the request at that moment. When I went inside, I found out that Bobby hadn't returned from his weekend with his dad, so it was just Pat and me at home for a couple of hours. I don't remember what prompted it but I remember Pat's observation.

"You're so somber, Nance. You're so serious all the time…"

I couldn't tell her how much effort it took to constantly censor myself. I couldn't let anything slip out that the father had demanded my silence on. I could never bring up a topic that I knew would upset her or discuss the fact that everything was upside down and weird since the mother died and we never talked about her.

She sat down on the couch and pulled me down next to her, hugging me to her side. "Before Mommy died," she said, "I told her I would take care of you. I'm trying, babe. I'm really trying, but I can't make you talk to me and I can't make you stay here…" Her voice broke.

I looked up. Tears streamed from both her eyes.

"I know something's not right," she continued, sounding unsteady. "What's wrong, babe?"

I bit my lip. She squeezed my shoulders a little tighter.

"It's okay. You can tell me."

Obviously she didn't know that it had been repeatedly shouted at me that I should never tell her. I hesitated.

"It wouldn't be like this if Mommy was still here?" she ventured a guess.

That was true. I nodded.

"You know I want you to stay with me?"

I nodded again, feeling like an absolute traitor against the father. I tilted my head back so I could look into her eyes again.

"What, babe? What is it?"

"I miss Mommy." That was all I could get out. That was all that was allowable, and even that felt a little risky. I wanted to rant, "And I can't tell you what happens when I go home, and I can't tell you that Daddy thinks I don't love him because I live here, and I only live here because Michael hurts me, and I can't tell you that either!" All I got out was, "I miss Mommy."

She nodded, tears running faster. "Me too, babe." She pulled me closer, resting her cheek on my head. I tucked my head and choked on all I couldn't tell her, including that now I was a huge disappointment to the father.

***

I never asked the father any more questions about Rusty. Her bowl and collar were gone by the time he brought me home that day, as if she had never been part of our family, as if we hadn't shared holidays with her and fed her people food when no one was looking and taken her to the park to run without her leash on. She was simply gone, along with the stub of this year's squeaky pork chop, and the father reassured me with his standard, "It'll be okay, Boo. Don't cry."

I told the father before the end of the school year that I would come back home. His initial response was warm; he was glad to hear it. Not too long after, though, he told me it would help him a whole lot if I would go to Mississippi for part of the summer to be with Chick and Jedda.

"But I thought you wanted me to come home?"

"I do. But it'll be too hard during the summer with you and Michael home alone."

"I'll just go to Aunt Connie's every day. I don't want to go away for the summer."

"Haaanh?"

"I said I don't want to go away."

"It won't be long."

Confused, I wasn't sure what to say. Hadn't I done the right thing by saying I would come home? Hadn't this been what he had asked about for so many months? So I was coming home, and he was sending me away again? And not even to Pat's, where I could see him on the weekends and go to Aunt Connie's house to play. Mississippi was hours and hours away. The only upside I saw was at least I'd have more time away from Michael.

"I'll make the plane reservations for you and Michael."

I sank down in the car seat. Would the good news ever stop?

One Mississippi...Two Mississippi

Chick had bought a boat. This changed everything about a visit to Monkey's Eyebrows, Mississippi, where I understood pretty much nothing that was said to me for eight straight weeks. Whereas the people I'd met in Hampton drawled, the people I met in Mississippi seemed to speak another language altogether, but who cared when there was a boat in the car port?

We arrived in late June. I immediately wilted from the heat and began making comparisons to when I had stayed in Virginia. Hampton had had bees and crickets and cicadas. Mississippi had lizards and enormous Gulf state cockroaches that popped out unexpectedly when you opened the shower curtain, or the garage door, or the linen closet. The lizards were tolerable, even cute, and they stayed outside. But those giant roaches were another story. I half expected one of them to greet me wearing a bandana around his forehead, wave and thank me for my contribution before making off with my socks. Taking a shower and opening the closet door to get a towel became an aerobic game of peek-a-boo, when I would –quick, quick!—fling the door open, and –quick, quick!—shake the curtain or the door to discourage wild life, and then—quick, quick!—jump back about three feet in case someone had been home who was now skittering around free range on the bathroom floor. These steps had to be followed at all times because the wild life was known to make an occasional appearance in the shower with you if you didn't rouse them and escort them to the county line beforehand and NOTHING was worse than coming nose to nose with a giant cockroach hanging on the shower curtain when you were all sudsed up and unarmed. What was I supposed to do then? Wash his hair for him?

Every Saturday and Sunday before dawn, we hooked the boat trailer up to Chick's Toyota and dragged it to the back bay and Chick took his two older kids, His and Hers, Michael and me out onto the bay to fish. Occasionally he took us out in the

Gulf of Mexico where we caught mackerel and snapper and sometimes poisonous eels instead of flounder and mullet. Jedda stayed home with their sixteen-month-old son, Ours, and every afternoon when we came back, we'd clean a pile of fish and Chick started the grill.

In early July, Chick took the four of us to see the new movie everyone talked about called *Jaws*. Things were going well until the scene in the movie when Brody and Hooper are out on the water at night and the whole theater was dark and creepy. They find Ben Gardiner's boat, and Hooper puts on a wetsuit and goes under the boat to investigate.

I sat there thinking that if I found a boat floating around in the middle of nowhere where a boat is not supposed to be, I'd probably go on the boat and look around before I threw myself in the water underneath it. But I didn't write *Jaws*, so I tried to go along for the ride. When that bald head with the mangled eye popped out of the ripped boat hull, my nephew, His, was definitely not going along for the ride with me. With popcorn in one hand and a Coke in the other, when that head popped out, His screamed and threw both his popcorn and his Coke over his shoulders, drenching the people behind us.

It was one of those episodes that can make you snort soda right through your nose and give you the giggles for twenty minutes. Chick was less than amused (probably because the guy in the next row threatened to kick his ass) and he swore at us most of the way home. When we got there, he demanded we go to bed right away. He needed a break from all of us. By that time, His was fully convinced a shark was in the closet, and he couldn't sleep in his room.

I was less worried about sharks in the closets than I was about giant cockroaches. I changed into some pajamas as Chick shouted and slammed things in His' room, trying to prove that no shark was in the closet. At the far end of the hall in Hers' room, I lay on my pile of blankets thinking, you're doing it wrong—it's open the door quick quick, shake it quick quick, and then jump out of the way quick quick!

Either way, if I had been a shark in the closet, I would have been afraid of Chick. Jedda said good night from the doorway and clicked off the light.

***

We had been home in shark-free Philadelphia just a few days and according to the father, Michael and I were supposed to be able to get through this short stretch of time before school started without getting ourselves into trouble. That was the plan anyway.

I went to the cellar to switch some laundry over. The cellar stairs ran along the north wall in the middle of the room. An old Hoosier cabinet stood at the bottom, a remnant of the house's previous kitchen. I shifted wet laundry into the dryer at the back of the cellar and on my second trip with my arms full, Michael bounded down the steps to wait for me by the old cabinet, grinning, hands behind his back.

Uh oh. Talk about a shark in the closet.

Whatever this was, it wasn't good. I dragged out the laundry process, not wanting to go near him. He waited without speaking, still with his hands behind his back. I considered ironing something. I didn't have anything to fold yet—it had just gone into the dryer. I considered going outside through the cellar door so I could re-enter the house upstairs but I wasn't sure the kitchen door was unlocked. It was five steps up to ground level, another five to the kitchen. Could I get up those steps before Michael could make up the interior steps to greet me at the door? If I locked myself out, he was not going to let me back in. I'd be stuck with no shoes, no lunch and no bathroom until the father came home. My other option was to walk barefoot down the alley, over the broken beer and soda bottles and rusted nails littering the alley floor and through the puddles of urine at the end to get to Aunt Connie's, where I'd spend the afternoon picking green and brown slivers of glass out of the soles of my feet. It was hard to tell which he'd find funnier, locking me out or making me bleed.

"You can go up," he said, grinning again. "I won't do anything."

I didn't believe him.

"Really. You can go."

I deliberated. Run for the door? Try to get upstairs without getting hurt? Slowly, I took a step in his direction. He just stood there. I took another step.

He moved one hand from behind him and gestured at the stairs as if to say, "Go right ahead!"

I closed in. At the bottom, I had to make a hundred and eighty degree turn as I passed him. The moment I did, he slammed me into the wall. My bare feet momentarily left the cool concrete floor. I whacked my head and his weight squashed the air out of my lungs. He wrapped his arms around me, pinning one of my arms between me and the wall. The other one was caught under his. Both of his hands closed over my face, the pinch familiar as he cut off my air supply by closing my nose with one hand and clamping the other one over my mouth. My knuckles scraped raw against the wall's rough surface trying to force a path to my face where I might pry a finger or two loose so I could breathe.

I don't know exactly how he managed it. I wouldn't have thought his hands were big enough, but he worked the hand that was clamped over my mouth upward until he could use the same one to pinch my nose closed. His other hand snaked behind him, scrabbling across gadgets on the Hoosier's shelf where he had set a small brown bottle and its lid. He pinned me flat to the wall with his forearm and elbow. Laughing, he shifted and swept the bottle up under my nose as he released the pinch holding it closed.

I sucked air in a desperate, pained snort, registering the odd metallic chemical odor coming from the bottle but unaware of its pending impact. My heart jackhammered. The room swam out of focus. My eyes started to roll back in my head and my knees gave out.

Michael helped me slide down the wall until I was in a heap on the cold concrete, with my head propped against the cabinet. The floor tilted and the walls funneled inward. He screwed the lid back onto the little bottle and sat down on his weight bench to watch, still laughing.

It passed quickly, whatever it was. When my brain could talk to my legs again, I sat up further, cringing against the wall.

"Howdja like that?" he asked.

"I didn't! What did you do?"

"The question is, what did *you* do?" He laughed again. "You just did Rush."

I scrubbed my hand back and forth over my nose, trying to get rid of the chemical smell. "I did not!"

"Yeah, you did! Whaddya think Daddy'll say about that? He's gonna be really pissed off at you!"

With focused effort, I was able to peel my head off the side of the cabinet. "But I didn't do anything."

"Did you breathe that in?"

"Well, yeah, but-"

"Then you did it."

I got to my feet slowly, holding on to the wall. The last thing the father had said was to stay out of trouble. I really doubted that sniffing drugs was what he had in mind.

***

The father met Marie that year. When Michael and I came back from Mississippi so I could start the fifth grade, his other girlfriend was notably absent. Not that I raised questions. That was definitely a let sleeping dogs lie situation.

"I met a lady-friend," he told me. "Her name is Marie and she wants to meet you."

Did it matter if I didn't really want to meet her? The last one was a disaster. Couldn't it just be us for a while? Not only had she been a disaster, but she'd been brought onto the scene just a couple of weeks after Michael and I had come back from Hampton—less than four months after the mom-sicle in a box was deposited at the cemetery. *Why didn't someone tell me she would be cold?*

I was never sure how much of that summer the first girlfriend had been around. The thought that the father had started dating only weeks after the mother's death weirded me out. He was moving on. I had turned eight that July and I just wanted my mom back. Sitting cross-legged in the recliner and facing the father now, I was acutely aware that my feelings on **that** topic hadn't changed a whole lot in two years. Of course, I said none of this out loud, looking at his hopeful, expectant expression.

"Where'd you meet her?" is what I said out loud.

Not a bar. Please don't say a bar.

"At the string band bar. We were listening to string band music."

I'm sure you were, I thought. *And downing …what…ten or twelve beers?*

"She has a daughter who's just a year older than you."

Great! We'll be the Brady Bunch! Did you tell her you have a son who's a total psycho?

Out loud I said, "Where do they live?"

He told me. It was twenty three blocks or roughly half an hour from us, and her daughter went to a Catholic school I hadn't heard of. I asked a couple more guarded questions, not because I wanted to know the answers, but I wanted ammunition to stop this in its tracks if I could. I didn't find any.

When I met Marie the following weekend, I was surprised when it started off okay. Unlike the first girlfriend, she didn't call me inappropriate names. She called me Nance. The first one had used terms of affection too soon to feel real—names the mother had once used, and were now used by Pat and Aunt Connie but to which she had no ground to lay claim.

She and the father watched a movie on HBO. Her daughter, Mary, and I watched something else on the tiny TV in my room and talked about our schools and movies we liked. On a commercial break, we started toward the stairs to get drinks, and I came to a standstill on the top step. From that angle, we could see into the living room below, where our respective parental units were…**oh no they were NOT**…making out on the couch, their untouched highballs on the end table steadily diluted by melting ice. I backed up and bumped into Mary, not sure if I should laugh or gouge my own eyes out.

Behind me, Mary began to giggle. Okay. We could handle this. I leaned over the railing and called, "Ahhh ha! Caught ya!"

The father and Marie split apart as if poked with hot irons, Marie laughing and the father looking disoriented and disheveled. Mary and I continued down the stairs.

"Sooo...." I said slowly, wagging my head back and forth. "What are you guys up to?"

Marie laughed harder. The father clearly wanted to disappear into the floor.

"Not to interrupt or anything," I said, meaning very much to interrupt.

"Nance," Marie announced, "you're a pain in my tomatoes."

True to South Philly, that last word came out as "tuhmayduhz".

"Marie," I said, equally serious, "where exactly do you keep your tomatoes?"

The father groaned.

Marie laughed out loud. "Ahhh...you're a real wiseass..." And she nodded at me, her eyes crinkling at the corners.

"Thank you."

***

The father said things would be different this year. Michael started high school. We wouldn't keep the same schedule or walk the same route to school anymore. He wouldn't come home for lunch. I don't know that the father had any specific plan for making things different. Wishful thinking on his part? He wasn't entirely wrong. Things **were** different starting that year, but probably not what he had in mind.

It was apparent early on that Marie wasn't the kind of drinker the father was. She might have one drink, maybe two, while they spent a Friday evening at our house. When she and the father went out on Saturday nights, she was almost always sober when they came home. Plus, she loudly and frequently expressed her disinterest in spending time with the I've Drunk Myself Stupid Father.

With his every weekend drinking routine now frowned upon, the father stayed sober for a few consecutive weekends, building up a little more each week toward blow outs that turned into entire weeks, staying drunk from Friday until the following Sunday. Each ten day stretch cycled through all of the various configurations of father, and time meant nothing to him with his days and nights mixed up.

As a freshman in high school, Michael smoked marijuana daily, having graduated from raiding the medicine cabinet for cold medication and inhalants like whatever was in that little brown bottle. Never the greatest student and —I suspect now—probably trying to get through school with an undiagnosed learning disability that caused him to struggle with writing and spelling, Michael treated the binges as personal invitations to take those weeks off and hang on the corner outside Dean's Bar. He usually put the pressure on me by Sunday afternoon.

"Don't set your clock tomorrow morning."

"I have to go to school."

"We're not going."

"I don't want to miss anything."

He slammed the fridge door shut and wheeled around on me. "Don't set your clock!"

"But-"

It rarely got any further than that.

Michael shoved me and I collided with the edge of the dining room table. He closed his hand around my neck and forced me toward the floor, where I landed less than gracefully, arms and legs in a tangle. He kicked me with the inside of his foot. The warning shot hurt, but I knew from experience that it hurt a lot less than when he kicked me straight on, toes out. He planted a knee in my back, wrapped his hands in my hair and pushed my head against the floor, raking back and forth so my forehead scraped the rough carpet. The brush burn started after only a couple of scrapes, and I clawed at the rug to find a hold.

The father snorted from the couch.

"Say it! You won't set your clock! You're not going to school!"

I had no direction to turn away. I curled my hands over his and dug my fingernails in. He yelped, his hands suddenly slick with his own blood. He let go of my hair on one side, yanking his arm upward so I lost my grip, and then he pried my other fingers loose. Now I was flat on the floor, and he was on my back like a jockey. He grabbed at my hands, one at a time, trapping them under his knees. He started rubbing against me.

"Get off me!" I yelled.

The father stirred. I wondered if I could yell loud enough to wake him. If I did, would he be able to help? Before the help stage, he'd have to get to the ambulatory stage. Maybe he wouldn't even be able to stand up. That wasn't unheard of.

Michael laughed, rocking against my back. My cheek ground into the floor, driven by his forearm against the back of my skull.

"Ow! Ow! Ow! Okay!" I gave in. "I won't! Just get off me!"

***

After having my face abraded on the carpet two or three times, I didn't argue anymore. If the father was still passed out on Sunday afternoon, I assumed we'd take part or all of the week off. I never understood why Michael demanded that I miss school too. It wasn't like he was dying to spend an afternoon with me. I couldn't get away from him fast enough. He never offered an explanation. He could make me do this. Maybe that was the only reason. This was just his freshman year. I lost track of how many weeks of school we ultimately skipped out on.

On top of missing for this reason, I continued to wrestle with various throat infections that also took a bite out of my time at school. Like the weeks when the father was too drunk to string a sentence together, when I missed school because I was sick, I was a sitting duck when Michael came home.

***

    I dozed in the recliner, wearing ill-fitting pajamas and wrapped in the fuzzy green blanket that I swiped from the father's bed. I lost track of time, foggy with fever, shivering with chills. I wasn't the greatest with the thermometer, but I thought it had said 102. I fell asleep again after lunch with a cup of tea cooling on the table beside me, crowded together with a bottle of nose drops, my glasses, a few crumpled tissues and some toast crusts that had been too hard to swallow. My left foot poked out of the bottom of the blanket, hanging off the recliner's footrest. Everything ached.

    The first time I opened my eyes, the TV offered blurred black and white reruns of some 1960s sitcom. I was alone. I drifted. The next time I opened my eyes, Michael had come in on a draft of cold outside air, shrugging out his jacket and draping it on the back of a dining room chair. Blink.

    It must have been a long blink. Maybe I drifted off for another few minutes. When my eyes opened next, Michael stood a couple of feet from the end of the recliner, twirling something between his hands. Without my glasses, I couldn't tell what it might be. He hadn't spoken a word. My weighted eyelids lowered again.

    When the wet kitchen towel snapped against the arch of my bare foot, pain rocketed up my leg and catapulted me awake. The shriek that jumped out of me felt like it ripped about six—no, ten—layers of skin from inside my raw throat. I howled, clutching my foot to my chest and writhing.

    Michael erupted into laughter. "You should see…you never saw it…Awww, that face you made!" He doubled over, hands on his thighs, the towel hanging harmlessly along his shin.

    Helpless, angry tears coursed down my face. My throat hurt too much to yell again. Desolate, I tightened the blanket around me, pulling it to my chin, ducking my head so I didn't have to look at him. How could I get away? If I made a move to stand up, he would be on me. I waited for the blows to start.

Michael threw the wet towel at me. It hit me in the head and landed with a plop on the fuzzy blanket. "Never saw it comin'," he repeated, still chuckling.

I cringed under the green fuzz pile, my foot still clasped between my hands. Hadn't I become aware of this years before? How could I forget Lesson Number Two? Never close your eyes. Or, if I listened to the father, I would know that if I **just left him alone, he wouldn't do those things!**

***

By the end of that school year, I don't know if the father believed his own advice as much anymore, although it didn't change the way he shouted it at me every time I mentioned that Michael had hurt me. He had no interest in and no patience for my whining, as he put it. Once in a while, he reminded me that tough guys don't cry, a variation on his message of how everything would be okay if I simply gave no indication that anything hurt me. Ever. For any reason.

I could say those beatings were the exception, but that would not be accurate. The bruises usually ended up somewhere covered by my clothes. If he hit me in the face, he opened his fist so it didn't leave marks. That changed later but in the beginning, he did make an effort to hide the marks. The locations of bruises and bumps that were harder to control were the ones I acquired when he hit me, and I bounced off something else. Maybe if I'd paid attention to those trajectories, I would be better at playing pool, but I usually closed my eyes before the crash.

He scared me. I hated him. The beatings followed a routine that I could predict. He arrived home from school half an hour before I did. When I got home, the "pre-game show" started when he blocked me from going to my room to change out of my uniform. Or having gotten changed, he blocked me from leaving the house.

Then the vile name calling started. I couldn't respond to it in kind. I learned early that if I responded similarly, it was what he was waiting for. It justified his hitting me because I had disrespected him. Girls shouldn't talk that way to boys, he informed me repeatedly. Obviously, girls were put on the planet for the specific purpose of being denigrated.

Unable to make a passage through the house and being degraded, I had a choice. I could stand still and let him berate me, or I could try to push my way through. If I attempted to push my way through, all bets were off and I was on the ground in seconds with him on top of me. If I stood there and said nothing, eventually he began to push me.

The pushing always started with one hand. They were little pushes, clearly not meant to hurt me. They were meant to annoy, to get a reaction. The pushes took me right back to the original choice: power through or stand here and let it happen. It was going to happen one way or the other.

If using one hand didn't get us to the next level, eventually he shoved a little harder and started using both hands. Again I was back to the original choice. Do I stand here and take this or try to push my way out of it?

We cycled through this nearly every day for too many months to count. It almost always ended in the same way when the urge to protect myself overrode everything else. The moment I put my hands up, Michael had all he was looking for. When you are hit in the head hard enough, you really do see stars.

***

I didn't actively consider returning to Mississippi until late in fifth grade when we crossed another threshold of who could attack whom. The father started drinking Friday night. By Saturday afternoon, he was well on his way to becoming The I've Drunk Myself Stupid Father, and I was in my room, wondering what, if anything, we had in the fridge that I could have for dinner. He wouldn't have dinner—eating was unnecessary for him during these stretches. Since he'd begun drinking yesterday, he also hadn't gone to the supermarket. I thought there were still some Reese's peanut butter cups on the fridge door.

I didn't hear what Michael said to the father that got the ball rolling. When Michael's voice started to rise, I turned the volume down on my tiny TV to listen. Ahh. Michael was going out and wanted money. I sort of believed the father when he mumbled that he didn't have any. He never had any when I asked for something, especially not when he was drinking.

Michael demanded again, louder.

The father mumbled.

"Then gimme your wallet!" Michael snarled.

That was met with an indecipherable comment, but I took it to be refusal from the tone.

"Gimme your fucking wallet!" Michael shouted.

"Heeeeyyyyyyyyyyyy!!!" the father objected.

The next sound was skin hitting skin and I thought for a split second that the father had hit Michael ("Shuddahellup! Immasmackyouinnamouff!") but the stumbling sound that followed was too big. The body associated with that was a larger person than Michael. I recognized the audible grunt when the body went down. Michael had hit the father.

I bounced off the bed, my breathing suddenly constricted, and went to the top of the stairs so I could see what was going on in the living room below.

"I'm not askin'," Michael said. "I'm goin' out. Gimme your wallet."

The father had landed on the couch in a sprawl. When he didn't answer right away because he was either too drunk or too surprised, Michael grabbed him by the hair and shook his head. The father groaned loudly. He'd had so much to drink already, I was sure he could barely keep the room in focus without having someone shaking his head around.

"Get off him!" I yelled, propelled down the stairs by my anger.

Michael barely glanced at me. "Gitouttahere."

Wild-eyed, I searched the room for something to hit Michael with or throw at him, something that would hurt. I grabbed a small statue of the Blessed Mother from the hutch, whirled around and heaved it at Michael's head.

Unfortunately, I was not the world's most athletic child. The statue sank steadily on its course and hit Michael on the back of his shoulder instead of on the head. He shifted, grunted and slapped the father across the face. The father's hands flew up to protect himself, except where Michael was holding him by the hair. Michael pushed him over sideways and snatched his wallet out of his pocket. He let him go, took what few dollars he found in the wallet, closed it and flicked it at the father with a twist of his wrist. He started to laugh.

"Hey, thaaaanks, Cholley-O." He reached down and patted the father on the shoulder. The father moaned.

To me, he said, "Nice try," and he walked out.

The father's shoulders shook. It took me a few seconds to realize he was crying and I thought I might cry with him. I approached him quietly and sat on the floor in front of the couch where he was still sprawled. I put one hand on his side and patted him gently.

He cried himself to sleep, with me sitting right there with him. I had peanut butter cups for dinner and Gulf state cockroaches were all of a sudden not as scary as they had been last summer.

The Road to Delaware

I didn't wait to be told. "Dad, I wanna spend the summer at Chick's."

"Haaaahh?" He glanced at me over the top of the daily paper.

"I said I wanna spend the summer at Chick's."

"Oh." He folded the paper and sighed. It sounded disgusted. "Why? What happened now?"

"I just wanna go."

"Because of Michael?" he asked.

You have to ask?

"Well...yeah."

"Leave the week after school is done?"

"That would be okay."

"You're gonna miss us."

"I'll miss you," I offered.

"Nah. You'll see. You'll miss Michael once you're gone."

Not bloody likely. I figured it was a joke because I didn't want to believe he could be so dense.

***

I had my own room at Chick's. His son (His) was away all summer. My arrival had a distinctly different feel to it this year, since I was the one who had asked to be here. My flight arrived late in the evening, and Jedda sat with me in the kitchen over some sweetened coffee-flavored drink and wanted me to catch her up on new stuff at home. I carefully avoided saying anything about Michael hitting the father. Without the father ever having said anything, I knew that topic fell into the category of things that ("For Chrissake!") we don't talk about in public.

Even without me saying anything about Michael pummeling the father, I quickly clued into some sentiment around the house about me not returning to Philadelphia. Nothing was said in front of me intentionally, but I noticed that when I'd walk into a room and catch the end of one of Jedda's sentences, "...and how can we send her back there?"...the conversation would come to a screeching halt. I wouldn't know for many years that these conversations were first debates between Chick and Jedda and then plans to approach the father and ask him to surrender custody of me so that I could live with them full time. I also wouldn't know that before they ever broached the topic with the father, Pat had already gone round and round with him and been refused. He wasn't going to just give me up, and if they thought so, they had another think comin'.

***

Every Saturday and Sunday started the same way. Chick woke me before dawn with a quick shake and a "C'mon, Boo, let's go fishin'," and I popped out of bed to make a peanut butter sandwich to take with me. Except for when we stopped to pick up bait, we drifted around the bay all morning and most of the afternoon. He showed me how to tie on leaders and bait the hooks with shrimp. He had plenty of opportunity to ask me about the father or Michael, but once settled, we just sat quietly with our lines in the water. I kept my eyes on the end of the fishing rod and said nothing.

The Montreal Summer Olympics started about a week before my birthday. Jedda's daughter (Hers) went to Georgia to visit family for two weeks, leaving me with Chick, Jedda and their youngest son, reducing "his, hers, ours and theirs" to just "ours and theirs." Chick did a lot of meetings that summer too, so Jedda and I spent our evenings on the living room floor with a bowl of popcorn, watching the competitions after Ours went to sleep. That was the year Nadia Comaneci swept female gymnastics and occasionally I overheard Jedda on the phone, talking about chasing someone named Jenner through the woods in a loincloth. When she realized I could hear her, that conversation, too, came to a screeching halt and a stilted replacement was immediately dragged into play. I guessed that was the Southern equivalent to, "Hey, how about those

Phillies?" It was a good summer, the first one since the mother died, until the end of July.

***

The Olympics were still underway and the East Coast had yet to be terrorized by the Son of Sam murders when the evening news carried the first reports of people falling ill in Philadelphia. Men who had attended the American Legion convention over the week of my birthday were being hospitalized with flu-like symptoms, and people were talking about pneumonia. By the first week in August, several men had died. The Bellevue-Stratford Hotel, the convention site, had been closed, and the news anchors talked about the city bracing for an all-out epidemic.

The father was in Philadelphia, ground zero for what the people were calling the most dangerous virus we'd seen in generations. I watched for signs of discomfort from Chick and Jedda. Nothing indicated that they might be worried. When the news bulletins said that the convention attendees had gotten sick, my ears perked up. When, within a few days, the bulletins changed to report that the men were hospitalized with fevers up to 107 degrees and no one understood what this was or how they had gotten sick, I started to get a little nervous. When they started dying one right after the other, I thought I would come unhinged.

I tapped on the doorframe of the master bathroom where Jedda was doing her makeup. "Jedda, can I call my dad tonight?"

She paused, drawing the eye liner away from her eye, and looked at me in the mirror. "What do you need, babe?"

"I just wanna call my dad."

"You just talked to Dad over the weekend."

"But can I call him again?"

Her eyebrows furrowed a little. "Why?"

"I just wanna talk to him." I couldn't say it out loud. I had to know if he was alive. I was so far away. What if he got sick? What if he got suddenly so sick he wouldn't even be able to call Marie? Or me? How would we know? Michael wouldn't help him, of that I was sure. What if right now, that minute, he was being taken to some hospital? Those other guys...had they had a chance to call their families? They were leaving a convention where they probably...I don't know...watched the Olympics and did whatever American Legionnaires did at conventions and then they were sick and then they were dead. It was very simple. And it was very fast. I remembered clearly how things had gone when the mother went into the hospital. She had a good day and then BOOM—she was gone the next day. I couldn't take this chance. I had to check on him.

"I don't think so, babe. You'd have to call him after eleven. Why don't we just wait until this weekend?" Perched on the edge of the sink, with one foot on the floor and one knee on the vanity, she swiveled halfway around so she could look directly at me.

"But..." I didn't know how to tell her how afraid I was. She would tell me I was being stupid. Chick would for sure. I could see no worry on her face. But he wasn't her father! "Please?" I asked.

"We'll do it this weekend, I promise."

I wanted to grab her sleeve and plead, throw myself on the floor and scream until she said yes. What if he got dressed this morning and packed up his thermal underwear like always and never made it to work? What if his thermal underwear, that he had had to fold himself because I wasn't there to help, was abandoned in its wrinkled paper bag in the parking lot of the refrigerated warehouse where he worked, and he was collapsed beside his car, sick and helpless? Didn't she understand that nobody else was watching out for him? That was my job.

"I'm fixin' to run out soon. Y'all ready to go?" she asked, changing the subject entirely.

It took a second to focus on what she had asked, caught as I was in my distress over the father's whereabouts. "Oh. Yeah. I guess."

"Good. Get me a Coke, would ya, babe? I'm just gonna finish puttin' on my face and we'll go. I can't go to the BX with all my ugly hangin' out." She swiveled back toward the mirror.

I nodded. Yes, I'd get her a Coke. I was not agreeing to this weekend being okay with me as good timing to call the father.

Six men were reported dead that night on the news. Over a hundred more were reported sick, with no word on the other estimated ten thousand attendees or of who else might be infected with this mystery disease. We sat at the dining room table, Chick, Jedda, Hers, and Ours in his booster chair, with the six o'clock news droning softly a few feet away. I shot Chick a glance. He showed no reaction. I looked over at Jedda. No reaction. I choked back fear and choked down dinner. They may not have been connected. Jedda was the first to admit she was not a good cook. We choked down dinner pretty much every night, whether Legionnaire's Disease was on the horizon or not.

***

As always, Michael and I cycled through a brief quiet period when I got home from Mississippi. As always, the beatings resumed when the novelty of having me back in the house wore off. As an added bonus, having to watch him beat the father became standard fare that fall. Any weekend could turn into a free-for-all, with Michael beating me, me defending myself, Michael beating the father, me defending the father, and the father yelling indecipherable comments and taking blurry swings at Michael. Marie's presence defused things but hinged on the father being sober enough to go get her and bring her to our house.

During the week, joining the father at Marie's was a welcome diversion. I could do my homework and watch TV, two activities I could not guarantee I'd get through unscathed at our house. Even as the father and Marie spent more and more time together, the father clearly did not want Marie to know any details about what was unfolding at home. I always had a feeling that she suspected things got violent between Michael and me, but as far as I knew, she had no suspicions that the violence extended beyond that. It must have been eye opening for her when she got her first real glimpses of the craziness.

The father's heavy, uneven footsteps woke me a couple hours after I'd dozed off. He'd been out with Marie to the string band bar where they'd met, one of their favorite places, and we were suddenly worlds away from when we'd all gone to see the movie *Rocky* a couple of weekends ago, and he didn't drink. As versions of fathers went, he was well beyond The Amusing Father but not as far gone as the I've Drunk Myself Stupid Father, which rendered him unable to complete full sentences. I heard Marie come up to the bathroom and for a moment, assumed they were on their way to bed. But he didn't follow. More alarming, I heard him in the kitchen, that rustling, trying to be sneaky but too drunk to realize how much noise he was making kind of sneak that put me on high alert immediately.

I slid out of bed and padded barefoot past the closed bathroom door and down the stairs. I found him with his back to me standing at the kitchen counter, chugging Seagram's 7 out of the bottle. I ran one hand over my head, disbelieving. God. That would take the better part of tomorrow to sleep off.

Without much thought, I snagged his car keys off the table where he had tossed them and looked for a good hiding spot. He still had not turned around. With his hearing loss, he probably didn't even know I was there. I set the keys quietly on the marble window ledge and let the curtains fall closed around them.

"M'rie!" he called, swiveling around sloppily. He pushed the bottle toward the back of the counter, then his head wobbled in my direction.

He smiled vacantly.

"Iz' Riestillu' stairs?"

I nodded. "Yeah. Are you goin' to bed too?"

"Ooohhhnoooo..." He pulled his shirt tail out of the back of his pants and held it out to his sides, trying to do the mummer's dance, but tripping over his own feet and stumbling up against the refrigerator. "Wegottagobackou'again."

I took his arm and supported him to his chair at the dining room table a few feet away. He more collapsed than sat, but at least he was down.

"Oh, Dad, please don't go back out..."

"Iddabefine!" He waved me off. "WherrzRie?"

"She's still upstairs."

"'Rie, hurr'up!" he called. He faced the table again. "Hey. Wherrzmehkeys?"

"Come on, Dad, don't go back out. It's late."

"Ohhh, youdon'tellmetogoout...I'mdafadder." He picked up a stack of mail and blinked at the tabletop when the keys did not magically appear.

If he was this drunk already, how fast was that quarter of a bottle of Seagrams going to hit him? And what would happen when it did? What if he were driving when it did? What then?

"Yeah, I know that but Dad...you really don't want to drive like this..."

"Li'whut? Iddabefine. 'Mokay. Gimmemehgoddammkeys."

Marie came downstairs. I was relieved for the backup. I knew she wouldn't let him leave in this condition.

"I don't have your keys."

"You *hid* them!"

That was clear as day.

"Dad, I really wish you wouldn't go back out."

"'Mfine!"

"You've had a lot to drink."

"You tink I'm drunk!"

Well, not to put too fine a point on it, but yes. I did. I also knew I couldn't say that. We had moved through The Amusing Father, and the Angry Father had been cleared for take-off.

"What's wrong?" Marie asked, finally joining us at the table.

"You guys really aren't going back out, are you?"

The father was not impressed with being left out of the conversation. "Inotgonnaputupwiddisbullshitfromyou!"

Marie eyed him cautiously. "You don't think he's okay to drive? He wanted to go down to Second Street."

"Gimmemygoddammkeys!"

Over his head, I said, "I just saw him chugging Seagram's out of the bottle—he just drank about a quarter of it."

"IDIDNOT! WHERD'UHIDEMYKEYS?" he shouted, spraying Seagrams spit on me.

"Dad! I just saw you!"

He got still and very red in the face.

I knew before he responded that I had said the wrong thing.

"You callin' me a liar?" he asked.

I didn't suppose that was rhetorical, and I was getting past the point of caring. "YES!" I shouted back at him.

If I had thought it through, I would have ducked. He reared back and punched me in the mouth, splitting the corner of my lower lip. Blood ran into my mouth and on impulse, I drew my own fist back and returned his punch, catching him on the cheekbone and rocking his head sideways.

His roar was wordless as he lunged to his feet with no coordination, his fists clenched. I took a step backwards, my own fists up, ready for him to come at me. Ready to get my ass kicked.

"Charlie! NO!" Marie knocked over the chair he'd been sitting in and scrambled to insert herself between us. "Charlie! Don't! Just stop!"

"Mykeys!" he shouted at me. "Gimmemegoddammkeys!"

Marie pounded on his shoulders, trying to keep him in one place as he pressed forward to try to reach me.

I wiped blood on my forearm with a furious swipe and retreated to the other end of the table, where I snatched the keys off the window ledge. "You want your keys?! Here! Here are your keys!" Wheeling around, I cocked an arm and let them fly. They smacked him in the chest with a jingly thud. "Go!" I yelled, thumbing more blood off my chin. "GO KILL YOURSELF! I won't stop you!"

He surged against Marie, determined to get by her. She stood her ground.

"Nance!" Marie said sharply, "Get out of here! Go! Go to bed! Let me deal with this!"

Sitting on the edge of my bed, I could hear his slurring voice disparaging me, telling Marie what a horrible kid I was, what a terrible, disrespectful, ungrateful person I was, and how could he put up with that? I clapped hands over my ears to shut him out, still tasting blood in my mouth where his knuckles had torn my lip. Ungrateful? I'd been trying to help. How did that make me ungrateful?

Fine, I thought. *Kill yourself. I don't need you--you're useless as a parent anyway. Go ahead.*

Sleep was elusive, and I tossed and turned long after Marie coaxed him to bed and he finally passed out. The next day, fully sober, he never acknowledged what happened. I couldn't tell if he remembered it. I said nothing. Marie barely spoke to either of us.

***

I wondered a lot why the people I was in contact with everyday didn't seem to notice that something odd was going on, but when the opportunity to tell someone outright finally appeared, I dropped the ball.

We had lined up to change rooms between classes. My English teacher, a gruff woman who intimidated most of us, waited by the back door with us. When the next room opened, thirty blue uniform shirts headed in one direction and another thirty headed in the opposite direction, and she put a hand on my arm and pulled me out of line. She waited until the tail of the line was out of earshot and then looked down at me.

"Is there something going on?" She didn't waste time.

"Going on?"

"Yeah. You know. Is there something happening that shouldn't be happening?"

I looked around, feeling trapped, hearing every warning the father had ever shouted at me about (for Chrissake!) not telling anyone our business. The hallway was empty. All the blue shirts had gone back to their assigned rooms and fallen into their assigned desks and were, right now, probably appreciating the forty-five second break from being told what to think, when to talk, IF we could talk. What could I tell her? I said the only thing I could think of.

"You wouldn't understand." I tried to angle around her.

She took a step sideways and planted herself in my path. "Try me," she said flatly.

"I…" I clutched my books tighter.

She put a hand up, resting it lightly on the top of the book closest to her. Contact, without making contact. My nerves tightened. (*Please don't touch me.*) "Let's try this a different way."

I stopped fidgeting.

"You miss an awful lot of time from school."

I nodded. I could admit that. She would know—they kept records of that.

"Why?"

"Why?" I repeated.

"Yes!" she said impatiently. "What's going on that you're missing so much time? You miss entire weeks…and then you come back and you take tests on materials you haven't even been in class for and get perfect scores. What's going on?"

I was frozen in place.

She tapped on the top of the book, again contact without making contact. "Talk to me."

"Sometimes," I whispered, unable to look at her, "my father drinks a little too much. When he gets sick…you know how people do…he misses work. Sometimes it's the whole week."

She lowered her voice to match mine. "So you don't come in when he's drinking? Is he stopping you?"

I shook my head, wondering if I might spontaneously combust for breaking such an important directive. "No. Not him. He doesn't get off the couch. My brother."

"Michael?"

I nodded.

"What does he do?"

"Beats me up."

Even as I heard myself say it, I thought it sounded benign. For all I knew, she took that to mean that he sometimes got me in a headlock and rubbed his knuckles on my head a little too hard. The truth was a shade different. While setting up the tree stand on Christmas Eve, he threw a hammer at my face when the point broke off a thumbtack he was trying to set and I happened to be in the room. I saw him draw his arm back, and I flung myself backwards, whacking my head on the floor. The hammer plunged deep into the cushion on the back of the couch. Looking up at it, I wondered how deeply it would have penetrated my skull had it hit me. The reality of those beatings was indescribable. I wasn't going to try. Not here. Not now. Probably not ever.

"What does your father do when he beats you up?"

"Well...nothing. He's drunk." I shrugged, not sure what else I could explain about the normal cycle of events at our house. I was staying doggedly away from the father punching me in the mouth and all the stories about Michael hurting the father. What would she think of me if I told her that kind of craziness? Would she even believe me? The father and Michael had certainly said enough times that no one would believe me if I did ever say anything. Not too long ago, the father had pinned me in an armchair and put his nose right at the end of my nose and said, "Go ahead...tell people...your father is just a bum...you think they'll believe you when they know I go to work every day? You go ahead and tell whoever you want...and they'll know you're lying." It just didn't inspire confidence that if I ever told someone that people wouldn't throw a butterfly net over me and cart me away.

She opened her mouth to say something but then closed it, frowning at me. I thought maybe I'd said something to anger her. She let go of my book with a sigh. "Okay. Go back to your homeroom."

When I reached the neighboring classroom where our next subject had already started, I glanced back. She was still staring at me, frowning. She came to the front door, waved at my teacher, which I took to be my admission ticket, and disappeared into her own class.

She never asked any other questions that year but every once in a while, I'd catch her looking at me with that furrowed-eyebrow expression I'd seen that day in the hall. Maybe I had offended her by telling her she wouldn't understand. Maybe she was contemplating the butterfly net. She never outright called me a liar, like the father had said would probably happen. When nothing more came out of the conversation, it was only a relief. I didn't want anyone at school chasing me with that butterfly net, and I didn't want to have to explain at home why I had been spilling family secrets to some nosy sixth grade English teacher.

***

"Who you talkin' to, you fat bitch?"

When the first punch landed, I wasn't exactly surprised. The beatings had become ritualized, with few deviations. I rocked with the punch and dropped to my knees on the living room floor. He'd caught me right in the middle of the back, and I struggled to get my breath.

I tried to get up. He shoved me down. He kicked me, with his foot twisted off to the side. I doubled over and tried to roll away. He grabbed my hair and dropped onto me with one knee, flattening me to the floor.

Of course. This was where we always went.

Then he was on top of me, my arms pinned under his legs, and he laughed. He slapped me. I bucked upwards. He laughed harder, moving against me almost convulsively. As he rocked, I managed to free one arm. On his next forward motion, I flailed.

It was blind luck. My forearm caught him in the throat and suddenly he gagged and clawed at his neck. I heaved sideways and he toppled off me, looking kind of green. I crawled away. He grabbed at my ankle. I kicked. He let go.

I got to my feet and ran for the stairs, too afraid to step over him to get out the front door. I raced to the second floor and locked myself in the bathroom. He was right behind me, pounding up the steps, and rattling the doorknob.

"Open the door, you bitch!"

Oh yeah. I was that stupid.

I glanced in the mirror. His handprint stood out clearly on my face. As always when the beating was over, I started to shake. I put my back against the door and slid down until I was sitting on the cold tile floor. When the tears came, I bit my lip and let them drip on my shirt. I made no noise that would let him know he had hurt me. At this point in the game, I knew better.

I didn't know how long he pounded on the door and shouted at me. He had a score to settle. He made sure I knew he would settle it. When he finally left, I crept quietly to the front bedroom that had been the mother's room. I pulled the phone down on the floor, propped myself against the side of the bed, and dialed Chick in Mississippi. I worked to still the tremor in my voice when he picked up.

"So...when you guys get transferred, can I come to Delaware with you? It's not okay here right now."

Maybe he was used to those calls. Maybe he was used to that sentence. He didn't hesitate.

"Yeah. Let's plan on it. You come here."

When I told the father later, he made it very clear in a disgusted tone that if only I had not hurt Michael like I had, I would not have to leave home again.

Breaking Faith

Chick's transfer orders came through, and they arrived at his new base in June. He expected this would be a longer assignment than at previous bases, and he and Jedda decided to buy their first house. In the meantime, they rented a tiny mobile home outside of Dover, jamming His, Hers and Ours into it along with some of their furniture and possessions that needed to move with them (instead of going with the moving company) and their exuberant Irish setter. When "Theirs" arrived, the only available sleeping space was on the floor in the pocket-sized bedroom that Hers already occupied.

After my first week, I emerged on Sunday morning and sat on the couch in the teeny living room where Chick sat reading the morning paper. I wasn't fully awake, so I sat there blinking and slowly coming to. Chick put down the newspaper, crossed the room with about a step and a half, and sat next to me. When I turned to look at him, thinking he was going to say something, he punched me on the shoulder.

I inhaled sharply, my opposite hand coming up to cover the spot he'd struck.

He grinned. "That's just so you don't miss Michael too much." His grin turned into a laugh.

I didn't know which hurt more—the punch or the fact that he thought what was going on with Michael was something to joke about. I looked down, unsure of what to say. When I looked back up, he put a hand on my head and tousled my hair like I saw him do once in a while with the Irish setter, then he returned to his paper.

All in good fun, right? We repeated that scenario every weekend for the first month I was in Delaware. The last time it happened, Jedda saw it. She didn't say anything in front of me, but it seemed like too much of a coincidence that she saw it and then it stopped. If she did ask Chick to stop, she never said anything to me.

It was difficult to picture Jedda stepping in to help, though, since on most days we were at each other's throats. I wrestled with the adjustment to living in a house I wasn't expected to take care of, however haphazardly one takes care of a house at twelve. I wasn't expected to change Chick and Jedda's bedding, as I was expected to change Michael's and the father's (especially if Michael had an accident)—on the contrary, if I got my clothes to the laundry room in a timely manner, Jedda actually did MY laundry. But it changed things and I struggled to catch on.

    Chick was gone long hours for his job on base and teaching a couple of evenings each week at the community college. Left alone with my sister-in-law, I went out of my way to get under her skin.

    Jedda and I had reached an uneasy impasse a couple of summers ago about my sense of humor and her inability to understand it. The moment of clarity for me came the afternoon I was reading an Erma Bombeck column to her about Erma's son handcuffing his ankles together and hopping behind her through the supermarket pleading, "Please, Mommy, take them off—I'll be good." I thought it was hilarious and could barely speak I was laughing so hard. I looked up to notice her panicky expression and realized instantly she thought I would do something like that. To her. Since that moment, it had just become sport to irritate her.

    I walked into the dining room of the new house, throwing a soccer ball up in the air and catching it. Jedda sat at the table, making a list of errands to do that afternoon. Without even glancing up, she said, "Don't throw that ball in the house."

    Pretending I didn't hear her, I threw the ball up in the air and caught it again.

"I said don't-"

Another throw and catch.

"... throw that ball in the house!" she said more loudly.

I tossed the ball up. "What ball?" I asked, innocently.

    The ball bounced into my hands as she lunged out of her chair at me, and I took off down the hallway, laughing. Jedda raced after me yelling, "I **swear** I am gonna KILL you!"

    With her Texas drawl, it took her about ten minutes to get that sentence out. By then, I was halfway down the street. I waited until Chick came home to go back in the house that afternoon. By then, she was harried over a mess Ours had made and trying to get dinner together and the soccer ball was forgotten.

About halfway through the summer, I found a pocket knife while I was fishing one afternoon and adopted it as my own. Jedda was not enthused about the idea of me carrying a pocket knife and immediately demanded that I give it to her. I figured she could go find her own pocket knife if she wanted one so badly, and I declined her repeated and increasingly loud requests. The last confrontation ended with an irritated, "Wait 'til your brother gets home!" which I assumed meant he would then want my knife because I didn't think he owned one either.

Chick breezed in between work and the class he was teaching for something to eat, and Jedda launched off into her story of my hoarding weapons of mass destruction, exhorting, "DO SOMETHING ABOUT YOUR SISTER!"

He slapped a sandwich together and spared me a glance. "What's with the knife?"

"I found it while I was fishing. That's what I use it for."

"Mmm. Mmm hmm. Mmm hmm." He nodded, ever logical and unemotional. "Did I ever tell you about the kid from our street who threw a knife at one of the telephone poles?"

"No." This approach did not surprise me; Chick was accustomed to people treating him as if he were Jesus Christ and often talked to us in parables.

"Well, he threw the knife and big piece of wood chipped off and flew back at him. Hit him right in the eye."

Dramatic pause. Wait for it...this would be the big finish, meant to scare me into giving him the knife.

"And do you know how he was able to ride his bike after that with just one eye?" he asked as if on cue.

I thought about it for a second. "Probably only on one side of the street," I offered.

He laughed, picked up his sandwich and walked out. Jedda followed him, and I could hear her badgering him about getting the knife and to "DO SOMETHING" about me.

I eventually lost the knife somewhere. Or maybe Jedda swiped it because she wanted it so badly. Probably not. I probably lost it. When I started sleeping with a butcher knife under my pillow in high school, I often thought about her discomfort over the harmless pocket knife and shook my head.

***

Jedda enrolled me in the seventh grade at the middle school and Elvis died. I was fairly certain those two events were not related. I'd never been to a public school and with my first experience, I wondered if Elvis had had the right idea. Even the year I'd lived with Pat, I'd gone to a Catholic school. I was nervous. I did not make friends easily, knowing after five years of Michael's rants about me that I was the dumbest, ugliest and certainly the fattest human being on the planet. Aunt Connie was forever thumping me between the shoulder blades and telling me to stand up straight, but I was much more comfortable curling in on myself, trying to disappear. I didn't expect to make friends at this school, but I didn't expect what I got, either.

Coming out of the highly structured Catholic school system, where we wore the same uniform every day, where our every move was monitored, and we were conditioned from the first day of first grade when to sit, when to stand, when to speak, and what to say, the chaos of the middle school put me on red alert right away. Sandwiched between the sixth grade class and the moody and unsupervised eighth graders, I went unnoticed for about the first couple of weeks. But during the third week, an unmistakable, unforgivable bull's eye was sketched on my back, and all expectations of civility ended. It started in the cafeteria.

I sat with two new friends I'd met in my PE class and a couple of their friends. I hated everything about lunch at this school and usually sat listening to conversations around me, rather than trying to shout to be heard above the noise to people I hardly knew. I had just finished my sandwich and was creasing and re-creasing the brown paper bag for lack of something more entertaining to do.

Someone tapped me on the shoulder. I glanced up. Behind me stood a girl I recognized from another class. Beyond her, directly in my line of vision was the table that she'd come from. She started to speak. Our surroundings were so loud that I didn't catch the beginning of what she said, but it ended with, "...wants to meet you," and she gestured at the table behind her.

I followed her gesture until I was looking at the table full of girls with whom she'd been sitting. They were the popular girls, the girls with the perfect clothes and perfect haircuts. I hadn't had a decent haircut since the father started taking me to his barber whose cuts looked like he slapped a Jell-O mold over my head and snipped around the edges with blunt-nosed scissors. Most days I wanted to shave my own head and be done with it. Who at **that** table would ever want to speak to me? Before I could ask what she was talking about, the entire table burst out laughing and one of the girls sitting there who was also in my PE class, exclaimed, "I told you she would look!"

Confused, I turned back to the girl who had tapped my shoulder. This seemed to require some kind of response but not being sure what she had said to me, I didn't know what to say in return. I had the sudden, troubling sensation I had just become a punch line. She saved me the effort of trying to figure out what to ask. She gave me a look of utter disgust and said, "Lezzie!" Then she huffed back to her table, where the other girls pounded on her back and screamed their laughter in my direction.

Still not understanding, I turned to the new friend from my PE class. "Nat, what **was** that?"

Nat set an empty milk carton on the table in front of her and smacked it flat. "She said there was a girl at their table that wanted to meet you. They were waiting for you to turn around."

"But she called me..." I had a vague sense of what I had just been called but had no idea what I had done to bring its vileness down on my own head. That was a word that was not spoken in my neighborhood—it was a word used in weapon-like whispers, and it meant something awful.

"Yeah. Don't worry about it. They're all like that." Nat dismissed the whole group of them and I fell silent. The table behind us was anything but silent.

The comments in the hall started by the end of the day.

"Dyke!"

"Lezzie!"

"Faggot!"

I'd been in this new school less than three weeks. I had done nothing wrong that I could think of; I hadn't crossed any social boundaries that I could identify. When they approached me, I hadn't been looking at them. I hadn't expected anyone to speak to me. I just wanted to sit quietly and fade into the background. I wasn't that, whatever that really meant. I was not whatever those whispers meant. I was…nothing. But my lack of identity didn't stop the comments, and I had no idea how to make the girls who had started this understand that I was just…nothing. Besides, it was too late now. This was already way beyond just the popular girls.

When the boys joined in and the physical harassment started, my lack of identity or my refusal to own up to what a worthless pervert I was (*Could I be a worthless pervert if I wasn't aware of it? Wouldn't I know that somehow?*) didn't stop that either. The halls were mostly unsupervised and anonymous hands frequently reached out of passing throngs of people and whacked me in the head or shoved me up against my locker, usually with an accompanying snarled, "Dyke!"

The whispers and snickers were incessant. When I attempted to confront them one morning, slamming my locker door closed and wheeling around to face the group of girls giggling at me several yards away, my adamant, "No, I am not!" was met with a bland, "For your information, we've heard that you are!" as if other people were certainly more expert on my orientation than what I knew of it, and I was an idiot for suggesting otherwise.

The weather turned. My winter jacket had a hood on it. It was a perfect tool on the bus for the kids in seats behind me to grab hold of and drag downward with an ominous muttered, "Like that, lezzie?" as the jacket slipped up around my neck and strangled me. Released, I looked around to see who had grabbed me, but several of them were laughing, so I couldn't pick one out as the instigator. While I might have gone up against one of them when we got off the bus if faced with no other options, I wasn't about to try taking on six or seven boys at one time.

I dreaded getting on the bus. I dreaded going to school. By mid-October, sitting on the bus with knots in my stomach yet again, I realized that I could have stayed in the father's house and put up with this kind of garbage.

It should go without saying, PE class was horrible. The other students split into camps. The popular girls led the verbal assault, and the girls I had managed to befriend because they weren't in the popular crowd stood by as silent witnesses along with the rest of the class. The class itself was not problematic, despite the fact that I was not terribly athletic. I was more comfortable with a book in my hand than I was on the uneven parallel bars. The locker room was another story altogether.

That PE class required showering as part of each student's grade. My school at home didn't even have a PE class, and here I was expected to undress in the middle of a group of hostile strangers bent on humiliating me at every opportunity. I went through every possible contortion to become invisible, waiting until the last possible minute, wrapping up in my giant towel, only showering in one of the two single stalls with curtains that the locker room had. The PE teacher sat at the edge of the shower room with a clipboard in her hand, making check marks next to people's names as they went by on their way out, post-shower. There was no way around the abasement.

Standing by my locker, wrestling my way back into my clothes without bothering to dry off, I glanced up at the wall clock to see how long until hell ended. As I did, one of the popular girls who had been at that cafeteria table when the bull's eye was drawn on me ("I told you she would look!") walked by on her way to get redressed. She paused, staring at me. I looked away and fidgeted, uneasy. She just stood there. I checked to see if she was still staring. When I did, she opened her towel and announced loudly, "Get a good look, why don't you?"

The teacher said nothing. She stood up, clipboard in hand, and retreated to her office.

My ears burned, and I averted my eyes immediately, grabbing the locker door and positioning it between her and me. What the hell was it with this girl and what she thought I should or shouldn't be looking at? I didn't want to see her. I was not THAT. The girls around me howled with laughter and a bra flew over the lockers to fall in front of me. I skittered away from it. What was wrong with these people? Couldn't they see that I was just...nothing?

***

By Christmas time, unwilling to keep fighting my way through every school day, I talked to the father about coming home for the spring semester. He was happy to oblige. Chick and Jedda said very little when I told them I was going home.

***

It was a Saturday afternoon in the middle of February. The father was running errands, and the jury was out on whether or not he'd be sober when he finished them. The first month I'd been home had been unremarkable, the usual quiet cycle when I returned from living elsewhere for a time.

Michael's behavior had gotten stranger in my absence. He was often jumpy and nervous and hurried and he sweated like a pig. He seemed suspicious of everyone, especially me. He accused me of taking things from him—his money (which he was taking from the father), his stashed drugs, and phone numbers he thought he had written down and left by the phone. This was all very odd because my belongings, sparse as they were, were disappearing at an alarming rate. The high school girls around our neighborhood worried about having gold chains snatched off their necks while riding a city bus. The few small things I had been given as Christmas presents disappeared from our house, no mugging on a city bus needed, presumably sold for drugs or drug money. I didn't know it then, but this change announced his shift from marijuana to amphetamines.

The argument started while the father was still out. When he hit me the first time, I was simultaneously surprised and resigned to the old, familiar pattern. He bounced me off walls and pushed me down the stairs. In the living room, he punched me repeatedly until I curled into a fetal position on the couch to protect my head and stomach. He hovered over me, slapping me randomly in the head to emphasize the names he called me.

I drew a foot back and lashed out. He doubled over, the wind driven out of him, and I jerked upright, pitching myself past him. He grabbed at my shirt but I was just far enough away to be awkwardly out of reach. I didn't stop to get a jacket. I ran straight out the front door.

ZZZZZZZZZZZZZZZZZZSsssssssssssssssss

Four houses away, a baseball zipped past my skull, just missing my right ear. I glanced over my shoulder. Michael was in front of our house, still too winded to chase me, but feeling well enough to try to take me down with a baseball to the back of my head. It sailed several more yards before it jounced down, skidded across the pavement and rolled into the gutter.

"I'll be here!" he yelled.

I knew what that meant. I couldn't return until the father came home and the father really needed to be sober when he got here or I couldn't go home at all.

Frustration welled up. I stopped running when I turned the corner and Michael was out of sight. THIS was what I had come home for. I bent over, my hands on my knees, drawing in a deep breath, my ribs aching from the pounding. My exhale was a cloud around me and I didn't have a jacket on. I couldn't stay outside long. I could go to Aunt Connie's, but I had just told her that things were going fine at home. I didn't want to drag this new mess into her house.

Our church would be open, I realized. Saturday afternoon confessions were about to start. The doors would be unlocked, and I could sit there for a couple of hours. It would be warm. Picking up my pace again, I headed toward our church.

Father Mazzotta heard confessions that day. He had just unlocked the massive front doors, and he invited me to come talk to him as he walked back down the center aisle, my sneakers soundless on the grey-white marble tile.

"Bless me, Father, for I have sinned. It's been three months since my last confession." I paused.

We sat face to face without the screen between us, a practice to which our church had recently transitioned. When I paused, he looked up. "Go on," he said in his high-pitched, almost cartoon character-ish voice.

I sighed. Was this really mine to have to confess? "I get angry, Father."

"Mmm-hmm. Why do you get so angry?" His eyes were back on the floor, and the lights reflected off the top of his bald head.

"I get angry at home. At my brother." Shades of talking to the sixth grade English teacher! That wasn't the best description I could come up with, but more accurate words escaped me once again.

"Why do you get so angry at your brother?"

I hung my head, ears burning, and I knew they weren't burning from the cold. Not right now. "He hurts me. He touches me."

"Mmm-hmmm...So he touches you and you get angry. What else?"

"I hate him."

"That's very powerful."

"I know. But I do."

It was his turn to sigh, and his eyes came up off the floor again. "You don't want him to touch you." It was not a question.

"No, Father, I don't."

He nodded. "If you pray hard enough, he will stop that. You must pray. You must pray very hard."

That's what it'll take? I sat there silent for a moment.

He took my silence to be acquiescence. "For your penance, say three Hail Marys and an Our Father. And an Act of Contrition now."

As the prayer tumbled out by rote, I understood that he had no idea what I was talking about, and he clearly wasn't concerned enough to ask further questions. I was not praying hard enough? How hard does one have to pray to stop being felt up by one's brother? What even would I say?

Please, God, I know You're busy and everything but can You smite this sick bastard just hard enough so he stops dry humping me? Get serious!

What else should I expect from a priest in a parish where men slapping and shoving their wives and their girlfriends seemed normal? How many times had I seen that? What intersection had we been passing last time we were down the shore and that guy had his girlfriend or his wife pinned to a wall by her hair while he slapped her and men who were passing by or crowding around to watch laugh and compliment the man who was doing the hitting? ("Yeah, man! Show the bitch...Teach the bitch...") Why was I expecting this cartoon character priest to see it any differently?

When I left the confessional, I sat in the wooden pews until the church closed. I didn't bother to say those prayers. I didn't think I had done anything wrong for which to ask forgiveness. For the first time, my thoughts about the church as a place of support coalesced. I thought that priest was an ass.

Not So Much of a New Start

I swapped one blue sack-shaped uniform for a different blue sack-shaped uniform and this time white shirts to start freshman year. The father had long since stopped making himself available when I needed new clothes, and the trip to pick up the new uniform was no different. He sat in the car, smoking, while I took his credit card and went into the store to get what I'd need—in this case, a Copenhagen blue, sack-shaped bundle of heavy polyester.

Wherever pollies are farmed, a lot of them gave their little lives for this.

Freshmen started mid-week, after Labor Day, alone in the building. For some odd reason, we had the very next day off, for the upperclassmen's first day. Then we were all to show up on Friday.

I hated that first day. Even with only the five hundred freshmen in the building, it was loud, chaotic, and the girls who knew each other through grade schools from other parishes were, in my opinion, too loud with their too thick South Philly accents. There was too much makeup and way too much hair. The buzzer between the classes annoyed me. The scheduling masterminds had assigned me a French class and a Latin class, and I was clueless why anyone was studying a dead language. What, exactly, would I be doing in my future that I'd need to speak Latin?

Released for the day, I stopped at Marie's, walking distance from school, before I caught the bus back to my neighborhood.

"Heya! How was the first day?" she greeted me.

I scrounged through the fridge. "I hated it and I'm not going back."

She laughed at me.

"Serious! It's too loud. It's too…girly. There are too many people. I hated it."

"Don't you drink out of that bottle!" She flapped a newspaper at me and handed me a glass off the dish drainer. "Are ya hungry? What can I getcha?"

I shook my head and put the used glass in the sink. "No, I should go home and let the dog out. Did my father call yet?"

The father worked second shift now and would call her on his break. You could set a watch by his calls. It would be a long winter of being stuck in the house with Michael until almost midnight every night waiting for him to get switched back to days. When that might happen was anybody's guess. Then again, if Michael would just get a job and get the hell out of the house, that would be a huge relief. *Yeah. Don't hold your breath*, I thought.

"Not yet."

"When he does, tell him I hated it."

"I will, and I'll tell him you're never going back and you were here drinking Coke right out of the bottle in my fridge! Pain in my tomatoes..."

She shooed me out of the kitchen and I headed for the bus stop. I wasn't sure how familiar the father was with high school. He had only ever mentioned trade school for sheet metal working, which I had always assumed pre-empted what should have been his high school sentence. Doubtful he'd be able to relate. Not like that was anything new!

***

The dog greeted me at the front door, a wiggly mess of black and white fur with brown shading on her face that gave her human-like eyebrows. The father had gotten her for me about a year ago from Marie's sister, who decided that a Beagle puppy mix wasn't really her thing. Dogs of any sort were definitely my thing, so the father brought her home when she was about nine months old, all floppy Beagle ears and long skinny legs of undetermined lineage that she tripped over. Our conversation as I changed clothes was, as always, fascinating if a bit one-sided, and I had the distinct impression she thought school sucked too.

I stayed in the house that night until just past six, fed the dog, and talked to the father on his mid-shift break. No school tomorrow. Time to go out. I met up with David and our friends Jimmy and Rita. We spent the evening sitting on parked cars until owners yelled at us to get the hell off, comparing first day of school notes, like we'd done since we were tiny people.

Our friends went home somewhere between nine and ten. Faced with returning to our house where I had no idea what would happen until the father came home, I dragged my feet. A quarter of the way down the street, I heard the music coming from our front door, which stood ajar on the warm, late summer night. The noise made my stomach clench. What was I walking into now?

I opened the screen door quietly and crossed the enclosed porch. The living room was crowded with Michael's friends, drunk and high, their words slurring together. A lighter flared in front of one of the guys on the couch as he lit the bowl in his hand. Last time Michael had a group of people together, someone threw up and lost control of himself on our bathroom floor. Michael then dumped him in his room and walked out, leaving me alone in the house—not just in the house, but next door trying to sleep, with no door attached to the doorframe— with some drunk man I'd never met before and hadn't seen since. The next morning, the father told me to clean up the mess as if I had been the one to leave it, and I spent an hour scrubbing vomit and dried feces off the floor.

I was not hanging around for the sequel. I turned quickly and left, slamming the door behind me. Resentment churned. Was this what the entire year would be like with the father working nights? Group after group of drunks either cheering Michael on while he kicked my ass or puking on our floors and leaving it for me to clean up? It was enough that I had to clean up when the father got drunk and threw up on himself and the floor. Cleaning up after some stranger who had more than likely been around to see—if not cheer on—Michael as he beat the shit out of me was intolerable. How was I going to be able to be home? I had tomorrow off, but what about next week? What about homework? Where the hell was I going to go every night?

I blew another half hour wandering around our dark neighborhood. It was too late to go to Aunt Connie's. Although she was likely to be up, a visit at this hour guaranteed some very negative comments about where the father was and why I wasn't home. The father got off at eleven. He'd be home very close to eleven thirty. I could last that long. Lights started to flick off around the street and the background rumble of too many televisions in too small an area began to recede.

I passed a beat cop sitting on the corner outside the dentist's office. I didn't know him by name, but I recognized him. We recognized most of the beat cops who patrolled our neighborhood.

"Kinda late, ain't it?" he asked.

"No kidding," I said.

"You goin' home?"

"Can't."

"Why not?"

I hesitated, not sure how much to say and what kind of problem it might cause. He just sat there, looking up at me with his elbows on his knees, waiting for an answer. "My brother's got a bunch of his friends in the house. I'm waiting for my father to come home from work."

"Yeah?" Expression of interest. "What are they doin'?"

"I dunno what all they might be doin'. Drinking."

"Anything else?" The gleam in his eye replaced boredom.

"They mighta been smoking pot."

Mighta...like hell. They had all been smoking.

"What house?"

I pointed.

"What time will your father be home?"

"Soon. Eleven thirty or so."

"Okay. I'll be sittin' right here."

As I rounded the corner, he turned toward our house and I heard him say, "...narcotics use..." Then I was out of earshot. It occurred to me he was on his radio. *Oh no. I shouldn't have said anything.* This was going to be a problem. I could already tell.

At eleven thirty, I returned home. I didn't see the father's car parked anywhere on the street, but the music was off and the windows were wide open in anticipation of his arrival. We were airing out. I made it to the middle of the living room.

"D'you tell that fucking cop we were in here smoking?"

I played dumb. "What cop?"

"I know you talked to that jerk off that sits on the corner—I know!" he shouted. "Call the fucking cops on me, slam out of here like you got something to say about my friends—you got NOTHIN' to say, bitch! I will destroy everything you fucking own! I will slit your fucking dog's throat, you wanna fuck around with me? You wanna see me kill that fucking dog?"

He backed me into a corner between the TV and the wall to the dining room. Trapped. I wasn't getting out of this without getting hurt.

"You stupid fucking whore—you want to fuck with me and my friends?"

I knew how this would end. I was going down fighting.

"I DON'T want to fuck with you—or your friends!" I erupted. "I don't want anything to do with you or your fucking friends! Why don't you just make EVERYBODY'S life easier and get the fuck out of here? Nobody wants you here—"

I didn't know what exposed nerve I hit but even in my tirade, I saw it. His face changed. It went blank first then wild-eyed.

"YOU'RE FUCKING DEAD, BITCH!"

The first strike was half slap-half grab along the left side of my head that ended with him using that ear as a handle to slam my head against the wall. My right ear caught on the raised edge of the light switch plate, driving the v-shaped point deep against the upper cartilage. My glasses flew off. Wrenched back, held upright, struggling on tiptoes to follow where my ear was being yanked, my weight was suspended now from that ear. Then the wall rushed up again and plaster crunched under my head. The room spun and lights twinkled. It may have happened a third time. It got a little fuzzy for a moment after the first blow.

He let go and my knees gave out. I hit the floor, face down. He took a couple steps away as I attempted to get to all fours, then he turned and punched me in the side of the head. He grabbed my hair, ripping part of a handful out as he pulled me onto my knees, then drove my head toward the floor again, the carpeted hardwood only slightly softer than the wall had been. My gag reflex kicked in, the muscles at the back of my throat clamping and unclamping.

He took more steps away. I managed to get to all fours that time, dazed and disoriented, drooling blood on the rug from biting my tongue. I caught a blurred glimpse of my dog cowering under the dining room table, as far back as she could get away from us. He would hurt her but I was even more afraid he was going to kill me. This time, he might really do it.

I started to crawl toward the front door. I made it about halfway, maybe five feet, when he turned back again. His kick caught me in the side, partly in the ribs, partly along the forearm that I shoved in the way at the last second. The force of the kick flipped me onto my back unexpectedly, cradling my arm, guarding my ribs, the pain an actual living being that moved through me. He punched me again, knuckles crunching at my hairline, my head bouncing in response.

"GET OUT!" he screamed. "GET THE FUCK OUT! I WILL FUCKING KILL YOU!"

I rolled back up onto my knees, still doubled over around the footprint in my side, holding the arm of the recliner for balance. Staggering to my feet, I threw myself out the front door and down the steps. I ran, if you could call it that, clutching my side, with one hand around the ear that had hit the wall. When I reached up to touch the other ear, warm blood smudged my fingertips where my hair had torn out.

The cop was no longer on the corner. It was almost midnight. He'd either moved to another street or his shift was over. I lurched past where he had sat and toward Aunt Connie's, unable to see much without my glasses, not sure where they were and not caring. Everything blurred together.

The living room lights at Aunt Connie's were still on. Rick had probably just gotten home from work. They heard me coming, the repetitive, strangled groan I couldn't hold in maybe announcing me two houses away. Aunt Connie was suddenly out on the porch with me, hands on my upper arms, intercepting me.

"Okay, okay, stop, stop, stop!"

My momentum carried us in a half circle, reversing our positions. I wrapped my hands around her forearms, pushed and pulled, shifting from one foot to the other, unable to remain in one place. I edged sideways, unwilling to have my back to the street, preferring the solid brick wall of the front of the house behind me, where I could see what was coming at me next.

"Hit me," I breathed, hiccupping. "Hit me." I tried once more. "He hit me."

That was all I could get out. My whisper sounded oddly screechy and wild. I didn't tell her about my head being slammed against the wall. Or the floor. Or my hair being torn out. Or being picked up by my ear. Or the kick. Or the threat to kill me. Or the threat to slit my dog's throat. I couldn't. I had no coherent sentences in my brain to share. Everything scrambled.

Aunt Connie tilted her head back to get a better look at me, one hand on the back of my neck, then glanced in the direction from which I'd come. The street was empty. "Oh baby..."

Rick's voice, from behind me, in the house, "Where is he? You want me to call Joe?"

She ran a hand over my head, feeling the bumps already forming. I cringed and twisted away, every muscle shaking.

"Come inside," she said to me, pulling on my arm. To Rick she said, "Get me some ice, would you?"

She sat on the couch with me, attempting to hold a kitchen towel full of ice to my ear and head. I wrapped both arms around my midsection, covering the ribs he had kicked, and rocked, trying to hide the shakes. Doreen and Rick hovered, unfocused shapes in the background, until Rick approached again, a glass of water and Tylenol PM in his hands.

"Will this help her?" He held them out to Aunt Connie. She took them and shook two pills into my wobbly hand.

"Take this."

I swallowed the pills and kept rocking, trying to ease away the pain in my side. The phone rang. Near midnight? Rick snatched it up to keep it from waking anyone.

"Ma. It's Uncle Charlie."

She stiffened beside me. "You tell that son of a bitch...no. Never mind. Give me that." She pressed the towel of ice into my hand. Rick sat down in her seat when she got up. He didn't touch me. He just sat close and was very quiet. His blond hair seemed fuzzy without my glasses. I trembled and fidgeted to cover it. From the kitchen, I caught an intense word here or there, but the room was spinning, and I was distracted by my insistent gag reflex. Then I heard:

"She is **not** coming home tonight! She's here, she's on the couch, she's fine!"

Wham!

She hung up on the father, who apparently thought it was a good idea if I would just come home now for the night.

The blood had stopped oozing above my ear. The swirly-ness of the room was nicely complimented by the Tylenol PM, and my shakes slowed. Rick got up, letting me have the couch to myself. Aunt Connie sat with me for several minutes without speaking. What was there to say? Then she leaned me back onto a pillow, running her hand over my head one more time, and draped an afghan over me. Then it was dark.

***

They let me sleep as long as possible the next morning. They probably had no intention of waking me, but seven people had to get up and out the door. I rolled off the couch, aching and my head pounding. In the bathroom, I found huge bruises on my ribs and arm, clear even without my glasses. My fingers tiptoed over painful, bristly patches of dried blood above my left ear.

Mid-morning, the father called to tell me it was okay to come home. Michael had gone out. As I crossed the east-west street between our blocks, a car honked, startling me, almost right on top of me. It sounded weird, as if it had beeped underwater. I waved to the driver to thank him for not running my dumb ass over. As he accelerated and passed me, I realized the acceleration didn't sound right either. It was muffled.

I put a hand to the side of my head. I could feel the swelling and my own exploratory touch hurt. Probing tentatively with cautious fingertips, I determined that my right ear, the one that hit the light switch plate, had swollen shut. My left ear, which I had been picked up by, was swollen mostly shut. No wonder I couldn't hear right.

That would certainly make it easier to ignore the father when he insisted that everything in our house was fine. Which, coupled with the question about what I had done to Michael to start "the fight" as he called it, took about a minute and a half once I got home. I found my glasses on the dining room table and remembered the out of focus black and white fur ball shivering her way through the explosion. I checked to make sure she was in the yard. When I opened the back door, she stood up, stretched and nosed my hand. He hadn't hurt her. That I could tell. I turned back toward the father, who sat with half a cup of lukewarm instant coffee in front of him.

"Dad, what do you think I did that would make my ears look like this? They're **blue**! Why can't you just tell him to get out of here?"

"I told you before, if you would just leave him alone, he wouldn't bother you. And besides, where is he gonna go?"

Was he asking me because he thought it mattered to me where Michael went? If "under a Septa bus" was an option, I was all for it. This was pointless. I clenched my fists. And my teeth. That sent shooting pain up the side of my head on both sides, and I grabbed for my ears as if I could get a grip on the burning sensation.

"I can't be here with him. He's crazy. He said he was going to kill me."

"He doesn't mean that."

"Dad! You didn't see this! You know what? I believe him!"

"Don't be so goddamned whiny. He's not going to hurt you."

Whiny. My ears had swelled shut, this was my fault and now I was being whiny.

"HE **DID** HURT ME!" I made myself wince. My jaw didn't open all the way. Yelling was not such a smart thing to do.

The father looked up for the first time. He started to speak and changed his mind. Very slowly, he nodded. "Alright. I'll take you to Marie's. You can stay there for a while."

I think he told her we had had a fight. "A while" turned into four months, the whole first part of freshman year, which only ended when Michael pissed off some drug dealer and had to leave the city because he feared for his life. Couldn't happen to a nicer guy.

***

Although I didn't ask why, the father informed me that something had gone wrong in a deal Michael had been involved in and now some people wanted to hurt him. From his explanation, you'd have thought that Michael was a businessman, and this might well have been a banking or real estate transaction. I wondered if the father really thought I was so stupid that I didn't know that the transaction was a drug deal gone bad. Michael had graduated in June, hadn't held a job longer than a few weeks since then or ever, but had been dealing for a couple of years. This was common knowledge. But who really cared what he did? It meant that Michael had to leave. I'd been sleeping on a rollaway cot at Marie's since September. It was time to go home.

Michael stayed with one of our cousins for a couple of weeks outside the city. Talk was that he would enlist in the Air Force and basic training would take him out of state. With the prospect of being shipped off for a number of weeks, he convinced the father to send him to Bermuda over the holidays. Always trying to maintain peace and not get slapped around too badly, the father agreed. Curiously, this was the same father who complained bitterly that I was bleeding him dry if I asked for five dollars to see a movie. I concluded that the father would be much more generous with me if only I'd start dealing drugs out of our house and piss someone off to the point where my life was in danger. I didn't know how I hadn't realized that sooner.

That was a quiet Christmas with just the two of us in the house. The father stayed sober until New Year's Eve, when we entered the 80s, and he checked out of his brain and into a bottle of Seagram's for several days. At least he was checked out here, not somewhere else where I couldn't find him.

"Dad?! Dad!" I yelled into his good ear, leaning over him where he had landed when he fell off the couch.

No response.

I threw a blanket on him. I could just step over him for the day or so until he came to sufficiently to get himself off the floor. I turned his head to one side so he wouldn't aspirate if he vomited and patted him on the shoulder. He snorfled but didn't open his eyes. I pulled his shoes off and set them on the stairs to go up to his room.

The next day, I rifled his pockets for money to go to the corner store for food. It felt like stealing, but clearly he would not be going to the grocery store any time soon and I was hungry. I doubted he would remember how much money he had when he sobered up.

When he woke, he had no idea where he had left his car. Nor could he explain the scrape marks down the passenger side or the missing side view mirror after we found it by playing the old familiar game of "let's walk the streets in a grid until we find Dad's car." It probably didn't even occur to him to ask about money in his pockets. He didn't ask if I'd eaten for the last three days.

Michael came back from Bermuda and, even though I'd been very cynical about it happening, he really did leave for basic training.

"Michael will be in San Antonio for eight weeks, then he'll find out where he's going to be stationed."

Just like that, he was gone. Had I only known that all it would take was someone threatening to kill him! He would be gone not just for eight weeks of basic training but then he could end up stationed anywhere, like Chick. Anywhere! I wanted to hug the father, but he'd have no idea why I was hugging him and besides that, he'd never been the huggy type. That had only gotten significantly more noticeable when my body started to change. I didn't touch him.

The recurring dreams about being beaten until my ears swelled shut slowed and then stopped. I no longer saw that crazed look on his face when I closed my eyes to sleep. The piano wire that ran through my intestines relaxed.

I came home every afternoon with piles of homework, plowing through it undisturbed. New friends from school could call without me having to worry that speaking anywhere in the house would end in getting the snot slapped out of me. With the father still working second shift, I could invite my friends to come over if I wanted. Unlike when Michael had invited his friends in to get drunk and high, my friends came in to listen to music or watch TV. If we could scrape up enough pocket change, we would get all kinds of crazy and call for a pizza. No one ever threw up on the bathroom floor.

Some nights I had so much homework that I couldn't ask friends over, and it was too late to go out by the time I got done. Even that was okay. I curled up in the recliner with the dog partly on my legs, partly on the seat, and reveled in the silence, stroking the sleek black fur on her spine and rubbing her floppy ears.

Maybe Father Mazzotta had been right. Maybe all I had to do was pray hard enough and sooner or later this would have to happen. He was gone! He wasn't coming back! Three years of high school with just the father and me in the house? I could do that standing on my head!

***

"What do you mean? What happened?" The father's voice was low and tight, not angry but far from pleased. "Have you called Chick?"

Why would Michael need to call Chick? My ears perked up.

"No. I'll call him. Don't do anything—just let me call him."

The father turned as he hung up. "Can you give me a minute here?"

I took the hint. The only place to go to give him some privacy was upstairs. Although I couldn't make out the words, I could still hear his voice and I knew by his tone there was a problem. Well...it was Michael...of course there was.

"Uuuuhhhh...Michael needs to come home."

I stared at the father, incredulous, for a few seconds. "No! Why? No, he's supposed to go somewhere else when he's done with training!"

"He ran into a problem..."

"What else is new? He **is** a problem. No! Dad, come on! You can't let him come home!"

"He got himself in some trouble and got arrested. He doesn't know if he'll be able to—"

"No!" I repeated more loudly. "Do NOT bring him back here!"

"I know you were thinking he was gone—"

"He **is** gone! Dad! He **is** gone! You don't have to let him come back here. Tell him to go someplace else. Get a job. Do something. Not back here!" I leaned forward in my seat.

"He doesn't have any place else to go."

"NEITHER DO I!" I yelled.

"Awww...don't get all upset..."

"Really? Don't get all upset?" I threw the fork I'd been holding on the table and stood up. My chair fell over backwards. "After everything that has happened, I can't believe you'd even THINK about letting him come back!"

"What else am I supposed to do?" He spread his hands apart, palms up.

Gee, let me think. Tell him NO. Tell him to get his own place and a job. Grow a backbone. The list could go on and on, I thought, furious.

"What about me, Dad? What am I supposed to do? How long do you think it will be before he's kicking the shit out of me again? Or you, for that matter?"

He sighed, disgusted with me that I'd even bring those things up. "Just stay away from him—"

"I LIVE here!" I shouted. "I can't just stay away all the time! It's not me-"

"Alright, *alright*!" he snapped. "Don't yell at me."

"Do you hear me otherwise?" I hadn't lowered my voice.

"Look, goddammit. He has nowhere else to go. He has to come home. It'll be fine. Just stay out of his way. Chick is trying to work it out for him that he'll go into the reserves, and then he'll have to be gone one weekend every month anyway."

One weekend a month! Great! What would I do to save my own ass for the other twenty eight or twenty nine days a month? I yanked the chair upright and slammed it under the table. I could not believe he was saying these words. We'd been out from under and now he was going to let us be dragged back in. This was not disappointment. It was catastrophic defeat. I turned away from the father as he uttered a few more meaningless words about how things would all be swell when Michael got home. Surely he must have learned his lesson in the military. He couldn't look me in the eye. I knew he didn't believe his own lies.

I stayed late at school on the day Michael was due home. The father picked him up at the airport and when I walked in, I tripped over his duffel bag on the porch. I assumed he had dumped his gear there waiting for me to pick up his clothes and do his laundry.

Oooooh no. Do your own goddamned laundry.

I kicked the bag out of my path and headed for my room. Behind the closed bathroom door, the shower ran. I hoped that meant he was going out for the night. Anywhere. Anywhere but here with me. I hung up my uniform and threw on some jeans before the shower turned off, usually a good indicator that I had enough privacy to change clothes even if an XY chromosome combination was on the second floor with me.

I was so nervous I felt a little queasy. How long would the good stretch last this time? Couple of weeks? A month? Had we ever gotten more than a month out of the good stretch before he erupted on one of us and turned the house upside down? I couldn't remember any longer than that no matter how long I'd been living elsewhere or he had been gone.

The bathroom door opened and a rush of Irish Spring scented air accompanied him into my doorway. He was wearing just a pair of jeans and had a wet towel slung over his shoulder. His head, shaved at the beginning of basic training, was covered with long fuzz, making his eyes stand out. I hated his eyes. I looked away quickly.

"Hey," he said.

I nodded. "Hey."

"How you doin'?"

"Fine," I said stiffly. I didn't want him in my doorway, especially not half dressed. In my doorway? Let's be honest, I didn't want him in the house. I was so angry I'd barely spoken to the father since he'd told me Michael was coming home. The father seemed oblivious to that fact. If I didn't know better, this would seem like one colossal bad joke.

The phone rang and I snatched it up, relieved for a distraction. Instead of continuing into his own room, he sauntered further into my room and planted himself in front of the mirror where he started to run my comb through the fuzz on his head.

Gross.

"Anne? Is he home? Is he there?" Several of my friends knew of the impending return, and this was my friend Robyn who lived several blocks away.

"Yup," I confirmed, keeping it brief.

"So what's happening? Is everything okay? What's he doing?"

I glanced behind me. He was still studying himself and trying to style his fuzz. "He's combing what's left of his hair."

He pointed at me in the mirror with the comb. "Hey!" he said, affecting an English accent. "I've got aaaalmost enough 'air to be a bloomin' Bee-tle." He started to laugh and put the comb down.

I wondered what he'd smoked. Or drank. He did not joke with me. We didn't speak. This was weird to the point of being creepy and I wanted him out of my room. I got off the phone with Robyn quickly, telling her I'd call her later, fed the dog and left the house, my skin still crawling.

The following night, I was doing homework in the dining room when he came in. He pulled out the father's chair at the end of the table and sat on the edge, leaning toward me to get my attention. I looked up.

"Can we talk?" he asked, rocking back and forth. Tiny beads of sweat stood out on his forehead, and his pupils were huge.

"For a minute. I have to get this done." I redirected my gaze so I was staring past him, not right at him.

"Look..." he started. "I know things haven't been the greatest..."

Ya think? I bit the inside of my cheek to keep the sarcastic retort from popping out.

"I've been a real asshole," he continued. "To you and to Dad. I can't keep doing those things."

For once, I agreed with him. "You have been a real asshole."

"I know I've hurt you. A lot."

I nodded, looking at the textbook in front of me. *Where the hell is this going?*

"I just wanted you to know that everything has changed since I've been gone. I know I can't keep hitting you. I can't keep hurting you like that."

I peeked up. I was sure he was going to start laughing any second, amused by his own acting talent. He didn't even smile. Again, I was struck by the size of his pupils; they occupied almost the entire hazel-colored iris in both eyes, making them appear black.

"Okay," I said tentatively.

"I'm serious. You can believe me. I'm not going to hurt you again."

"Okay." This time it was a little louder and I wondered if it sounded more convincing.

"Can I give you a kiss?" he asked.

I hesitated, thinking of the sour milk smell I always detected on him.

"C'mon," he coaxed. "New start."

I leaned forward, every muscle coiled, ready for him to punch me or knock me out of the chair or spit in my face. Likewise, he leaned in. I turned my head to make my cheek available to him. He tried to kiss me on the lips. I jerked backwards, revulsion pouring into my throat, his sour milk-Michael smell in my nostrils.

He smiled. "New start!" he declared and stood up, swiping his arm across his forehead.

I remained in my chair. Was that intentional? Jesus Christ, what kind of game was he playing?

***

It took about two weeks. Our new start ended almost before it got underway. It was a warm afternoon in the middle of May and school was out in less than a month. The argument between the father and Michael was in full swing when I got there. I'd been home already and changed clothes and gone back out for a short time. The father had recently switched back to day shift and was home for dinner every night, so I came back to eat with him. Michael didn't usually eat with us and seemed to be dropping more weight. I had no idea what they were arguing about, nor did I care. I said nothing, ignoring the words flying between them, and sat down in the recliner with the dog on my lap.

The father snapped at Michael, picked up the newspaper and headed upstairs. He was going to camp out in the bathroom, a process that took half an hour on a good day and on a day when an argument was happening, could be endless. It was the only place to go to avoid.

As he stomped up the steps and disappeared, Michael turned on me.

Not to me. On me.

"And you, you fat little bitch..."

Whoa. I knew that tone. I knew that expression and that stance. I quickly put the recliner's footrest down and pushed the dog off my lap. "I'm not in on this, Mike," I said. "Your argument is with him. Leave me out of it." I turned away from him and went to the kitchen, praying that would signal my disinterest in a confrontation. *We don't even have to start. I give up—just leave me alone.*

The father had left a package of chicken on the counter that he'd want me to get started. I took a steak knife from the utensil drawer and slit the plastic wrap along the length of the Styrofoam backing.

Michael appeared behind me. "Who you walkin' away from? You think you can just turn your back on me, you fat whore?"

I gritted my teeth and said nothing. I would not do this with him again.

"Fat…stupid….bitch." Each word was emphasized with a sharp jab to the back of my shoulder.

I ignored him and pulled the plastic wrap off the package. *Not now. Not now! Go **away!***

"BITCH, I'm talkin' to YOU!" He punched the back of my shoulder and my whole body jerked.

My reaction was just instinct, honed by six years of constantly being ground down. I wheeled around, the knife handle flat in my palm and my arm extended, and lunged at him. He backpedaled quickly, running into the front of the refrigerator, with me pressing the tip of the knife to his stomach.

I don't think I hurt him. I don't think I even broke the skin. But the surprise of finding myself holding him at knifepoint was jarring. Would I? Could I? At that moment, I wasn't certain I could. I also wasn't certain I wouldn't. I pressed a little harder and he winced, his hands thrown up by his shoulders in a gesture of surrender. He looked a little afraid.

"Leave me **alone**!"

He nodded. "Yeah. Yeah. Okay."

I held him another few seconds and then dropped my arm. I had made my point. As I turned back to what I was doing—as if we could all just go about our business and pretend I had not just done that—he let out a short barking sound that was half laugh, half gasp.

Then his clasped hands descended on the base of my neck. I sank like a bucket of rocks, stunned wordless, trying to focus on the dog's water bowl a few inches from my nose. It wavered. That was troubling. He kicked me in the back. Once. Twice.

"Next time, don't stop, you stupid fuck." Then he walked out.

When the father finally came downstairs, I was sitting on the floor next to the dog bowl. "Why the hell didn't you get dinner started?" he asked, throwing the newspaper on the table.

Hey, Chuckles, I thought, still a little blurry. *How's this working for you to have him home?*

***

It was a no-brainer to tell the father I would leave that summer to return to Delaware. I resented him for perpetuating this senselessness, and I was not quiet about how much I detested Michael. I didn't want to have to go. I seethed over having to leave—yet again—my home, my dog and my friends. Yet it was the smart thing to do, and smart decisions were few and far between in this family. Somebody had to make them, so I did. I left. Again.

The weeks dragged. The father and Marie visited over the July 4th weekend. Seeing him again after the break, I noticed his chronic cough had worsened. He wheezed a lot. He didn't look healthy, but then he hadn't for a while. His diagnosis of emphysema had come to light a year ago after yet another brawl, when he had had to explain to one of my cousins why he was unable to keep Michael from hurting me. It was no longer just a matter of him being unwilling or unobservant. As his ability to breathe deteriorated, he was no longer capable of restraining Michael. He managed to gloss over the fact that if he attempted to help, Michael turned on him and he wasn't capable of stopping **that** either.

The holiday visit was odd. The father and Marie sat in the kitchen, drinking coffee with Chick and Jedda, talking. When I wanted to sit in with them and actually spend time with him, Jedda asked me to give them space and go "be with the other kids." I had thought the point of the visit was because he wanted to be with his kid. I retreated to the family room. We all had dinner together later, and then the father and Marie left.

Sad and disappointed, I watched him go from the front steps, wondering what made it so easy for him to keep walking away, driving away, sending me away, looking the other way. Today had hurt almost as much as being beaten, despite the fact that no punches had been traded. I closed the door literally and figuratively when they turned the corner.

As I had in Mississippi, after that visit I occasionally interrupted conversations that hinted at me relocating to live with Chick and Jedda permanently. It took a couple of weeks, but Jedda finally opened up the topic with me one afternoon, driving me home from the dentist.

"You know, babe, the more I hear about Michael, the more adamant I am that you should not go back there."

I didn't answer, but I turned to face her.

"Chick tried to help him..." She hit the turn signal and eased the station wagon into the left lane. "He did everything he could think of to keep him out of jail."

"Nobody told me what happened," I said, realizing she was using Michael's recent military experience as the springboard for wherever we were going.

"He got caught selling drugs."

Are you surprised?

"Once he came home, he was supposed to go Reserves instead of full time. He never showed up for his duty weekends. Chick can't do anything else to help, and things are getting worse."

I scowled and shifted away. "I don't know how things could possibly get any worse."

"Do you want to go back?"

"No, but I have to."

"Why?"

"Who else is gonna to take care of Dad?"

She tapped her fingertips on the steering wheel. "You know you can be here with us."

Come back here to go to school again? I covered a laugh. *Yeah, that went so well the first time!* She pulled into the driveway and I reached for the door handle. She put her hand around my other wrist and I stopped, one foot on the garage floor, the other on the floorboards.

"We won't make you stay," she said. "But I think you should give it some thought. You don't have to go back there."

Message received. I'd been bouncing from home to home since the second grade. I knew how to read between the lines. This was code for "We discussed this and we agree, but Dad won't give you up. If you want to get away from that mess, you have to make the choice. It's your decision." It had been my decision since I was eight years old. Why couldn't home just be safe? Why couldn't the father just do something—anything—that normal fathers did? Why did Jedda want to talk about this? Angry at her but not sure why, I got out of the car.

I did consider the offer over the next few days, even as angry as I was, but it felt like a dead end. Returning here for school was out of the question. Chick was going to be transferred again next spring; Tennessee, Hawaii and Florida were the options on the table. Even the thought of a single school year in Delaware as a complete social reject was intolerable. The thought of school in some mountainous, non-urban area of Tennessee was just as intolerable. No one in our family could be lucky enough to be stationed in Hawaii. I didn't waste time thinking about that.

The phone rang late Saturday afternoon. I was on the floor in the family room, reading and listening to the new Billy Joel album I'd bought for my birthday when Jedda called down from the kitchen. "Pick up the phone—it's Dad!"

I grabbed the extension receiver. "Dad?"

"Heeeyyyyy, Boo..."

Sigh. He was half drunk.

"Whaddaryadoin?"
"I was just reading."
"Iwazdoinsomelaundry. Miss you."
"I miss you too."
"You come home in a couppa weeks." He seemed very pleased about this and his enunciation improved.

The thought crossed my mind that maybe I should mention Jedda's offer. I pushed it away and tried another approach. "Is he still there?"

"Who?"

Are you kidding? Who do you think?

"Michael! Is Michael still there?"

"Yeah. He missezyou."

"Right. Dad, look, about me coming home..."

"Justacouppa weeks!"

"It can't be like it was, Dad."

"Likewatwas?"

"It can't be like that with him."

"You donwannacomehome?

"I didn't say that."

"You **can** come home!" He sounded indignant. "Do you wanna?"

I sat cross-legged on the floor with the phone cradled against my shoulder and measured my words carefully. *How can I explain this?* "I'm trying to tell you...there's a difference between wanting to and being able to. So can I?"

"Sure you can—you're the one who decided to go there!"

"No, I mean...I know I can—I know you want me to, but it's not safe. That's what I mean by being able-"

"Ahhh...dongibme dis bullshit now! You wanna come home or you don't?"

My hand tightened on the receiver. It pissed me off that I had to be the one to explain the difference between having the ability to and the circumstances being safe enough to do this. My irritation at having to figure out **how** to explain it morphed into irritation at the fact that I had to explain it at all. Half drunk or not, I was certain he was playing dumb intentionally. "I do—am I gonna be able to?" I glanced up. Chick leaned in the doorway, listening to my side of the conversation.

"Yeah, you can."

"Can you make him stop? Make him leave me alone?"

"Hesezhewonbodder you."

"C'mon, Dad, how many times has he said that?"

"No, hemeanzit. You can come home."

I put a hand on my forehead, squeezing my temples. *Oh, he **means** it this time...well, that makes all the difference...*

"So yoube home 'n tw'weeks?" he asked.

I rubbed hard against the pounding pressure coming from inside my skull. This had gotten me exactly nowhere. "Yeah. I'll be home in two weeks."

When I signaled the end of the conversation a couple of minutes later, Chick righted himself off the doorframe and approached me. I had just gotten "Bye, Dad," out and he reached down and took the receiver, picked up the base off the floor and slammed the handset into it. Then he slammed the whole phone down on the end table so hard that the phone rang out loud as if someone were calling.

He pivoted toward me. "How dare you?" he snarled. "The father I grew up with would have beaten the shit out of me for talking to him that way—who the hell do you think you are?"

Taken aback, I could think of nothing to say right away.

"Could you **be** any more condescending? You have no idea how lucky you are!"

Okay, I agreed, the call had not gone well. I would even admit that I had probably not been the most pleasant person to speak with. My head spun from the mixed messages of "grow up and make the smart decision because (wink, wink) we all know the father can't" and "don't show any sign of distress, especially not frustration, over that fact that he can't". I still couldn't think of anything to say.

Chick sat down on the couch across the room from me and took a deep breath. "I have a question," he announced gruffly.

I hadn't spoken yet so I just continued to sit there.

He glanced up the stairs toward the kitchen, presumably making sure we were alone. When he spoke, his tone had changed and his voice was lower, which I suspected was meant to make me want to converse with him after he had just bitten my head off. Nonetheless, I was totally unprepared for his question. "Has Michael raped you?"

If he had walked into the room and kicked me in the face, I couldn't have been more surprised. I shook my head and stammered, "No, no, not that—he does other things—"

"That's not what I'm asking!" he snapped. "I asked if he has raped you!"

"N-n-no."

His eyes narrowed. "He has not raped you?"

I shook my head again. "No."

"Then you have no goddamn reason to be so afraid of him. Make up your mind about where you're going. If you're going home, go home. He's not going to hurt you."

I couldn't believe my own ears, the same ears that had been turned blue a little less than a year ago by this person who was not, according to Chick, going to hurt me. On whose authority could he make that declaration?

Chick leaned forward on the edge of the cushion. "But whatever you do, if you ever speak to our father that way again, I'll knock your goddamned teeth down your throat." He stood up and walked out.

My thoughts raced. It was not okay for me to disagree with the father but everyone was perfectly okay with Michael beating the snot out of him? Being raped was not okay, but being held down while Michael dry humped me was not a problem? Where the hell was **that** line? It was okay if I wanted to come and live at Chick's to get away from the craziness of the father's house, but if I gave any indication of how angry I was about that craziness, Chick was going to hurt me? Make the decision, but don't feel anything! If you do feel anything, you sure as hell better not let anybody know it!

("It'll be okay. Just don't cry.")

***

Was I overreacting? All brothers and sisters have disagreements, right? Chick was so convinced that I had nothing to be afraid of that I doubted my own assessment of the situation. Things could not possibly be as weird as I thought they were.

I'd been home just a short time when I found the empty syringe with the hypodermic needle still attached to it under the couch when I vacuumed. The house looked like the father hadn't vacuumed since I'd left in June. Even if he'd vacuumed, obviously he had not moved the couch! I picked up the syringe and needle. Only one drug dealt in our neighborhood required a syringe. Michael had moved on to heroin.

I opened the end table door. The tray of marijuana and rolling papers was right where it had been, next to where the father sat to watch TV. Okay, so this was just added to whatever else he was already on. I didn't know how those combinations worked nor did I really care. I snapped the needle off under my foot and threw the whole thing away. My nagging doubts about my own judgment disintegrated. Chick was not the expert here. Things were, indeed, as weird as I thought they were.

School was a welcome relief. Although not thrilled about another year of Latin, I did like the nun who taught it, so even that wasn't a hardship. I suspected that she liked me too, but in a room full of twenty five of us in a sophomore class of five hundred, she played it safe and didn't let on too much.

"Sister," I told her one afternoon, "as an act of patriotism, we have all decided to sacrifice doing our Latin homework until the hostages come home from Iran."

She started to smile, then caught herself, and told me to sit up and pay attention.

On another day, after we finished the Our Father in Latin, on my cue, half of the students stood up and recited, "Sometimes you feel like a nut!" They sat down and the other half of the room stood up and said, "Sometimes you don't!" I ducked my head behind the girl in front of me so Sister Emily didn't see me laughing. If only we had thought to say it in Latin!

The next afternoon, after the requisite Pater Noster, we all stood up and turned our desks around to face the back of the room, took out our textbooks and began class.

That was when Sister Emily finally laughed. Score: humor one, Catholic school structure zero.

***

It was still warm in the late afternoons when the first beating after my most recent return happened. At first, I blamed Michael's bizarre behavior on the fact that he was shooting heroin; I was unaware that another drug had made its way into our neighborhood. What little I knew of heroin's side effects, though, didn't match what I saw happening at home. He was awake for three days at a time and when he finally came down, he was crazed with paranoia. Even the father's intoned, "Just stay away from him" didn't apply anymore, because I didn't have to be anywhere near Michael for him to come after me. If I opened a door, answered the phone, (or didn't stop someone from calling me whose call I was not expecting) walked through a room, happened to be in the house...those were all reasons.

Michael was sleeping on the couch, crashed out after three days of sleeplessness. I woke him accidentally by closing the front door. He screamed something garbled at me, and I responded, "I didn't know you were there."

He came off the couch in a blur of swinging fists and dingy, droopy white Jockey shorts. I dropped all of my books and threw my arms up to cover my head. Backing away, I took most of the punches on my forearms and shoulders. He pounded on me as I tried to maneuver to a place where I could make a break for the front door. His advance, though, forced me farther into the house. When we reached the dining room wall, he pinned me there by my throat and leaned against me to hold me in place.

"Fucking little bitch..." He slammed a fist into my stomach. I couldn't double over with him pressing against me, but the air was driven out of my lungs. "You wanna see how bad I can hurt you, bitch?" Another punch.

He straightened up, removing his weight from against me, and pulled me away from the wall by my neck. Then he smacked me against the wall, headfirst. I was nauseated by the smell of him—the ever-present sour milk smell coupled with the fact that he hadn't showered in three or four days.

"You wanna know about hurt?"

Was I supposed to answer those questions?

"I'll show you hurt, bitch. I'll rape you and we'll see how you like that."

I froze against the wall, his hand around my throat. He leaned more weight against me, and I felt his erection rubbing against my hipbone. Oh Jesus. Fight? Don't fight? Play dead? Eight years past the mother's death, we had certainly proven that screaming would have no effect.

"I'll ram my dick in you over and over, you little pig." He pushed against me. "And when I'm done, I'll go upstairs and get that curling iron…"

I fought a scream anyway.

"I'll plug it in and then I'll jam THAT inside you over and over and I'll laugh while you scream, bitch. I'll laugh. You know what that's gonna sound like? Hot metal inside you? DO YOU? Tttttssssssssssssssssssssss." He mimicked the hissing sound of burning metal on something wet and grunted a laugh. "You know what that's gonna smell like?" Another grunted laugh and another push against my hipbone.

I couldn't stop the sound that escaped. Nor could I stop the tears that were running down my face and dripping on his hand. I could not venture down the path of pondering why he might know those things. Ants. Bugs. Pigeons. Stray cats? He liked to burn things.

I still don't know what stopped him. I doubt my tears had any impact. I'm not even sure how much of him was even present that day. Perhaps this behavior was the remnants of his new crystal meth habit. As I cowered and waited for the next punch, he took a step back, pulled me off the wall and shoved me away from him. I stumbled, my knees just a little weak, but found my footing quickly and ran out the door.

Standing on the front steps of my friend Robyn's house blocks away, I repeated part of what he had said. She looked at me, horrified. "Anne…you can't go back there. You know that's not normal, right?"

"I know. I know." I hadn't even told her half of it.

***

The father took me to Marie's that night. I wouldn't be able to close my eyes in the same house with Michael. The next day at school, I was irritable and distracted. Sister Emily zeroed in on that almost as soon as class started, as I was not feeling up to our daily joke. Standing by my desk, she said softly, "Anne, do you feel alright today?"

I shook my head, out of sorts. "Not really, S'ster."

"Do you need a pass to see the nurse?"

"No, S'ster."

"Is something wrong?"

I turned my head, not wanting to look right at her, fearing I might start to cry right there in class.

She put a hand on my forearm. "Okay, let's talk afterward."

When she dismissed the rest of the class, she sat down in the vacant desk next to me. "Can you tell me what's wrong?"

"I don't know if I should."

She nodded. "I wish you would try."

"Yesterday…" My voice dropped. "Yesterday my brother beat me and threatened to rape me."

I heard her sudden inhalation beside me. "Are you hurt?"

"No. He didn't do it. He just threatened to. He's got kind of a problem…"

"What kind of problem?"

"Kind of a drug problem."

She sighed and her expression filled with understanding. "Is your father able to help?"

"No. He keeps telling me Michael didn't mean it and he's sorry."

"He's **sorry**? That's not a threat someone makes and then says that they're sorry."

"Yeah, I know."

"He can't help you, can he?"

I shook my head, my fingers curling around the edge of the desk, gripping tightly.

She set her hand on my forearm where my sleeve was rolled up and cuffed. "Anne, I'm going to get you a phone number. I think there are some people who can help."

The next day, a messenger from one of the offices brought a call slip to my class. Sister Emily wanted to see me. I found her at the room number specified on the call slip, a tiny room no bigger than a broom closet, with two chairs jammed inside it. She gestured to close the door behind me. I had no option but to sit down as the only other place to put my feet would have been on top of her feet.

She extended a piece of paper with a phone number on it. "This is the number for Child Protective Services. When you have a safe place to do it, call them and tell them what's going on."

"What will they do?" I asked, taking the paper.

"I don't know for sure. But they may be able to help your father get your brother out of the house before he hurts you. They can at least talk to him about options."

I stuffed the paper in my uniform pocket. When I had a safe place to do it...that criteria alone might take me days.

"Anne, when you talk to them, I want you to tell me. Will you?"

I nodded. "Okay, S'ster."

It took more than a week before Michael was gone when I got in from school, and the father wasn't home yet. I dialed the number on Sister Emily's little piece of paper, shaking just the slightest bit.

122

The man who answered identified himself as a caseworker. He was polite, listening without asking a lot of questions. But the plug was yanked at the end of the call when he said, "I'd like to be able to help you but this is all happening because of your brother. If it was your father, I could help. For your brother, I can't do anything."

I thanked him for his time and hung up.

Sister Emily was appalled.

I was just grateful he hadn't told me that if I prayed hard enough, Michael would stop.

Part 2

January 1982

I arrived in the office, rolling the call slip to summon me into a tube, relieved to see my neighbor at her desk behind the counter. Mrs. Diamond lived directly across the street from us and worked in the main office. "Mrs. Diamond, do you know who sent for me?" I asked.

She looked up. "Hi, Nance. Your father called and asked if we would send you home."

"Why?" That was weird.

"He didn't say. He just asked that we tell you to hurry, that it was important. I called for a cab for you. It'll be out front on 10th Street."

That was even weirder.

"He just wants me to come home? In the middle of the day?"

"Yes. Just go. I've already let the attendance office know."

I ran to get my jacket from my locker and found the cab waiting at the curb just outside the main entrance, where Mrs. Diamond said it would be. Low steel skies threatened snow at any moment. Reaching our house, I threw money over the seat and made a beeline for our front door. I found the father sitting on the edge of the couch, waiting for me. Dressed as if he had started to go to work and gotten interrupted, his face was grey and sweat glistened on his forehead.

"Dad?"

"We have to go."

Go? I had just walked in. "Go where?"

He stood up, wincing. "I don't feel well. Take me to the hospital."

"Yeah?" I was very confused.

"Let's go. Now. Get the car. Bring it out front. I'll be right out."

"Okay." I picked up his keys from the table. The car was parked just a few doors down the street. By the time I pulled out of the parking spot and slid up to the curb, he had come out of the house, still sweating. He did look sick.

It started to snow.

He dropped into the passenger seat with a grunt. "Broad Street Hospital."

"Okay." I eased off the brake and angled away from our house. Snowflakes drifted against the windshield and dusted the cars lining the street. "What's wrong, Dad?"

"Nothing. I'll be fine."

But we were going to the hospital? He sat quietly with his eyes closed, sweat trickling down his colorless face.

A few minutes later I tried again, keeping one eye on the snow-slick street and one eye on him. "You been sick all morning?"

He grunted once. I assumed that meant yes.

We straddled trolley tracks and slid haphazardly over them. I narrowly missed the parked cars on either side of us. Turning a corner, the Pinto's back end went wide and for a split second we faced one of those parked cars at an aggressive angle, then the front end straightened out. I knew from being the passenger that there was no tidy way to ride trolley tracks in the snow, but I'd had my license only a couple of months, and this was my first time navigating them. The father kept his eyes closed. It was probably better that way.

"When we get there, don't park," he said. "Just drop me at the front doors."

"But you don't feel good. I can walk you in."

"No. Just drop me off."

I glanced over at him. This was getting stranger by the second. Drop him off, and he'd just walk in? What was this—a hotel? "Dad..."

"Just do it."

By some miracle, I found a small parking place I could fit the Pinto in right in front of the hospital. He opened his eyes and turned to me. They didn't look right. "And don't tell anybody I'm here."

"What about Marie?"

"Okay, you can tell Marie. But don't tell Chick. Or Pat. They don't need to know." He swung the door open and stepped out into scrunchy snow. "Just keep your mouth shut."

I nodded. What the hell would I tell anyone, anyway?

"Go home." He slammed the door.

I sat at the curb to make sure he got up the walk okay. He moved slowly and the snow didn't help. When he was out of sight inside, I turned the car around and slid toward home.

He called that evening. I thought he'd request that I come to pick him up and hoped he could be patient. We had a few inches of snow on the ground. It would be a long, messy trip back up Broad Street. It turned out he didn't need a ride home; he just wanted to let me know that he was staying overnight. He still wasn't feeling well.

I realized I had to break the news to Michael when he got home and my stomach rolled into a ball at the thought of talking to him. Surely the statement that no one needed to know didn't apply to the other person living in the house who would probably notice that our father wasn't sitting in his usual spot on the couch when the news came on. I made it as short as I could. "Dad's at Broad Street Hospital. He's staying tonight and he doesn't want anyone to know."

I wasn't sure Michael had heard me. I didn't particularly care. I went to bed, trying to squelch the dinosaurs blundering around in my stomach from having to speak to him.

I had to close at work the following day, having taken a job at McDonald's at the end of last summer when I returned from visiting Chick and Jedda in Florida, so I took the car to school in the morning. Technically, the Pinto belonged to me. I had paid for it but when faced with the cost of insurance if we registered it in my name, we registered it under the father's. In true Mullen fashion, what was mine was his and what was his was his. He paid the insurance on it, a much more reasonable cost for a fifty six year old man, and he had daily use of it. I got it when he didn't need it. Since he worked every day, that wasn't terribly often. When I questioned this, he told me I should be grateful I had an old man who still went to work every day, not like some of those other lazy bastards he knew about. Having the car to go to school was an anomaly, but having the car to go to work after school even more so.

Before I clocked in, I called the hospital. "Hey, Dad. What do they tell you? What's going on?"

"Aahhh," he said dismissively. "Everything's okay. They're a little worried about my heart, but everything's okay."

"Yeah? When can you come home?"

"They haven't said yet."

"Is it a no news is good news thing?"

"Hope so. They ain't sayin' much."

We talked a couple more minutes, then I had to punch in. I promised I would call him tomorrow for an update. He sounded more normal than he had in the car yesterday. Maybe things were on the upswing.

When I stepped out the door at almost midnight, the Pinto leaned decidedly to the driver's side rear, sitting as it was on a flat tire. I didn't know if it had a spare. Even if it had a spare, I didn't know how to change a tire, and it was dark on that side of the parking lot. Swearing to myself, I went back inside. I could probably get a ride from someone. I could probably even call my aunt's house and see if one of my cousins was up who wouldn't mind terribly coming to pick me up. Rick often got home around now anyway. The bigger problem was how to get that tire changed.

The following morning, Michael got up close to the time I was getting ready to leave. He was working a day shift. He didn't ask. He demanded. "Gimme the keys. I'm taking the car."

I almost laughed but that would have been incredibly stupid. "You can't take the car."

"Bullshit. Gimme the fucking keys."

"It's sitting in McDonald's parking lot with a flat."

His eyes went hard and the snarl appeared. "You fat, stupid fuck! How d'you get a flat?"

I should have predicted that. I turned away to avoid eye contact. *Please do not feed or tease the animals.* If I could just get out the door before this went ballistic...

He shoved me. I dropped my books. He slapped me across the back of the head, bringing immediate tears to my eyes. "How am I supposed to get to work, you stupid bitch?"

"I don't know—take the bus like I'm doing!" As if I cared how he got to work or anywhere else, for that matter.

"Who you talkin' to, bitch?"

Don't answer that. At this point, anything I said would not matter. Nothing would de-escalate this. I grabbed for my books. My work uniform sat folded on the end of the table. I reached for the pile.

This time he punched me, his fist bouncing off the back of my head, jolting me forward. "You dumb, useless fuck!"

I caught myself on the edge of the table and involuntary tears ran from my eyes—part pain, part fear, part just having someone slam his fist against my brain. Here we go **again**. I wouldn't give him the satisfaction of hearing me admit he'd hurt me. I scooped up my uniform, smashing the pile against the books I held, and ran for the front door. He didn't follow. About halfway to the corner, I paused long enough to pull my jacket on, my breath hanging in a fog around me on frigid air. He wouldn't chase me. Once on the street, I was safer than I was inside the house but that was our secret. As far as I knew, our neighbors thought Michael was a great guy. They had no idea.

Pulsing adrenaline blocked most of the pain but I could already tell I would have a lump on my head later and probably a headache to go with it. Thankfully, I didn't have to wait long for a bus at the corner, which might have given him time to finish dressing and get out the door. He would have to walk right past this stop to get to the one he needed. Stepping over the frozen snowbank at the curb, I drew in a breath that hitched and hesitated as I climbed onto the bus. *Don't cry*, I told myself. *Nobody needs to know.*

I got through my first couple of classes, head pounding. In homeroom, Sister Richard, the IHM nun who moderated the period, approached and said quietly, "Anne, are you okay?"

"Oh, yeah, yeah, I'm okay, Sister."

"You don't look okay."

I shrugged one shoulder and absent-mindedly rubbed a fingertip over a blister I'd acquired while cleaning the grill last night. "Ehhh....I just had a fight with my brother this morning."

"I see. No one else was home?"

Could I lie to her? I decided not to. "No. My father is in the hospital, so it's just the two of us home."

"Why is your father in the hospital?"

"He wasn't feeling well the other day." That didn't exactly answer the question, but I didn't have any other information to offer.

"Is there anything I can do to help?"

"No. But thank you, Sister."

I called the father at lunch time. No news. I wouldn't tell him what had happened that morning. What difference would it make? He could do nothing while he was in the house when Michael exploded. What could he possibly do from a hospital bed on the other side of the city?

"You haven't told anybody, right?" he asked.

"Pat and Chick don't know anything," I replied, choosing my words very carefully. I thought he'd be angry if he knew I had mentioned him being there to Sister Richard. Like the situation with Michael, I didn't see the point in telling him. When we ended the call, I told him I wasn't scheduled to work the next night so if he was still there, I would come visit. He reminded me not to tell anyone, and we said goodbye.

The Pinto was gone from the parking lot when I reached McDonald's after school. I doubted the general manager would have had it towed. She knew it was mine. Michael must have come for it. I hoped he got frostbite while working on it. I wished him four more flats to go with the first one. In a blizzard. I hoped they'd end up cutting his fingers off—from the elbows. The GM was at the manager's desk when I walked in and Rod Stewart's "Young Turks" poured from the break room, signaling the shift changeover from the day ladies to the high schoolers.

"Hey, did you see my car out there with the flat?"

"Yeah, I saw it. Your brother came and changed it. That was nice of him to do that for you, huh? Listen," she said, extending a sheet of paper in my direction, "when you do inventory tonight..."

I spaced out and stopped listening. Figured. I wouldn't be getting that car back while the father was stuck at the hospital. I'd have to take the bus to the hospital to see the father, while my car—**my** car—sat in the parking lot at Michael's job all day. I realized the GM was still talking about inventory. I tried to tune back in but I did a slow burn all night.

***

The next day, I called the father's room from the pay phone in the cafeteria, hunched forward, covering my other ear to be able to hear above the noise even inside the glass booth. No answer. *Would they have taken him for tests?* I waited a bit, using the delay to get something quick to eat, and called back but still no answer. Thirty minutes later, I had not reached him and was getting nervous. I checked the other number he had given me and called the nurse's station.

"I'm trying to reach Charlie Mullen. I've called his room a couple times and there's no answer. Can you tell me if he's out for some kind of test or something?"

There was a pause on the other end. "Who is this I'm speaking to?

"I'm his daughter."

"Oh. Well...Mr. Mullen had another heart attack and was transferred to ICU."

ANOTHER heart attack?

"What do you mean—**another** heart attack? Is he okay? ICU where? There?" Panic shot through me and my own heart accelerated.

"I'm sorry, that's all I can tell you. He's been moved to ICU."

"No—tell me if he's okay!"

"I'm sorry. I can't tell you any more. I don't know-"

"But you said 'another heart attack'! When did he have a heart attack?"

"I'm sorry..."   The image struck me of the father sitting in the car with me, sweating and colorless, breathing funny. His eyes didn't look right. How stupid could I be? THAT was his first heart attack! When I had been driving –or rather, sliding—across trolley tracks in the snow to get to the hospital.

Why wouldn't he have told me? And why was he so insistent that I not tell anyone else?

Why the hell wouldn't he have called 911?

The panic spilled out of my mouth now as I loosed a barrage of questions, and probably a few accusations, on the nurse while she kept repeating that she couldn't tell me anything more and that she was sorry. I had to get to the hospital immediately. ANOTHER heart attack? How many did we think he could withstand?

My friend Beth, with whom I'd just been sitting, waited for me outside the phone booth. "What's wrong, chick?"

"I gotta go. They moved him to ICU, but they won't tell me anything."

"Wait, you can't just go! It's the middle of the day!"

She was right. Attendance had been taken, and I was on record as being here. I couldn't just disappear. I had to let someone know I was leaving. The buzzer sounded to end lunch. Five hundred students scraped chairs and turned as one toward the cafeteria doors. Had I been able to think at that moment, I wouldn't have been able to hear myself doing so. Ahead of the tide, we ran up three flights of stairs to my French class and I barreled into Mrs. Eustace's classroom with Beth right beside me.

"Mrs. Eustace, I gotta go. They sent him to ICU. I gotta get to the hospital."

She balanced her open textbook on one palm as she wrote something about today's assignment on the board. "Who's in ICU? What are you talking about?"

I was on tiptoes and rocking back and forth, my French book in one hand but completely forgotten. "My father. I gotta go." Notice served, I started for the door. It was possible that I overestimated those words as an explanation. It was definite that I underestimated her reach.

I heard a clunk as the chalk Eustace had been using landed on the blackboard's metal ledge. She grabbed my arm just before I got to the door. "Anne, wait!"

My momentum pulled her forward and her grasp on my arm tugged me backwards and we bumped into each other. I turned around. In my head, I was already breathing diesel fumes on a northbound bus to Broad Street Hospital. She steered me toward her desk, away from the door and other incoming French scholars. Her voice lowered. "You can't just walk out of here. What's going on?"

"I just called the hospital. My father's been moved to ICU. She said he had another heart attack, but they won't tell me anything else. I gotta get up there!"

Information processed quickly across her expression, probably starting with the part where my father was in the hospital. "I can't let you leave."

"But he's all alone! I can't leave him there alone!"

The classroom behind us had filled and the buzzer signaled the start of the period.

"Okay, listen, he's where he needs to be. If he's in ICU, they're doing exactly what he needs. You can't do anything if you leave right now."

"But I-"

"No." She shook her head. "I can't let you just walk out." She still had hold of my elbow. "Take a breath. Calm down. He's where he needs to be. This is where you need to be right now."

"But-"

She squeezed my arm. "No but. I have to start class. Why don't you take a minute and go to the restroom and get yourself together." Her tone was warm.

I stared at her. She stared back at me. My adrenaline level dropped a fraction of an inch. She released my arm and put her hand on my shoulder, nudging me toward the door. "Go. And come right back here."

I wondered for a second how much trouble it would cause if I left under the pretense of going to the restroom. But was she right? Was there anything I could do if I showed up at the hospital now? I had no idea what visiting protocol on ICU was, but I guessed it would be rigid. What if they wouldn't let me in? *But he's there alone!* If I walked out now, Eustace was probably going to be pissed off. Detention pissed off? Or suspension pissed off? I didn't know anyone who had ever walked out in the middle of the day—hard to tell. What if I got all the way to the hospital and they wouldn't talk to me? Would they talk to a sixteen year old? *No one else knows he's there— who else **could** they talk to?* But if they wouldn't talk to me, how could I help?

As if she were tracking my thoughts, she interrupted. "Go," she repeated quietly. "And come **right back here**." Each word was carefully emphasized.

Was I that transparent?

Eustace had a planning break in her day after this class. When everyone left, no new students would appear to replace them. My attention flitted from home to hospital the entire time and she didn't bother to call on me to answer anything. When the end buzzer rang, she gestured to me. "Don't leave yet."

Already on my feet again, I waited by my desk, anxiety simmering.

She took a seat in one of the empty student desks nearby. "Okay, you. What is going on?" Thankfully she had abandoned the third year classroom rule that we could only speak to her in French, so I gave her the English version.

"... I didn't know he had had a first heart attack and now he's had another one!"

"And you? Where have you been staying while he's there?"

"Home."

"With your brother?!" Her eyebrows shot up. Last year, Eustace sent us home one day with our usual homework. That night while the father was still at work, Michael had beaten me around the house, and I had run out to get away from him. I spent about three hours roaming our neighborhood waiting for the father to return, then collapsed into bed exhausted. I got no homework done. When Eustace checked homework the following day, something she rarely did, I explained that my brother had hurt me, and I simply had not been able to stay at home long enough to do the assignment. She hadn't said a word; she gently put a hand on the back of my head and then moved on. It had never come up again. But clearly, she remembered who Michael could be.

"Yeah."

"All week?"

"Yeah."

"Where's your sister? Where's your other brother?" She had met them both at the beginning of this year at my induction into the National Honor Society. At my request, Chick had worn his dress uniform. He stood out among the dads and other brothers with their open shirt collars and heavy gold chains tangled with body hair.

I shuffled my feet. She waited. I looked at the wall.

"Okay, I'll ask again. Where's your sister?"

"She doesn't know."

"Why not?"

"My father didn't want me to tell anyone."

"He **what**?!" Eustace shifted in the desk suddenly. She stood up, walked a few feet away and then circled back towards me, her head tipped to one side. "So they don't know anything?"

I shook my head.

"Not even that he's in the hospital?"

Another head shake.

"So you've been dealing with this alone all week?"

"Yeah."

"Oh, Anne."

That came out in the tone usually reserved for when my teachers had hands clapped to their foreheads. I immediately thought of a conversation in religion class when we were exploring morality issues, and we derailed into a discussion about the Atlanta Child Killer. From the time those

134

murders were made public until Wayne Williams was arrested, people bought small green ribbons to wear on their lapels in memory of the kids who were killed. In an attempt to rein in that conversation, the teacher asked my class who we thought could possibly be capable of committing such crimes. Mine was the only hand up. The teacher acknowledged me and repeated her question. I said, "The green ribbon salesman." The other students burst out laughing. The teacher put a hand to her forehead and gave me that same, "Oh, Anne..." that Eustace had just given me.

"You have to tell them."

"No! I can't do that. He wanted me to promise that I wouldn't tell them." I was filled with an awful sense that I had done something wrong.

"He wanted you to promise?" I couldn't mistake her note of disbelief. Or was it disgust? Or maybe both? "You can't promise that—that is not acceptable. Your brother and sister need to know."

Michael's voice was a silent shout in my own head. ("You dumb, useless fuck!")

I couldn't look at her.

"Anne, you have to tell them he's there. You have to tell them what happened. It wasn't okay for him to ask you to keep that to yourself. Listen..." she said gently. "If he's in ICU, you know this is serious. They have a right to know—to come see him. And you shouldn't have to deal with this by yourself."

"I'm fine," I mumbled, miserable.

She started to say something and changed her mind. She let that one go.

***

I never made it to Broad Street Hospital. That afternoon, the father was moved to a different hospital, one just a few blocks from Marie's house with a... newer???...bigger???...cardiac care unit, where the docs now wanted him. He wasn't coming home any time soon. I called Pat that night and filled her in. She agreed to visit him Saturday and suggested I meet her there.

When I arrived, she had just given him a shave, and she held his plastic bedside cup so he could drink through the straw, avoiding the oxygen tubing wrapped around him that ended with prongs in his nose. He was still grey but he looked in less pain. I kissed him on the forehead and rubbed his shoulder. He pressed my hand in his, capturing it against the hospital gown that resembled a large dinner napkin.

"How you doin', Chuckles?"

"I was better before your sister had a razor to my throat."

Pat smiled at me when I caught her eye and nodded at the door. "Come outside for a minute."

She wasn't angry at me but she was less than enthusiastic about the situation. "Look, I don't care what he told you to do—he's my father too. So when the dumbass tells you to do something that stupid, don't pay any attention!"

Alright. Chalk one up for Eustace.

Pat put her hand around the back of my head and pulled me to her to hug me. "Now that we have THAT out of the way, what's with the circles under your eyes, girl? And how much weight have you lost?"

I elected not to tell her that the weight loss might be related to the caffeine loaded over-the-counter diet pills I was taking because I was working until close a lot and kept falling asleep in Algebra 2. "Why, you gonna call me a dumbass too?"

She laughed and squished me tighter. "I might, babe! I just might!"

***

Someone must have confronted Michael about returning the car to me because he gave me the keys back that weekend. My bet was on Chick. Pat's opinion would mean nothing to him. With the father at a hospital nearby and the car back in my possession, I was able to squeeze in quick visits between school and my work shifts.

On the day the father told me that he'd be discharged the following morning, I left the hospital in a particularly good mood. He was coming home. Everything would be okay. He looked so much better—almost pink! This year, pink fathers were all the rage.

I climbed into the Pinto, warmed it up and engaged in the Battle of the Non-Power Steering wheel to position the tires so I could sneak out of my tiny parking spot. I tapped the accelerator and went exactly nowhere. I revved again and the tires spun on the ice beneath me. I hopped out, scanning the sidewalk and low banks of icy snow along the curb for something cardboard to jam under my back wheel for traction. I found a battered corrugated box a few car lengths away, probably used by someone else who had gotten stuck on the ice. I worked the edge under the driver's side rear tire, the very same over which I'd been punched in the head a few days prior, and got back behind the wheel.

I revved it again, but the car didn't move. Hadn't it caught? I'd felt a momentary "hiccup," and I thought I would be on my way, but I wasn't moving. Maybe I'd be spending the last night at the hospital, bedside with the new and improved pink father.

Someone knocked lightly on the driver's window. Just beyond, a middle aged African-American man stood, laughing to himself, pulling his glove back on and waiting for me to look up. He gestured at me to open the window with the universally understood circular motion. I rolled it down.

"Baby, you gotta stop spinnin' your wheels so hard. Your box is halfway down the street!" He pointed.

I checked the side view mirror. My do-it-yourself escape tool flapped end over end in the wind, on its way to the intersection of 5th and Reed Streets. I sighed and hoped the new pink father wouldn't snore too much.

"You know how to rock this?" the gentleman asked.

I could figure it out.

It must have been iffy from his perspective, looking down at a young driver who was now stuck **and** frustrated. He decided to explain it to me. Since he was the one about to place himself in my path if I put the transmission in the wrong gear, I could hardly blame him.

"Don't rev it. Just touch the pedal lightly and then stop. And touch it again and stop."

I nodded, feeling pretty silly. I could conjugate any number of verbs in Latin but couldn't get my car off the ice.

He got behind the Pinto and put one hand on the back quarter panel and one on the sloped window. He could have used the back bumper, but the Pinto sat so low to the ground it was like driving a turtle. He would have had to get down on his knees or pick the back end up off the ground like a Pinto wheelbarrow. I revved lightly. He pushed. I revved again and he pushed again, and the Pinto rolled unceremoniously off the ice into the street. As an added bonus, no one was coming because I was so caught up in our revving and rocking, I hadn't looked.

At the corner, I glanced in the rearview. He was still standing in the street, laughing. I reached out the open window and waved. He waved back. I could conjugate the verb "wave." Pink fathers and nice men who unstuck your car from the ice, even if they did laugh at you—what a good day!

October 1982

I called him in sick that morning. It's usually the other way around, the parent calling the kid in sick, but that would be really unlike us at this point. The call itself was uneventful.

"Pennsylvania Refrigeration, may I help you?"

"I'm calling Charlie Mullen in sick."

I'd never met the women in the office but they were always pleasant. Were they the same women who had worked in the office all of these years? On a lot of past mornings, I wondered if they knew I lied.

"Okay, thank you."

That was that. He really wasn't feeling well; no lie today. I knew that. He had mentioned not feeling well the night before. The fact he wasn't doing shit to take care of himself wasn't lost on me. A small "I told you so" floated on the edge of my awareness. *Try giving up smoking like the doctor told you,* I thought. *Try not eating the stuff they told you not to eat. Maybe you'd feel better.*

As I returned the handset to the cradle, the phone rang. I grabbed it again. My friend Kathy asked if I had been given the message that she had her parents' car this morning and she was driving us to school. Could I be ready in ten minutes?

Of course I hadn't gotten the message. I'd been off making a 10 p.m. dog food run. I ran from dining room to basement, searching the dryer for a pair of my uniform socks, and then back upstairs to the bathroom. I wasn't in too much of a hurry to pause at his bedroom door, though, and ask, "Did Kathy leave me a message that she was picking me up for school?"

He grunted, half awake. "Oh, yeah. Last night."

"Awww...Dad, you are such an asshole!"

He didn't answer.

I showered, spooned out some of the dog food rallied on the emergency Alpo run, kissed the dog and met Kathy on the front steps. We lived in a neighborhood of one-car families. It was a big deal to get the family car for school, avoiding the hassle of a Septa bus, or—God forbid—the Grays Ferry school bus. I was not going to miss this. We were seniors! With a car! As I picked up my work clothes, I contemplated calling out a goodbye. He was probably asleep again. Besides, Michael might wake up and bitch about being disturbed—or slap the shit out of me. I didn't need that. *Never mind.* I locked the door behind me.

Kathy greeted me with her usual morning announcement. "School blows." She turned toward 29th Street to pick up Robyn.

I could only agree. Six weeks into senior year, we were already counting days mostly unremarkable in their sameness; same uniform, same nuns, same resented expectation that we not think for ourselves. The good part of the day started when my work shift at McDonald's did.

October 18th was a beautiful day in South Philadelphia, still warm, with shortened sunshine slanting earlier, heralding fall. By October we had golden sun, not the white sun of midsummer that made the asphalt melt and heat shimmer up off the pavement, playing tricks with your eyes. The walk from the bus stop to McDonald's was pleasant, even enjoyable, and my leftover irritation with the father softened. I hadn't missed my ride, hadn't been late to school, all was well.

I changed into my uniform and clocked in without a minute to spare. I loved closing shift. I especially loved coming in directly from school, skipping that whole going home part. This was my second year at this job, my part-time, as-close-to-forty-hours-a-week-as-I-could-manage job. I had been promoted to manager last spring. Maybe it was being able to exchange the nasty polyester crew uniform for the cotton button-downs that the managers wore. Maybe it was not having to wear the crew hat that never looked right no matter where I put it on my skull, earning me the nickname "Helmet Head" from the regional manager. Maybe it was just that the regional manager **had** a nickname for me. Whatever it was, this was my favorite place.

A few minutes before 8 p.m., the phone by the manager's desk rang and one of the guys on grill called me to pick it up. I expected the father and was surprised to hear Marie's voice.

"Have you talked to your father today?"

"No, I came right into work from school. Why?"

"I've been calling the house and it rings and rings but nobody answers."

"Okay. Let me call and see if he answers. I'll call you back."

The phone in our house rang endlessly, surely long enough that even with his hearing loss he would have heard it. He would have rolled over or coughed or something, and the ringing two rooms away would have pulled him the rest of the way into consciousness. My stomach tightened.

Turning to the other manager on duty, I said, "I gotta go. Something's up."

A friend from my neighborhood had just clocked out at the end of her shift and she offered me a ride. We didn't think to turn off the radio as we drove. As it had been for weeks, the theme song from *An Officer and a Gentleman* played.

My house was dark. Not a single light shone, despite it being full dark outside now. The front door was locked. Chills ran down my back and arms. Above me, the dog jumped down to come greet me. From the direction of the thud, she was in the father's room. I relaxed a little. Navigating a few steps around the couch arm, I flicked on a lamp and went up to see how he was feeling. The door was closed halfway. I pushed gently, reaching for the wall light switch.

"Dad?" I stepped into the room. "Dad?" I stopped beside the bed, put one hand on his shoulder and shook once. "Dad?"

The information flooded in all at one time.

Sight.

Sound.

Touch.

Overload.

He lay on his back, with his feet crossed at the ankle and his hands folded together on his stomach. His fingers were waxy white. Bloodless. I was the only one breathing in the room. His shoulder under my hand was cold. When I shook him, his head rocked slightly to one side but the muscle did not recoil. I looked down into his face: the slack jaw, the pallor, and a detail that I didn't speak about until more than fifteen years later. Oh God. His tongue was black.

    I backed away, shut the light off, closed the door. I learned later that one of the neighbors heard me scream, although I was never aware that I did. This was it. I had known for months it would happen exactly this way. Years ago last night, I went on a dog food run so I'd have something to feed her this morning. Upon arriving home I sat in the car, idling at the curb, staring at our front windows and thinking, *It won't be much longer. He's so sick.* I knew. I always knew it would be me that found him. And years ago last night, I did the familiar, unwanted practice run in my head that I had been doing for months. Now it kicked in automatically.

    I dialed 911. "I need an ambulance."

    "What is your emergency?"

    "My father has had a heart attack."

    A few more questions followed that blurred together. I didn't feel any emotion, only hands shaking so badly it was hard to dial the phone. I called Chick's house, where my sister-in-law answered. I called Pat's house, where my brother-in-law answered. Both siblings were out. I left the same message. Send them—I think our father is dead. Still disconnected, I called the father's girlfriend. Jesus, had it only been half an hour ago I'd spoken to her? How could that be possible?

    "The paramedics are on their way, but I think he's dead."

    "Oh no. Oh no. Oh no." She was crying. Why wasn't I? "We'll come. I'll find a ride."

    Marie was half an hour away, even if she had a ride and walked out the door right now, but I agreed she should come. I wanted her here. After seven years of dating the father, she was a part of this. I refused to call Michael. Him, I didn't want here.

    "Okay. Come."

    Hanging up, I knew I couldn't stay there alone. As I had practiced in my imagination, I made one more call to my aunt's house. "My father has had a heart attack. I think he's dead. Can someone come and stay with me while I wait for the paramedics?"

I don't remember who answered the phone, but the first person in the door was my cousin Doreen. She was eight months pregnant. *Oh God. She's gonna have that baby right here!*

The paramedics arrived next and I took them up to the father's room. I hovered in the doorway to see what they would do, but they asked me to wait downstairs. My Uncle Dick, definitely no fan of the father, and Joe, my cousin Maureen's husband, came in on their heels and Uncle Dick went upstairs with the paramedics. *Why him but not me?* They announced they would take him to the hospital.

"He's not dead?"

"You should get ready to go to the hospital."

My cousin David came in, out of breath. He took one of my arms and Doreen took the other. David said softly, "Let's walk up the block to Maureen's." We needed to figure out how I was getting to the hospital, who would be taking me and staying there, since Chick and Pat were both at least an hour away.

A few houses away, Mr. Forsythe, summoned to his front porch by the flashing ambulance lights called to us, "Are you okay, Nance?"

David answered. "She'll be okay. We have to go to the hospital with Uncle Charlie."

Maureen greeted me with a hug and stood with me as I splashed cold water on my face. I didn't know where she and Joe had been when my call came in, but she obviously already knew what was happening down the street. "Here, take this. You need a' be calm if you're goin' to the hospital." She handed me a Valium, pressed a glass of water into my other hand and prodded me to sit down at the kitchen table.

I was just placing the water glass on the table when the phone rang. It was Joe. Maureen relayed his words. "He's been pronounced dead. The paramedics had to wait for the doctor. No one's going to the hospital."

David, sitting on one side of me, held my right hand. Doreen gripped my left. I didn't hear anything beyond that. No nonononononono. I couldn't tell if I was saying it out loud. I wasn't making any sense. Someone said they were sorry. No nononononono. David and Doreen held my hands, squeezing them, kissing them. Maureen stood behind me, her hands on my shoulders and the back of my head. No nonononononono.

Of course he was dead. He was **cold**. I had known. They hadn't wanted me there when they took his body away. His fingers were bloodless. How could he not be dead? I had known. But he had looked asleep. He had looked peaceful in his boxers and his strappy tee shirt with his hands folded on his belly and his feet crossed, and it didn't matter what I had known because I wanted to believe we were going to the hospital. It should hurt, shouldn't it? Dying should hurt. He looked asleep. His fingers were bloodless. I squeezed my eyes shut as hard as I could, but I could still see them. I had known. No nonononono. They were never going to take him to the hospital. It's possible I howled. Don't all wounded animals?

Within the hour, Marie's daughter and son came, accompanied by his wife. Marie didn't come. I understood. If I could opt out on this one, I would too. We stood on the porch, and they wanted to know if I was okay. Could they do anything? Did I know they were there if I needed anything? Yes, no, yes. What could I ask for that would be remotely humanly possible?

It was close to 10 p.m. when Pat arrived. I sat with a comforter wrapped around me and a cup of hot tea in front of me, so cold my whole body shook. Just two hours ago, I had been comfortable wearing a hooded sweatshirt, unzipped, with the sleeves pushed up. This was cold like the middle of February, and the comforter and tea kept my shivers at bay with only marginal success.

I tuned into some of the back and forth about where I might sleep that night. Did I really want to go sleep in the same house where my father had just died? Would I be okay? I didn't belong at Maureen and Joe's. I needed to go home.

Pat walked with me, retracing the steps that Doreen, David and I had taken just a short time ago, hoping I was wrong, knowing I was right. I thought I was ready. I hadn't anticipated the surreal feeling, walking into the living room, seeing the father's shirt draped over the back of a chair and his shoes on the steps where he had left them.

Overload.

Disconnect.

The room spun. I staggered two steps and my sister caught me. The lump in my throat exploded and an animal-like sound swelled out. Pat sat down on the couch, pulling me with her. My head rested against her shoulder, the father's shirt in my line of vision. The noise kept going, that animal sound. It took several moments to become aware that I was making it. No doubt about it this time. I was howling.

Chick offered to stay in the house with me that night. At some point, Michael showed up and announced he would stay at his girlfriend's house.

Good. Go away. We don't need you here.

I was afraid I wouldn't sleep, but the next disconnect came and I welcomed it. I prayed for it. Please take this away. Please make this stop. Several times during the night, I started to surface toward consciousness. Each time I became aware of an overpowering pain in my chest, quickly followed by no nononononono, words I saw in neon print on the back of my eyelids. My vocabulary was gutted. It was the only word I could manage.

***

For variation on a theme, the next morning I called myself in sick. Again, one would suppose that to be the parent's job, but as of last night, I was fresh out of parents. Someone had to do it. I reached one of the nuns in the attendance office, but I didn't know her. I tried to be business-like. "This is Anne Mullen," I said, giving her my formal name. They had no record of my nickname. "I won't be in today. My father died last night."

"Oh dear. I'm so sorry." It could have been an exclamation of surprise or an unexpected term of endearment. I had no idea how many times students called themselves in sick with dead parents. Maybe this was out of the ordinary. I was on the phone with a nun I didn't know at 7 a.m., with no idea how or if I'd be back in school, so it felt a little out of the ordinary for me too.

The mechanics of the morning took over: let the dog out and feed her, make nasty instant coffee in the green pot with the loose handle, shower, stay blank. Chick woke up in time to join me for the nasty coffee. Pat would return soon. Today's agenda centered on funeral plans. I wasn't sure I had anything substantial to offer to that. When Pat asked if I would rather go see Marie for a couple of hours and take a break, I hoped that would help. My brain seemed shut off and trying to answer even basic questions felt delayed and sticky.

I made it halfway to Marie's house when the wave hit. I pulled over to the curb, hunched over the steering wheel, my arms wrapped around my stomach. I screamed until my throat was raw, just as animal-like as the night before, but without the buffer of shock and Valium to subdue it. No one bothered the crazy kid screaming in the beat up Ford Pinto. My fists wrapped themselves in my shirt, pressed into my legs. What now? What now? As I screamed my fear and my loss, the next question formed. Where was I going to live? I rocked slightly, now screaming despair at the steering wheel until I choked, and the screams began to quiet. Lifting my head, I glanced out the windows, half expecting to find myself surrounded by curious expressions. The neighborhood was deserted. No one had witnessed the crazy kid's meltdown. I pressed the tail of my tee shirt against my face for a moment and pulled away from the curb.

Tears came to Marie's eyes as soon as I walked in. "Oh, Nance..." She hugged me. We sat in her kitchen, drinking generic cola, and I replayed as much of the preceding night's events for her as I could, starting with when she had called me at work. She cried intermittently through the details. She had loved him. Even when I didn't understand how anyone could love him when he was such a train wreck, she had loved him.

Of course she would be there for the wake and the funeral. Of course if I needed anything, I knew I could call her. Being this numb, I couldn't imagine anything I might need. Ever.

I was ready to leave but not ready to go home yet. I stopped by Robyn's house on the way back. Robyn and her mother were both home, Robyn having arrived only a few minutes before I did. The awkward question hung in the air so I just ran with it.

"You know?"

Robyn nodded. "Yeah. It was announced during homeroom."

"I found him when I came home from work."

Her mother looked appalled. "You found him?"

I nodded, numb. No tears.

Robyn spoke almost tentatively. "We saw it."

"What do you mean? Saw what?"

"Billy and I were walking home and we saw the ambulance. We saw them wheeling someone out all covered up, but I couldn't tell from the corner that it was your house. I didn't put it together until I heard today that it was your dad."

I couldn't say any more. I couldn't tell them how I had known the night before, how I knew when we drove up to the darkened house, what I saw when I walked into his room. I couldn't speak. I simply nodded, claiming him...claiming the event and the ambulance and the body she and her boyfriend had seen.

"What will you do now, Anne? Where will you live?" her mother asked.

I shook my head. I didn't know. We sat quietly for a few more minutes, then it was time for me to leave. I arrived home to chaos; Pat and Michael yelling at each other, Chick yelling over both of them, something to do with drug use.

"Fuck you! You don't want to be around it, get the fuck out! This ain't your house!"

Pat didn't back down. I could have told her that would only escalate things.

"Stupid bitch! You don't like it, don't do it! But don't fucking tell me...I'll sit here in my quarter of this house and smoke my joint and do whatever the fuck I want!"

Ah. That explained it.

I didn't catch what Pat started to say. It didn't matter. I knew how it would go from here. Michael lunged at her, swinging. Chick dove between them, holding Michael off. Michael feinted in one direction, lunged in the other, swinging at Pat's head again. He forced them toward the wall with the momentum of his punches. He would hurt her when he got to her. He was good at that.

"I'll fuck you up, you stupid bitch!"

"Mike! Mike! Mike, stop! Pat, shut up!" Chick shouted over all of it, trying to regain some amount of control.

"I'll fuck her up! She doesn't fucking tell me! Nobody's gonna fucking tell me what I can do in my house!" He swung at her head again. The only thing preventing him from cracking her skull was the length of Chick's arms, pushing him away. She slapped at him. He swung again. Chick shoved him, and he backed off a couple of steps. Chick got right in his face.

"Alright. Alright. Alright! Leave her alone!"

"She's not gonna fucking tell me what to do."

Chick and Michael faced off for a few seconds. Then Michael started to laugh, that soulless laugh that had made my skin crawl for ten years. He started to mock Pat. He had won. Of course. If anyone questioned his power over any thing or issue or person, he smashed it, or stole it, or beat it, or manipulated it until he got what he wanted. And then, when the object of his anger was on the floor in a heap, then he would laugh. I could have told her that.

We didn't speak until he left the house. Some things were just never going to change. Pat turned to me, incredulous. "Is that what he's like with you?"

I nodded and kept my lip buttoned on the statement, "Yeah, but he actually punches me when this happens."

"Why the hell didn't you ever tell me?'

How could I tell her that I had been trying to explain that irrational, inexplicable behavior for a decade and that no one had ever believed that it was that crazy?

***

"You can't stay here. You have to go."

The "you" in question was me. I stared at Chick across the table. "No! Dad said he left the house to me. Let Michael leave."

"But you can't stay here. I can't leave you here alone."

"Why? You think I can't take care of this house? Who do you think takes care of it now?"

"No, that's not it. You're too young. It wouldn't be safe."

I almost laughed. Was he really under the impression that it had been safe? At any time? Had we not just seen Michael go after Pat like a rabid dog? After ten years of being beaten, groped, threatened with rape, forced to watch animals being tortured, dragged into fistfights to defend the father, the father dragged into fistfights to defend me—the concept of this house as safe was an absolute joke. Was it not his house I had run to summer after summer because living in this house was so dangerous?

Was it really my age? Or was it my gender? Was it that Michael warranted more based on his gender? Impossible to tell, but probable. Females existed solely to make my brothers' lives easier. When they didn't, the routine response in our house was to injure them, however, wherever, with whatever happened to be nearby.

"Look, we need someone here who can deal with the realtor when the house goes on the market. You'll be in school."

"Michael works. Occasionally. When he can hold a job."

"You can't stay here."

"Where am I supposed to go? I am not leaving my school."

He sighed. "We'll have to figure that out."

"I don't want to leave. This is my house. I live here. I take care of it. Dad told me he left the house to me."

The father and I had been in the car when he told me that, driving to Marie's house. Shortly after his first heart attack, he wanted me to know that he had changed his will. Everything had been left in my name. He had said that the new will was hidden in a place Michael would never to think to look for it. He had repeated this information to me just a couple of months ago. This probably wouldn't have meant much coming from me, but Marie told Chick and Pat the same thing. The will was hidden where Michael would never think to look for it. The house was mine. Everything was left in my name.

Chick cleared his throat and glanced away. "We…uhhh…we can't find the will."

I covered my mouth, partly to keep my lip from trembling, partly to keep from screaming again. Below my shaking hand, I could feel cords standing out on my neck. "You can't **find** it?"

Chick shook his head. "We've looked everywhere. We can't find it here in the house. We can't find a safe deposit key or any lawyer's name that might have drawn it up for him. Unless we have that, the house has to be split four ways. Everything does."

"I'm working. I can stay here." I tried quickly to calculate what I made in a month and what I thought it would cost to live here.

He shook his head again. "Even if you could afford it, I can't leave you here alone. You're seventeen. We need to leave Michael here."

Okay, I was seventeen. Irrefutable. He knew how old I was. But in my pained reasoning, I had been on my own in that house since the mother died. I had been working close to full time in the same job for a year and a half, had been promoted twice while maintaining my honor roll status at school through most of it. Michael never worked more than a few weeks at a time before he either quit or was fired, and then spent weeks creating havoc at home. This is what they thought was a good solution to the house sales issue? Michael? The answer did not appear (to me) to be moving me out; I had already proven I was more responsible than he was. I also doubted that affording it was the problem since I estimated that I made more money than Michael did. My suspicions solidified that being asked to leave had nothing to do with my age. Being male, Michael simply deserved to have the house. As always, Michael won. Michael would take whatever he wanted and I knew Chick would back him up all the way. The boys in our family stuck together. I was on my own.

"I'm **not** leaving my school."

***

They picked out a brown suit for him with a white shirt. He wore a tie. *Since when?* We'd more recently begun having exchanges that started with, "Dad, you can't wear those together," and ended with the universal Dad question, "Why not? It's clean!" He was certainly no slave to fashion. When we arrived at the funeral home for the wake, I paused in the door, stunned at his appearance. He didn't even look like the father. It took me months to figure out why. He wasn't a tall man, but he had a round beer belly that retained water and gave the illusion he was in his third trimester. Upon embalming, all of that water drained from his body, shrinking the familiar round belly.

I approached the casket, knowing this time what temperature to expect when I touched him. Pat and I stood shoulder to shoulder and I put a hand over his. He was cold, but this time there was no shock, no poke with an ice pick. I closed my eyes, held his cool hand for a minute. "You look good," I whispered to him, opening my eyes and taking in his slicked back, greying black hair. "But you look a little like Bela Lugosi."

Cousins, friends from work, and neighbors from our street filtered in. My homeroom teacher, who had taught my freshman Algebra class, came. I wasn't expecting that. Every once in a while, Pat called for me to come and speak to someone—a relative I hadn't seen since the mother's funeral, and former next door neighbors who had moved away when I was five or six. My friends kept squirreling me away, inviting me into a conversation in various rooms or asking me to step outside with them while they had a smoke, and then surrounding me, wanting to talk, to make sure I was okay.

They made me laugh. I caught myself time after time, snickers turning into full laughs, and I would remind myself I was at a wake. Not just any wake—the father's wake. The innocence of the mother's wake was long gone. I knew I shouldn't be laughing. Yet, there I was, listening to ridiculous stories from my coworkers about the Stea twins hiding inside the doors where the trash cans were supposed to be, and when unsuspecting customers approached to dump their trash, they would take hold of the tray from inside the trash receptacle and call out, "Thank you!" It's surreal how funny that can seem when your father is laid out in a brown suit and a tie he would never wear, his beer belly having been stolen but not reported missing, just feet away.

***

The offers started at the wake. The first one came from my cousin Joe, extended to Pat, while I was outside with my friends from work.

"You know, if Nance needs a place to stay until she graduates, she can stay with us."

Pat thanked him. We hadn't made the decision yet about where I would land.

Before the end of the evening, Marie repeated the offer. "Nance, if you need a place to stay, you know you can be with me."

I thanked her and told her I hadn't figured out yet where I was going, but we would talk. It made some sense to go with Marie but I couldn't think about it then. Not yet.

The following morning, I dragged myself out of bed and through the shower with only one thought in mind: this would be the last thing I had to do for the father. I had to say goodbye. Fewer visitors came to the morning viewing. The minutes crept by. I noticed Pat wasn't around and I found her crying in the bathroom. I went in and put my arms around her. It felt eerily reminiscent of the mother's funeral when I hugged her head because I thought I was helping her cry.

In the main room, I sat on the wooden folding chairs in front of the casket. People came and went from beside me. Michael sat down and made a show of putting his arm around my shoulders. Every muscle in my body went rigid and my teeth ground together. I stood up and took a few steps away. I wasn't up for that game. *Not anymore. We're done*, I thought. *You don't touch me again.*

When Michael moved, I sat back down. Bob, my sister's son, sat down beside me next. He, too, put his arm around my shoulder, minus the overly demonstrative show Michael had made. "Hey, Boo," he whispered. I leaned into him, let my head rest against his cheek for a second, his scruffy college moustache tickling my forehead. He didn't ask how I was. No need.

Unlike the mother's funeral, we weren't asked to wait outside at the end. I had front row center view for the funeral director and Chick starting the final preparations. Someone slipped the ring that Marie had given him off the father's little finger. Chick found seven pennies in the father's pocket that visitors had left for him to pay Charon to ferry him across the river. He pulled the sheet up and rested it gently over the father's face. The funeral director helped him close the lid. My eyes burned and a giant hand fastened around my chest. Every breath, shallow as they all were, was effort.

Again, we took the slow walk across the street to our church. Again, the daylight gave way to the dimness of the vestibule, the cool marble floor, and musty smell of old incense. Neighbors nodded and muttered to us as we pressed past them, Pat and I once again huddled together. My limbs felt stiff. It took conscious thought to get my arms and legs to cooperate.

The priest who did the mass had no idea who the father was. He had never met him. He spoke of him warmly, as a child of his God called home, a good man, a good father. I glanced at Pat a couple of times, noted the same "are you kidding me?" look on her face. Okay, I wasn't the only one. I surfaced for a few minutes at a time, then submerged again in overwhelming pain and fear. Submerged, I had to concentrate to follow the mass, sit, stand, kneel—choreographed movements I'd been making since I could walk but suddenly couldn't remember. Submerged, the lump in my throat interfered in swallowing and breathing. The pain in my chest was knife-like. On the surface, nothing felt real. I bobbed throughout the mass, unable to fasten myself to one place.

Chick, Pat and I rode in the limousine to the suburban cemetery, my first visit there since we'd buried the mother ten years earlier. Once inside the limo, I whispered to Pat, "Did you hear that eulogy? Who the hell was he talking about?"

Pat nodded. "I know. Didn't that man know we're burying Archie Bunker?"

We fell silent, holding each other's hand. The prayers at the graveside were uninspired and uninspiring. Climbing back into the limo, Chick leaned over sideways, rested his head in Pat's lap and sobbed. We both held him until he quieted. It was October of my senior year of high school. My parents were dead. I had no home. The brother who had assaulted and terrorized me and the father for years had possession of my home and everything in it, including my dog. And I held Chick until he stopped crying.

***

Chick and Pat had decided to have a lunch at a restaurant after the funeral instead of the traditional *faux* celebration of the deceased's life, which most folks I knew took as an opportunity to get drunk. It seemed they had settled into the decision that I would leave the house and go somewhere else. I was not so settled. Chick was stationed in New Jersey now, not far from Fort Dix, where I caught the bus to go back and forth to his house for occasional visits. Pat lived an hour southwest of Philadelphia. Staying with either of them, while an option, would require changing schools. On this point, I dug my heels in. I would do anything—live anywhere—but I would not leave my school. It was the last remnant of familiar territory and, sitting at lunch surrounded by relatives I loved but didn't want to talk to, it was non-negotiable.

With this question still up in the air, Pat asked me to come to her house for a few days while we talked things through. Again, we went through the questions. Why was I the one expected to leave? How about if someone moved in with me? Doreen and her husband? What about Rick? Her answers weren't any more satisfactory than his had been. They needed someone to be responsible. They needed someone who could deal with the realtor, and they were determined to have Michael take this role. Nothing I said made any difference. Yes, they both understood that I had been taking care of the house. Yes, they understood that I had been working as close to full time as I could manage, and yes, I had certainly proven myself responsible. When all was said and done, though, the message remained clear: we are going to give the house to Michael, never mind his drug problem, never mind the fact that he's batshit crazy and can't hold a job, never mind the fact that the house was to have been left to me—please stand back while we this fucking ship to ground and get it done. At first incredulous, it took little time for the exchanges to grate on me. I withdrew from both of them and kept conversations as short as possible.

Several days into this, I had not been able to convince Pat that their plan would fail. I wanted to return to school and work the following week, so I needed to make a decision. I'm sure now that I couldn't have come up with a better solution had I been them, but at the time I was furious at both of them for this intolerable situation. I told Pat I would go with our cousin Maureen. She lived only a block away from the house where I grew up. Aunt Connie didn't have enough space. Marie didn't have enough space. This choice allowed me to stay in my neighborhood and my school. This was the option. Pat agreed to make the call.

I sat across from her as she dialed—she had an upscale push button phone-- and listened to the one sided conversation. "Hi, Maureen, it's Pat. Yeah, we're okay. Everything okay with you? Listen, I wanted to get back to you about what Joe said. Nance would like to accept." She paused.

Her eyebrows furrowed. "Joe didn't tell you? He offered at the wake that if she needed a place to stay until graduation, that she could stay with you." Another pause. "Ooooh. Okay. Well, I assumed you knew. No, sure, I understand that you'd want to talk it over with him."

My shoulders tightened. Maureen didn't know. Joe had made the offer and never said anything to her. Panic. Panic! This wasn't going to work. He hadn't meant it. He was just being nice, the way people do at funerals when they don't know what else to say. Had it been a serious offer, his wife likely would have known that he had offered their guest room to a relative for the next eight months.

Pat continued. "Well, yeah, you talk it over and then you call us. Yeah. Yeah. No, it's okay. I just thought you already knew."

I clenched my teeth. This was not what I wanted, living with Maureen and Joe and their two kids. They were my family but I didn't belong there --or anywhere else. I couldn't think clearly. I must have smacked my head on the floor when that proverbial rug got pulled out from under me.

Pat hung up. "She didn't know Joe had offered for you to stay with them. She needs to talk to him." She sighed. "Babe, you know you can stay here..."

"No! I know I can, but I want to graduate from **my** school! I don't want to change school halfway through my senior year. That's where my job is. That's home." I didn't want to go through this again. Any second now, I was going to stop making sense.

When Maureen called back the next day, the answer was yes. The thoughts came and went quickly. Did he talk her into this? Did she try to talk him out of it? I pushed them away. I had to. This was the option. I closed my eyes and jumped.

Resettled and Unsettled

Maureen and Joe set me up in the third of three bedrooms in their house. Roger, Michael and Joe had moved the bedroom furniture from the father's house down the street into this room, piling it into the back of Roger's truck and hauling it to the next block. My bedroom furniture and my clothes were all I took from that house when I left. The Pinto was mine, everyone agreed, because I had paid for it.

My cousin Maureen, who is ten years older than I, is the second oldest of my Aunt Connie's kids. Although I depended on my cousins for what most kids depend on their parents for since they'd started driving, like taking me for haircuts and sometimes medical appointments (Rick), and taking me shopping when I needed girl clothes for some event or school function because I was clueless (Doreen), I wasn't particularly close to Maureen. I loved her as people love family members that they don't know very well. They're still family. Like Chick and Pat, she was an adult by the time I was a social being. We weren't friends. We didn't have mutual friends or even have mutual interests. Once in a great while, I babysat for her son. Unlike David, Rick, and Doreen, I'd never spent an evening just hanging out with her, gone to a movie with her, or…as much as I could remember, even just watched a movie on TV with her except when she babysat me thirteen or fourteen years ago when the mother was hospitalized. In more recent years, she and Joe had interceded with the father a couple of times on my behalf when I'd show up bruised, bleeding or crying—or all three—from yet another encounter with Michael. She and Joe had been supportive before. This had to be right.

I tried hard to fit in when I couldn't avoid participating, but mostly I wanted to be left alone. I stayed in my room, feeling like an intruder in their lives. I didn't belong there. We didn't speak about the father's death or the circumstances that brought me there. I felt responsible to be a good guest, but it didn't take long to find out I was doing several things wrong. Accustomed to working nearly full time and going to school, I operated on auto-pilot. The father had shown decreasing interest in my plans over the last few years. As long as the police didn't bring me home, it didn't seem to matter to him what I did or where I was. Complicating this, I wasn't looking for a family and the fallout from the father's death, about which we weren't speaking, was an enormous drain on my energy. I was tired and miserable most of the time.

Before I had even moved in, Pat and Chick both put me on notice that I'd have to "do something" about my dog. They were never specific about what they wanted me to do, but time after time they made the point that the dog had to be removed in order for this elaborate scheme of Michael escorting realty people through Mullen Manor to work. They offered no suggestions. Neither one of them would take the dog. Just, "You have to do something with the dog." Shortly after settling into my new space, I begged Marie to take my dog. "I'll pay for everything. I do now anyway. I'll come visit her as much as I can." The only other option was to take her to Morris Animal Refuge where I feared she'd be put down before she found another home. No one wanted a six-year-old dog. They wanted puppies. If I surrendered her, she'd likely be euthanized. I couldn't let her be killed, alone and scared. I had to find her a home.

With no support or suggestions for resources, I was desperate. After some more begging, Marie eventually agreed to take her. At Chick and Pat's prompting, I went to the house when Michael wasn't home, packed her up and took her to Marie's. I missed her horribly. I squeezed visits into my schedule as often as I could to sit on the floor with her, kiss her ears and rub her belly. Each visit, Marie would comment on how much the poor dog missed me, as all she did when I wasn't there was pace the house and look for me.

It didn't take long, maybe two weeks, maybe three, before Marie told me that it wasn't working. The dog wasn't adjusting to the change and Marie couldn't take another day of her pacing and whining. Please take her out of here. I'm sorry.

What's the next step beyond desperate? I would have done anything to keep her. Maureen and Joe had a dog and didn't want another one. No one wanted her except me and I had no leverage to make that happen. I hated the thought of it, dreaded having to talk to him, but I had to ask Michael if she could come back until I could figure out what else to do with her. To my surprise, Michael didn't make jokes and didn't insult me. He agreed that she could come back until I knew my next step. I wonder now what he was on when I asked him.

    Chick and Pat both went ballistic when I told them the dog was back at the father's house. The pressure ratcheted up to a ridiculous level. Get the dog out. Get the dog out now! They didn't care where I took her. Just out. Again, they made no suggestions, just gave me directions about following the grand plan to make everything easy to put the house on the market.

    I hated what they were asking me to do. She was a young, healthy dog, and I agonized over her life being shortened because of these unbelievably shitty circumstances. I dodged their phone calls. This wasn't THEIR dog. They didn't care what happened to her. They hadn't spent the last five years with her sleeping at the foot of their beds.

    I stayed at work long hours to avoid everyone. I went in early and on nights when I wasn't closing, I hung around in the break room long after my shift was over. Sleep evaded me even on nights when I did go to bed at a decent hour. When I did sleep, I dreamed often about finding the father, replaying walking up the steps, touching him, finding him cold. Awake, the thought of having to give up my dog or possibly kill her tormented me. Asleep, I couldn't get away from the slack jaw, the colorless skin, and waxy fingers dressed peacefully in boxers and an undershirt. Awake, I clenched my teeth and thought if I let anything surface, if I felt **anything**, it would drown me. Unconscious, it got the better of me and I came to, already crying.

    Playing multiple roles of intruder on Maureen and Joe's family and potential dog murderer wore on me. About a month after the father's death, I woke one morning with a fever and sore throat. I called myself in sick and fell back to sleep. When Maureen woke me to ask what was wrong, I explained I was running a temperature, and I had called school and gone back to bed.

"Really?" she said. "You should have gotten me up. I would have called you in."

The thought had never crossed my mind. I took only one day off. I couldn't afford to lose any more time from work. I had just been gone for two weeks. Fast food jobs do not wait for you. I went back, still achy, still feverish.

The pressure from Chick and Pat did not let up. Chick was angry that I wasn't following the plan. After weeks' long litanies of "Do something," and having no ideas about what else I might do or where I might take her, I finally reached the conclusion that I would have to surrender her to the animal shelter where, I had no doubt, she would be destroyed. Without her person.

I wasn't going to sentence her to an anonymous death. I would go with her and stay while they put her down. I would do that for her. It wasn't for Chick and Pat, and it wasn't for that house. It was for her. If she had been miserable at Marie's where she knew people and they were kind to her, how could I expect her to make a transition to some stranger's home, if even I could find someone who might want her? Was I going to let her go another five years or more being miserable without her people? Was I going to drop her off at the animal refuge and run like a coward? I had no other answers. I loved her. All I could do was to help her die so she wasn't stuck in this anymore. It was a shattering decision.

I woke up sobbing every night that week, first trying to reach the answer, then trying to reconcile myself to her death sentence. I was going to kill an animal I adored simply because she was an inconvenience. *Was it not enough I had had to move out of my house? Was it not enough that I took care of our father until the day he died and then got tossed out on my ear? Was it not enough that I am living with strangers?No, let's make this even more intolerable, please comply when we ask you to get rid of your dog. Do not look to us for suggestions, do not expect our help. And please do not argue with our euphemism "get rid of." We all know that she is going to have to die, that you are going to have to kill her, but for Chrissake, let's be polite about it and never say those words out loud.*

I needed not to do this alone. In past years, my French teacher Mrs. Eustace had played sounding board. But this time, it felt like more than a sounding board. She didn't even have me in class this year so it wasn't as if she were dealing with the potential disruptions to her class as when the father was hospitalized. Plus she was the only person I could think of to ask. When I approached her, she didn't wait for me to ask. She offered to come with me while I did it. I couldn't agree fast enough. We named a day, and I was to pick up the dog, then I'd pick her up and we'd go together to take the dog to her death.

I was sickened by what I was about to do, tortured by not knowing how the process worked, how much it would hurt and if she would know I was the one causing it. How much would she feel? How much would she know? How long would she suffer? The day she had run from Michael and tried to hide under my bed, only to have him pick her up by her tail with one hand while punching her with the other as she flailed and yelped pitifully suddenly felt like nothing to be concerned about. She trusted me. I was going to kill her. Had I ever been able to protect her?

The guilt was unbearable. I was an immeasurable failure. When Michael had beaten her, I had put my head down and charged him from behind, catching him with my shoulder, knocking him down. He beat me senseless when he got up but he left the dog alone. I couldn't even offer her that much now.

On the designated afternoon, I went to the father's house to get her. Michael was home. I assumed he had lost yet another job and was on a binge. I would have to be careful. This could get ugly.

"What the fuck do you want?" he asked. "You're in my house, bitch. My house!"

"I've come to get the dog."

"Fuck you. You ain't takin' my dog."

"I have to take her. Chick and Pat—"

"Fuck Chick and Pat! Get the fuck out of my house."

"This is my house too."

"Bullshit, bitch. Get the fuck out."

"I have to take the dog. They want her—"

"I don't give a fuck what they want. That's MY dog! Get your fat fucking ass out of here. This is MY house, you stupid whore."

"I can't go without—"

I didn't get a chance to finish. Michael closed the distance between us and punched me in the head. I reeled, momentarily stunned. He shoved me and I stumbled backwards. He grabbed at the end of the dog chain hanging from my hand and yanked hard. The chain shot through my hand, a jagged, broken link gouging a furrow into my palm and fingers as I tried to hold on. Blood dripped out of my fist. He slapped me in the face. I let go, my ear ringing. He shoved me again, this time with both hands. I slammed against the front door, cracking the side of my head against it.

Bleeding, with a lump forming on my head, I fumbled to get the door open. I reached quickly for the screen door handle, partially turning to see where he was. In my last glimpse of my little black and white friend, she was again cowering under the dining room table, ears plastered to her skull. Michael kicked me in the stomach. The latch gave on the screen door when I fell against it. I bounced down the concrete steps outside on my back.

He stood in the doorway, five steps above. "It's my fucking dog. Don't you fucking come back here." He closed the door.

***

"Where's the dog?" Eustace leaned in the passenger door.

"No dog. Michael was home." My voice was unsteady, and I was still shaking. "When I told him why I was there, he started screaming at me, then he hit me and kicked me down the steps."

That made it sound so calm. I could never accurately describe Michael in one of his rages. That kind of craziness defies description. You understood it when he turned on you. As I had just seen with Pat, that was an eye-opening moment.

"Park the car and come on in," she said. "You need a few minutes to pull yourself together."

As I pulled into a parking spot just across the intersection, the song "Ebony and Ivory" came on and I flicked it off impatiently. The idea of anyone living in harmony was a goddamned joke. When Eustace stepped back to allow me into her home, she saw the blood and brought me antibiotic cream and Band-Aids for my fingers. I couldn't do anything about the gouge running across my palm. It wasn't deep enough to need stitches so I just waited for it to stop bleeding. She directed me to her kitchen table and put tea in front of me. I didn't say anything about the lumps on my skull, but I had a vicious headache.

I hiccupped, trying to slow my breathing. "I don't know what to do now. I can't believe this."

"This has been going on a long time," she pointed out pragmatically. "What did you expect?"

I didn't know quite how to answer that. I didn't want to do this in the first place, but getting punched in the head to boot had never been part of the scheme. All of the time I had spent making myself sick over this decision...now it wasn't my decision to make. He had my dog. I had lumps on my head, blood smeared across one hand, part of a footprint forming on my stomach, and my glasses were bent from being slapped. So far, the master plan to leave Michael in the house was going smashingly.

***

December dragged. The dog remained with Michael but at least Chick and Pat had stopped pressuring me to do something about it. When I'd shown up at Pat's house with my palm still oozing blood and my glasses bent and explained to her what had happened, the world shifted yet again. She had picked up the phone and called Chick, and they had ended up in an argument, with Chick refusing to do anything to confront

Michael, refusing to consider that perhaps this wasn't the smartest plan. I missed most of the call, but I did get to the kitchen in time to hear her snap, "Fine! The next time my sister shows up at my door bleeding because that son of a bitch went after her again, YOU bandage her goddamned hands!" She hung up on him.

The dog was alive. I couldn't say for sure she was safe. No one was safe around Michael but I hadn't killed her. I resumed responsibility for scheduling at work and scheduled myself to work every possible minute. I opened. I closed. I opened and closed on the same day. If anyone called in sick, I wanted their hours. School and McDonald's were the only places I felt even remotely normal.

By mid-December, those hours started to show. A class I'd taken just to fill my schedule came with a number of assignments—all easy and not terribly interesting. It was fluff. I couldn't get motivated to complete them and suspected I might fail the class. I didn't care. One morning, I dozed off in typing class on top of my typewriter. The teacher paced the room with a pointer and when she passed, she whacked me across the shoulders. I jerked awake, ready to hit her. I didn't care if I failed this class too.

I scheduled myself to work on Christmas Eve. Regrettably, the store would be closed Christmas Day or I would have worked then too. Pat invited me to come to her house for Christmas. I didn't care about the holiday. In fact, I dreaded it. I was so tired all the time, I wouldn't be good company. Work, school, sleep. Work, school, sleep. That was all I needed and some days, school didn't fare so well.

I worked with several friends from school that day and my friend Charlie, who was an assistant manager. At the end of my shift, not looking forward to walking back to Maureen's, I hung around the break room. Charlie poked his head in.

"Hey."

I looked up. "Hey."

He stepped into the doorway. "How you doin'? I mean, with this being the first Christmas and everything? How are you?"

How was I? This was a great question. I was still crying in my sleep once or twice a week. I was tired all the time. If anyone looked at me sideways, I wanted to take their head off. I was failing at least one class and I didn't care. How was I?

"I'm fine," I finally said.

"I got you something." He ducked out and came back carrying a Christmas gift. "I didn't know where you'd be for Christmas..." His voice trailed off.

I understood the unspoken, "...or if you'd be having Christmas at all..." Surprised and very touched, I took the gift from him as a couple of my other coworkers who were also friends from school came into the room.

"Where ARE you gonna be for Christmas, Nance?" one asked.

"My sister's."

"It's okay? I mean, you want to go? You could come to my house."

"Yeah, it's okay. I'll be back right after."

Inside the wrapped box lay a shirt-y, sweater-y kind of item. It was purple and very soft, and I was moved that Charlie had done this. He sat sideways in his chair, watching me. I kissed him on the head and hugged him.

"Thank you."

He nodded. I'm sure he had no idea he was the only person who had asked me how I was faring through this first holiday without the father. He'd never know how much that meant, or that I would take this memory out every year afterward and think of him fondly and wish him well.

I boxed the sweater-y item back up. Maybe I'd wear it tomorrow. It was time to go. Pat expected me early evening so I could join her, Roger, and Bob at a friend's home for their Christmas Eve tradition. I gathered my belongings, including my new sweater-y thing, dug my jacket out of the pile and started out the door.

That Christmas Eve, the temperature hovered in single digits in the late afternoon. By midnight mass, the forecast called for it to sink below zero. I walked along with my head down, my nose running and numb at the same time. I didn't bother to zip my jacket. I actually felt very little. The wind whined, and my attention came to rest on the odd burning sensation on my right cheek. I reached up. Two tears had escaped. I went into lock down.

***

Christmas Eve with Pat, Roger, and Bob was pleasant enough. I can't say anything went wrong but I felt like an intruder into their holiday plans. If I hadn't been so exhausted, I might have cared about that more, too. As it was, I tried hard to smile and be cheerful and just get through the night. I had to fight to keep my eyes open.

Christmas afternoon, I excused myself from the middle of a conversation and went to the living room to watch TV with Bob and fell asleep. I got up long enough to have dinner, then fell asleep sitting on the couch. Whenever I sat down, my eyes closed.

"Babe, do you feel alright?" Pat woke me from my umpteenth nap, and I joined her at the kitchen table to have some tea.

"Yeah, I'm fine. I'm just a little tired."

"Not sick?"

"No, just tired."

"I think maybe you should stay until tomorrow and I'll take you to see one of the docs at the hospital."

"Nah. I'm fine."

"I'll feel better if you go. You don't look right. You're sleeping an awful lot."

"That's because I'm tired."

"Uhhh....yeah...." She gestured like she was going to give me a tiny smack in the head. "So stay one more day and come with me."

I doubted I was sick. I was just working a lot. But I agreed I'd stay another day or two until she could get me in to see her doctor friend and he gave me the all clear.

***

"Mono? I can't have mono! I have to go back to work!"

She nodded. "Sorry. The blood test says you have mono. You're bordering on it affecting your liver. Have you been sick?"

"No." I thought for a minute. "Wait. Yes. I was sick in November—about the middle of the month. I thought it was the flu or a bug. I took a day off."

She stared at me. "You've been sick for six weeks and you haven't said anything?"

"I just thought I was tired. Once the fever and sore throat passed, I didn't think anything of it."

"You're lucky you're not sicker."

I contemplated how lucky I felt.

"Doctor says you're out of school until further notice. Work too."

"I can't take more time off!"

"If you keep pushing yourself, you will end up damaging your liver."

I was still contemplating how lucky I felt. "How the hell do you even get mono? I don't know anyone who has it!"

"He said you can be more susceptible to it if you get run down. And then you can pick it up from drinking out of someone's glass or other kinds of contact like that. Why? Who did you kiss?"

I snorted. "Yeah, that's it."

"Okay, babe, you're out for a while. I'll call Maureen and let her know."

I didn't need to be around to hear this conversation, thinking it unimportant. Yeah. Unimportant like a canary in a coalmine.

Pat was upset, I could tell.

"What did she say?" I asked.

"She doesn't want you in her house until you're better. She's afraid you'll infect her kids. She says you can't come back until you're well."

"I can't go back? Where am I supposed to go?"

"No. You're here until the doctor clears you."

Merry Christmas, go away. Was I still supposed to be contemplating how lucky I was?

Much later as an adult, I came to understand Maureen's perspective. At the time, though, it felt only like a giant rejection. Already afraid I was intruding on their lives, I felt out of sorts in their home. When I returned a couple of weeks later, I couldn't shake the feelings of guilt for being an interference. I was angry about being pushed out over something that I could not control. Most of all, I resented being in this situation and neither she nor Joe had anything to do with that. Was this supposed to be my home? Wasn't that the whole idea? The message was now clear—whether Maureen and Joe intended it to be the message or not—this is not really your home, and you're not really family, so don't get comfortable. That was how it made sense to me and it stung deep.

The canary had fallen.

Winter 1983

Report cards for the second marking period came out and I was back in time to claim mine.
It actually didn't hold any surprises. I failed the fluff class with the extra assignments. My homeroom moderator, whom I'd been surprised to see show up at the father's wake, commented on the failing grade when she handed me the report.
"That's a little unlike you, don't you think?"
I grunted and took it from her. *Don't start with me.* In the comment section, the teacher of the failed class had indicated that I had been careless with my assignments. Above that, a nun had commented that I handled her class, in which I had an A, with great care and responsibility. I almost laughed. Well, I guess if you have to be careless and not do your assignments, the least you can do is to do it responsibly. In fact, I had gone from an A to an F in that class. Can't be more responsible at failing something than that. I dropped like a responsible rock. I just couldn't decide if I was carelessly responsible or responsibly careless. *Saw that coming. Who cares? Next?*

***

The following week, a scuffle in homeroom resulted in the entire class being invited back for detention. I never saw what happened. I rolled with it and showed up when we were expected but about half the people in our homeroom skipped it. If I had been scheduled to go to work that day, I wouldn't have been so understanding. Someone else's detention would cost me money. As it was, I had the day off, so hanging around school wasn't a big deal.
Bored, I sat through the half hour wondering what was going on at work. When the teacher, Vivian, ended detention, I stopped at my locker and ran into her on the stairs on the way out. She still looked angry.

"Looks like your day sucked," I observed. "Sorry they couldn't be bothered to show up."

"Yeah. About as much as your year so far."

I agreed that so far my year did, indeed, suck. Talking to her reminded me a lot of my sister. "It's not you," I said. "You know that, right? They act like that every day."

"I do know that but thanks for saying it."

She still looked so upset, I hugged her quickly. She seemed surprised.

"Gotta go. See ya tomorrow."

"See you tomorrow."

If I'd been paying closer attention, I would have seen yet another canary topple over.

Monday evenings were the best. On Monday evenings, I slept over at Doreen's house when her husband Danny worked an overnight shift. The nights at Doreen's felt more homelike than anywhere else I could have been. Not a bedtime went by that I didn't think about my siblings' choice to leave Michael in our house when I could have been living there with Doreen and Danny full time. As far as I knew, Michael had so far refused any access to the house by a realtor or even by Chick or Pat.

How hard would that have been in October? Tell Michael to get the hell out, much like what had been said to me, and have Doreen, Danny and the baby move in. The house had plenty of space. But similar to when no one consulted me about telling the mother she had cancer, no one wanted my opinion on this either. I lived with Maureen and Joe. What was wrong with me that I wasn't making the adjustment? Something was clearly not right; I assumed it was me.

Not that Michael could have been trusted to stay away and leave us alone. Why was he the one still alive? My life would have been so much easier if he would just overdose and be done with it. It happened sometimes in our neighborhood. Guys who used to be nice kids in the neighborhood starting spending a little too much time on the corner, family ties got strained, the mainstay friends were the ones who were also using or the ones who were holding, the weight loss, the scarred skin, the rotting teeth ...and then eventually, you'd see the ambulance in front of their house. Michael, with his bizarre outbursts, was usually only a step or two removed from that scenario. The whole family would be better off without him.

Those long January nights, even the Mondays, were nothing but time to replay October 18th and its unending questions: how the call had come in, how I had rushed to get home. Would things have gone differently if I hadn't gone directly into work? What if I had gone home between school and work? Could I have helped? Would he still have been alive? Could I have called 911 then? Gotten him to a hospital? Would he be alive now? Why hadn't I gone home?

Chick decided to forego an autopsy of his body. He had already had at least two heart attacks and his nightstand was covered with his medications. It followed logically that it was another heart attack, this time fatal. Except...except...

No. No. no nonononono

Don't look.

***

Viv was in her classroom with one of the girls from homeroom when I walked by. I waved. She waved. I poked my head in the door. She was gathering papers to grade. The other student had stopped in, as I was doing, just to say hi. The exchange among the three of us was fast and light and I was ready to leave when Viv commented, "You go ahead. One of these afternoons, though, I'm going to kidnap you and find out what makes you tick."

I found that unusual but let it go. People intended to do lots of things...even good things...that never got done. Don't give it a second thought.

The following week, she invited me over on my day off. This invitation was not out of the ordinary at our school or among my friends. Teachers spent personal time with students. They gave them rides home after basketball or softball games, had them and/or their parents over for dinner, and went out for pizza after special events at school. No one thought anything of it. Last year, I had ended up at a graduation party for a friend with a teacher from the science department. He was dating my friend's sister. Another teacher lived down the street from the father's house. I'd known him my whole life and he gave me a ride to school one morning in his vintage Mustang when I needed to be in early. He still joked about the time I bit him when I was four and left a scar on his arm.

I was curious enough about why she wanted to bridge this gap with me that I agreed to go. I had no intention of letting her find out "what made me tick." If she asked anything I didn't like, I'd leave. For all of her jokes, though, she asked me nothing. We talked about school and her freshman algebra classes, and I watched MTV. No secrets were revealed or even pursued.

The following week, I stayed late at school one afternoon for a prom committee meeting and again met Viv on the stairs on my way out. It was freezing outside and she offered me a ride to Maureen's. Pat had asked me to use the Pinto as little as possible. She worried that I'd run it into the ground before graduation. Most days, I took a city bus to school. When Viv offered me a ride, I appreciated not having to stand on the corner in the cold and wait for the bus. I accepted.

Most of the conversation in the car was casual. She asked me about work, then about school. When she pulled up outside Maureen's, she turned to me. "You know if you ever want to talk about serious stuff, I'm here."

"Serious stuff?" I repeated.

"Yeah. Serious stuff."

"There's nothing to talk about."

She laughed. "The year you're having, there's nothing to talk about?"

"Everything's fine."

Now she repeated me. "Fine?"

I waited to see if a question was coming.

"That's all. Just that. If you want to talk, I'm here."

"Okay. Thanks." I was polite, even while I sat there thinking *no fucking way*!

I opened the passenger door and stood up, the cold air rushing into the car. I glanced at the front of Maureen's house. The blinds moved. What the hell? Was she checking on me? What was so exciting about me talking to a teacher?

"Thanks for the ride!" I slammed the door and she pulled away. I briefly considered asking Maureen why she was peeking through the blinds at me—why not just come out and say hi? I'd introduce her to my homeroom teacher. Then I wondered if she'd admit she'd been peeking at me through the closed blinds or if she'd be embarrassed because I saw it. Maybe she didn't want to meet Vlv. I sighed. *Oh Christ, who cares?* I went into the house and up to my room.

Unlike the nights spent at Doreen and Danny's, the evenings at Maureen's were always hard. Feeling as if I had somehow guilted them into taking me in, I tried to stay out of everyone's way. Alone in my room, I'd make an effort to read or do homework, but it never took long before the questions arrived to distract me.

I thought a lot about dying. I wished for it. It would be okay to be dead. On those cold, quiet evenings, I'd sit at my desk with my arms around my midsection, hunched over whatever textbook I'd brought home, eyes closed, teeth clenched, rocking slightly to quell the screams threatening to well up from my chest. (*It'll be okay. Just don't cry.*) Being dead had to hurt less than this. It didn't take long before the wishing for it morphed into contemplating how I could make it look like an accident.

Why hadn't I gone home? Could I have helped? What if he was still alive at two-thirty when I was on my way to work? What if he'd known something was wrong then and I could have called 911? Or what if it had just happened and he was still conscious?

(What happened?)

No. No. No.

I shoved aside images of the beatings, images of cleaning up after him when he'd had too much to drink. I allowed one lone image to remain. I was twelve years old, going to bed, just starting to drift off when I heard his footsteps on the stairs. He stopped to use the bathroom before coming to my bedroom doorway. I waited for him to speak. He stood for a moment, silent, maybe thinking I was already asleep, then brushed past the dresser to stand by the top of the bed. He bent down in the dark, kissed me quickly on the forehead and turned around and left. He never did that while I was awake. I held on to that image, that one night in the semi-dark, when it was inarguably clear that no matter was going on in our house, he loved me. *Dad, what happened?*

I might have been able to help. (His fingers were bloodless.) I might have been there to call 911 instead of flipping burgers at McDonalds. (His skin was cold.) I should have been there. Jesus, I should have been there. (But he looked asleep.) Why wasn't I there? (His tongue...)

Don't look.

I missed my dog. And oh God, I missed my clumsy, standing-there-in-the-dark Dad.

He had looked asleep. He had looked—

NO! Don't look!

He had looked **posed**.

I bent double, my arms wrapped around myself as tightly as I could. Yes. That was it. He had looked posed. I knew it when I found him, knew it that whole night. It should hurt. Dying should hurt. I had seen him when he'd had his first heart attack. He didn't look relaxed, and he wasn't going to lie down with his hands crossed on his belly and his feet crossed at the ankle. He didn't look right because he **did** look asleep—and dying would hurt. Oh God. What happened that day while I was gone? And why wasn't I there to help him?

Don't look.

***

Guilt and fear battled it out to see which one would be top dog. Unable to move past the image of the father and the way his head rocked to the side when I shook him and the utterly chilling silence in the room when my own exhalation hung up, I returned day after day to the question about why I hadn't gone home to help. I couldn't put words to anything beyond that—just that I should have been there to help.

Help what?
Just help.
Do you think...
NO! Don't look too closely. Don't look.

The cyclical thinking was exhausting. Every path of it ushered me to the same conclusion: I had failed him. I had left him alone. Not only had I left him alone, I left him to die alone. He depended on me, and worse than not being there to help him, my parting words to him before I left that day were to call him an asshole. He was sick. He was worn. He was about to die. And I called him an asshole—the last thing he would ever hear from me. Afraid of waking Michael and getting beaten, I hadn't even said goodbye to him. I was, without question, the most vile person on the planet.

Some days, phone calls from Chick or Pat interrupted the cyclical thinking. They touched base periodically—Pat more than Chick—to ask similar questions. "How are you?" typically led the list. How could I even begin to answer that? Well, if you don't count the fact that I have terrible dreams, and I let our father die alone, and our psycho brother is holding my dog hostage, and people are expecting me to think about college next year but I usually think about driving my car into a bridge abutment several times a day, I'm fine. All that ever came out aloud was, "I'm fine." For all I knew, they really believed it.

***

I couldn't overdose. That was something we'd expect from Michael. I couldn't cut my wrists. The cuts would have to run up the insides of the arm and how much of an accident could that be taken for? There were no garages where I lived, so carbon monoxide poisoning was not an option. Even in our neighborhood, people were likely to notice if I taped a hose to the tailpipe and ran it in through the Pinto's window with the engine idling. That, too, would be hard to pass off as an accident. In addition to it looking like an accident, I didn't want anyone in my family to find me. Especially not Pat, but not even Maureen or Joe. Replaying that soundless room and cold skin, I couldn't do that to anyone else.

    Years later working in the HIV field, I would come to have conversations with men who were exploring physician-assisted suicide. A gentleman named Doug told me about his chosen method one day over coffee. "Take a handful of muscle relaxers," he said, stirring slowly. "Put a plastic bag over your head with a rubber band around your neck, lay down and hold the rubber band out from your neck. As the muscle relaxers begin to work, you'll fall asleep and your grip on the rubber band will loosen. You'll already be unconscious when the rubber band pulls the bag closed around your neck and you'll never feel a thing." Doug ran a hand over his receding hairline and joked about having once been young and cute, and now he was planning his own death.

    I can only wonder what I might have done with this information when I was seventeen.

***

    Another Sunday off in early February, another visit to Viv's house, but this one came with a turn I wasn't expecting. The first visit and the drive to Maureen's had been so uneventful, when Viv finally introduced her questions, they surprised me.

    "So how are you...really?" Before I could speak, she added, "And don't tell me fine, okay?"

    I took my foot off the coffee table and shifted further into the corner of the couch. "I'm okay."

    "You don't talk about what happened."

    "There's nothing to talk about." I crossed my arms around myself.

    "It's pretty big, what happened."

    I said nothing.

    "Everything's changed for you. You still want to tell me you're fine?"

"I am fine."

"You're not fine."

"Well," I countered, "even if I'm not fine, there's nothing you can do, so there's nothing to talk about."

"Most people wouldn't be fine."

"I'm not most people," I pointed out, irritated. I didn't want to be pumped for information.

"Why don't you tell me what happened that day?"

"What day?"

"The day your father died."

I grabbed the half empty glass of Coke on the table beside me and took it to her kitchen. Oh no. Hell no! We were not having this conversation. "I'm gonna go now."

She leaned forward. "No, don't go. I think it would be good if you talked about this."

"I don't **want** to talk about this!"

"Talking might help." She sighed. "Come on. Sit back down." She gestured at the far end of the couch where I'd just been sitting.

"Why? So you can ask me more questions? You can't handle the answers, so why are you asking anyway?"

"I can't handle the answers?"

"No! So just leave it alone!"

She stood up, stepped around the coffee table and came to stand in front of me. She was now in my path, blocking my way to the front door. "Come on. Sit down."

I didn't move in either direction. I didn't want to leave just as much as I didn't want to talk about this. "I'm not talking to you about anything."

"You really don't think it will help to talk about it?"

"Jesus Christ!" My hands, claw-like, came halfway up between us. "No! I don't want to talk about it!"

"Okay then, tell me why you think I can't handle it."

"What difference does it make? I said I don't want to talk about it!"

"At some point, you're gonna need to talk to someone."

"No!"

Her voice never changed volume or tone. "Come on. Sit down. Talk to me."

My fists clenched. She was still standing between me and the door. "No! Move!"

"I'm not moving. Talk to me."

"I'm not talking to you!"

"Then I guess we're not getting very far."

"Okay, then we're not getting very far."

"Except you're going to sit down and talk to me."

"I AM NOT GONNA TALK TO YOU!"

"Tell me what happened that day."

I saw two choices. I could tell her something to make her shut up or I could knock her out of the way. I backed away a step. Every word came out between gritted teeth and my fists were still clenched, held in front of me. "I went home from work and I found him. He was dead in his room—in his bed. I shook him and he was dead. He was grey. He was dead. The ambulance came and they took him away. Okay? He was dead and they took him away."

That was as much as I could say, and even I didn't think what came out had made a whole lot of sense. I didn't have words to tell her about my nightmares or my endless guilt over having left him alone to die, and nothing could ever do justice to my fear that maybe it wasn't a heart attack.

She looked horrified. I don't know what she was expecting, but my freaked out, repetitive explanation didn't seem to be it. "You **found** him?"

That little detail must not have been mentioned in morning announcements when the father's death was broadcast all over the school. I hadn't said anything when I called myself in that. Of course no one knew. I nodded.

"Oh my God...you need a hug!"

This was not a question. I took another step backwards. "No! Don't touch me!"

"It's okay. You need a hug."

She reached for me. I punched her in the jaw. Her head snapped backwards and she covered her face, turning away from me. "Goddammit!"

I angled toward the door, trying to get past her before she threw me out or called the cops, but she snagged my sweatshirt sleeve.

"Okay, okay, don't go."

I hesitated. Was that only so she could call 911? I pictured myself being led away, handcuffed, stuffed into a squad car like when we got arrested for drunk driving when I was eight.

She let go of my sleeve and went back to the couch. She gestured again at the far end. "Come sit down."

I just stood there.

"It's okay. Really."

My fists unclenched but my breathing was still fast and ragged.

"You don't want to talk to me."

"No."

"Can you tell me why?"

No, but thanks for asking! I shook my head.

She rubbed her jaw where I had hit her. She was quiet for a minute, then said, "You're carrying a lot for being seventeen."

I couldn't argue that. I half-nodded, half-shrugged. It probably looked like I had a twitch.

She kind of squinted at me and said, "Come on. Sit down."

There weren't any more questions that afternoon but I turned it over and over in my head on the drive back to my neighborhood. What did she think she could possibly help with? There's no cure for dead. There wasn't any place else to live. All I wanted was to graduate and get a job and be done with this situation. Why would I want to rip open those topics I was barely keeping a grip on? Talking about it was only going to make it worse.

An image hovered just beyond language of what I feared happened on the day the father died. If I got too close to it all, mental brake lights came on and I was propelled away from it. I saw hints of it in dreams, woke up crying, ran from it while I was awake. The only sentence I could put together in relation to it was, "Leave me alone." I applied that to everything. Sometimes, the more congenial "I'm fine" got airtime, but the message was always the same.

* * *

"What does she want with you?" Maureen's tone was suspicious.

"Whaddya mean? She doesn't want anything." I wasn't sure where she was going with these questions.

"Why would she want to spend so much time with you?"

"She spends time with a lot of her students, it's not just me."

"Well, that's weird. Why?"

"I don't know. Lots of teachers do it." I could name a handful of teachers I knew right off the bat who were spending personal time with their students.

"She wants something from you."

What did I have that anybody could possibly want? I shrugged. "I don't know what she could want."

"I'd rather you didn't spend time with her."

"Why?"

"It's weird."

I thought Maureen's suspicions were a little weird. So far, all Viv had done was ask me some questions about a topic no one else discussed with me. Although I didn't want to talk about that topic, I failed to see the harm in spending time with someone who was displaying an interest in how my life was going. This line of questions left me unsettled. Maureen was clearly concerned and I tried to read between the lines. She was afraid that somehow Viv was going to hurt me but I couldn't figure out why. Having just punched her in the face a couple of days ago, it seemed that Viv was at much greater risk of getting hurt than I was.

"We talk about school and stuff. I've helped her grade papers or I watch TV while she does her grading."

Maureen insisted that Viv wanting to spend any time with me was so out of the ordinary, I should steer clear. I was getting annoyed. The whole family knew Michael was pounding the snot out of me on a regular basis up until a couple of months ago. Did anyone think THAT was weird and out of the ordinary besides me (and now Pat)? But someone spending time with me without pounding the snot out of me was weird? That made no kind of sense.

***

I couldn't wrap my thinking around college. I couldn't imagine past June and being able to get a real job and get out on my own. The topic came up regularly and it mystified me. Did these people not understand I needed a real job? How was I going to survive a four-year college with no place to live during breaks and summers off? The idea of four more years with no real home was unfathomable. How was I going to pay for it? It could wait. I needed a job.

I stopped in to Mrs. Eustace's classroom to say hi a few days after my confrontation with Viv and my disturbing conversation with Maureen. I wondered if Maureen would find **this** weird too—you just can't be too careful around those Catholic school faculty members who show an interest in their students. They want to say hi to you? Well, what is it that they really want?

"Have you talked to Jo Canning about scholarships?" Eustace asked.

Jo Canning, the director of guidance, wouldn't know me if she fell over me. In four years, I had never felt compelled to be guided by her, had never been inside the guidance office. "No, why?"

"She has some scholarship information you should know about."

Now seemed as good a time as any to introduce my decision. I shrugged. "It won't make any difference. I'm not going to college."

"What do you mean, you're not going? Of course you're going."

"I need to work."

"This is why you need to talk to Ms. Canning."

"There's no point. I can't go away next year."

(If I was even still here next year...)

She glanced up at me, packing her materials to leave for the day. "So what is it you will be doing—slinging hash at McDonald's?!" She waved a hand in my direction. "Don't be ridiculous. That's no future!"

I didn't know whether to laugh or get defensive. "It's an option!"

She straightened up to look at me, leaning against her French book set spine down on the desktop. Her next words were slow and enunciated clearly, making me wonder if she thought I had turned into the main character in *Flowers for Algernon*. "You not going to college is not an option."

"Me not having a job is not an option," I shot back. "I'm. Not. Going!"

She came around her desk quickly, more quickly than I cared for. "Do **not** speak to me like that. And you **are** going!" She grabbed my shoulder and pulled me around so we were both facing the same direction. "I'm not having this conversation with you!" She thunked me on the head with the textbook.

"Hey! Ow!" I protested.

"Get out of my classroom!" She pushed me toward the door, thumping my shoulder with every step. "Get out. Go! Right now!"

"Okay! Okay!" I went, half-willingly, half-propelled out the door. Apparently not everyone saw the logic in postponing my college entrance. *That went well. Damn. Did she really just hit me in the head?*

***

The note arrived in homeroom, delivered by a messenger from the Activities Office. "Anne Mullen needs to see Sister Clarence immediately on an urgent matter."

"Anne," Sister Clarence greeted me, "there's a problem with your tuition and until you pay it, you can't attend prom."

After twelve years of Catholic school and nuns who used only my formal name, it hardly registered with me anymore. I waited a moment before I spoke. This was the third time this same nun had initiated this conversation. Each time, I had to remind her that Pat and I had met with the principal within days of the father's death to talk about my tuition, and he had waived it for the remainder of the year. "Sister, you asked me about this already and I told you that Father Slane waived my tuition."

"Father Slane would not waive your tuition!" She glared at me over the counter as if I were some new specimen of insect.

"But he did."

"There is no reason why he would do that! You **must** pay your tuition!"

It wouldn't take a rocket scientist to realize that this woman, who had to be somewhere near eighty, was unable to remember this conversation from one day to the next, so every time a new senior activity came up, we had the same conversation again. Each time, she implied that I was lying to her. The last time, I had even encouraged her to call Pat and to please speak directly to Father Slane, with whom the arrangement had been made.

"Sister," I said, wanting to grab her nun-collar, "the **reason** my tuition is waived is because my father just died, there's a problem with his Social Security benefits, and I'm working to support myself."

"Don't you take that tone with me!"

That was a popular theme this week.

"We've had this conversation three times already! I've asked you to call my sister. I've asked you to confirm the agreement with Father Slane!" I stopped short of yelling at her

183

to write it down, for Chrissake, so she could remember it for the rest of the year. "Is he here? Can I speak to him?"

She hesitated. "No, he's not here."

"When he comes in, can we talk to him together? You keep asking me this same question and I keep giving you the same answer. "

"Don't you get smart with me."

"Sister, I'm not trying to get smart with you. This is what we agreed to."

She slammed a book on the counter. "I will call your sister! You are not going to stand there and talk to me like this!"

"Fine! Great! Please call my sister!" I grabbed the Bic pen stuck on the shoulder of my uniform where everyone carried them. "Here's her number. She's home after six." As I exited, Sister Clarence slammed something else and yelled that she was not going to put up with me.

***

Maureen had just left to run an errand, taking the kids with her. Already dressed in my work uniform, I tugged my jacket on, checked for car keys in the pocket and opened the front door. Champ, Maureen's two-year-old boxer, shot out between me and the door frame, jumping the front steps and darting out into the street.

The oncoming car's driver saw him and stamped on the brakes, but the car's front end slammed against Champ's shoulder. Champ yowled, holding one front leg in the air. My mouth went dry—I couldn't even yell to him. I got my feet engaged and lurched after him where he shivered under a parked car. I couldn't tell if his front leg was broken.

I had no idea who they used as a vet. I had no idea how long Maureen would be. Joe was at work and wouldn't be home for hours. I ran back in the house, snatched up the phone and called Aunt Connie's house. Rick answered.

"Rick, Champ just got hit by a car!"

"Where is he?"

"He's right outside. But he's hurt. He needs to go to the vet—I think his leg might be broken."

"I'll be right there!"

Rick came running around the block and I pointed him to the car where Champ was hiding, whining softly. He coaxed him out and Champ crawled forward in obvious pain. My breathing hitched a little and I felt my lower lip quiver. I felt horrible. Rick lifted him up, cradling him against his chest. "I'll take him in." He glanced at me. "You were going to work?"

"Yeah."

"Go ahead. I'll tell Maureen when she gets home. Did he just run out?"

"He bolted when I opened the door. I never saw him coming."

Rick nodded. "It's okay. I've got him."

Enormously grateful for Rick's sense of calm, I locked the door and went to work. I had no clue that Champ would bolt—he'd never done it before. Had he seen something? Smelled or heard something?

Champ was home when I got back after work. His shoulder was injured but nothing was broken. Maureen was strained and cold. I couldn't tell if she was angry that Champ had gotten out, or that I had called Rick to take care of him and then gone to work. I didn't think it mattered.

***

Pat phoned the next day to say she'd had a positively uplifting conversation with some forgetful old nun from the Activities Office. I hadn't even had a chance to let her know the call would be coming.

"I'm tellin' ya," she said, laughing, "they need to put that woman out to pasture."

"Did you talk just to her?"

"No, I talked to Father Slane again too. He said he would handle the problem in the Activities Office, and you won't be asked again why you aren't paying tuition. But do yourself a favor, babe. Don't piss her off. She's not all with us."

***

When Viv invited me to visit that weekend, I was going regardless of Maureen's preference about not spending time with her. My presence in their house created an incredibly tense atmosphere. I was starting to think that she hated me. I didn't think Joe did but I was fairly certain that Maureen did and it made my insides wither. Joe made occasional friendly overtures toward me, sometimes giving me hints about what I was doing wrong, what he thought were the source of the tension between Maureen and me.

"You don't talk to us, Nance. Sometimes you could talk to us."

Could I? That would be new and different after 12 years of "Nobody needs to know".

"Maureen says you went to bed with the dryer running. She doesn't feel comfortable sleeping with the dryer running, in case anything goes wrong."

I went to bed with the dryer running because I worked until midnight most nights. When I needed a clean uniform or something for school, that was one of my few chances to do laundry. That's how I'd done it at home. I had no idea she didn't like the dryer running after I went to bed. Okay. Now I knew. If that's what it took to make her happy, I'd wait up. Unfortunately, I hadn't found out exactly what else would be needed to make Maureen happy to have me there. So when Viv asked if I wanted to come over, I was going.

Two weeks had passed since my last visit. I guessed my point had been taken. We are not going to talk about—**couldn't** talk about—certain topics. And don't touch me! Those things seemed perfectly clear to me. The first hour or so went without incident. I had just finished telling her about the Activities Office problem when it started.

"So," she said, "tell me why you think I can't handle hearing about what's going on with you."

"Because I don't."

"Don't you think you could let me decide?"

"No."

"You have an awful lot of control over your life for someone who's seventeen."

"What's your point?"

"You need someone to depend on besides yourself."

"For what?" I scoffed. "I'm doing just fine."

"You're not fine."

"I **am** fine!"

"You're working too many hours, you just failed a class, you look exhausted all the time! You're not fine! I tried to hug you and you hit me. That's not fine!"

"What do you care if I fail a class?"

She rolled her eyes. "Somebody needs to take you in hand."

"Well, that won't be you."

"You are too young to be carrying the responsibility you're carrying."

"That's none of your fucking business. I'm not a kid and I can handle it."

"It **is** my business. I care about you. And don't talk to me that way in my house."

"I don't need anything from you. I don't need you to care about me."

"I didn't ask your permission. This is what happens when people care about you."

"I can fucking take care of myself. Mind your own fucking business."

This was going nowhere I wanted to be. I stood up to go. She stood up too.

"Okay—reminder. You are seventeen. You **are** a kid. So who died and left you boss?"

"My father!"

She clapped one hand to her forehead. "I understand you better if I take everything you say and turn it upside down and inside out."

I should have left. It would have gone so much better if I had just left. I hadn't invited this line of questioning, and I wasn't going to let it go any further. It was time for her to step back. "Go fuck yourself!" I yelled.

"Do you know what you need?"

I needed nothing from her. I didn't want to talk to her about the father, didn't want to talk about living in a house with strangers who didn't want me there (nor did they want me **here** for that matter), didn't want to talk about my awful dreams or how badly I missed my dog or how much I thought about dying. She couldn't do anything about any of that. No. I needed nothing.

"You don't worry about what I fucking need! I'll decide what I fucking need!" Once again, my fists were clenched, my shoulders tight.

She took a step closer to me. "You need somebody who will grab hold of you and not let go, no matter what you say or what you do."

Now she was in my space. I jabbed her in the collarbone. "And YOU need to back the fuck off!"

"Stop poking me!"

"You don't fucking ask me those questions! You stop it!" Poke, poke, poke, poke. Harder. I was probably leaving bruises. I didn't care. I was going to make her stop.

"Don't talk to me like that!"

I stopped poking, and my hand flattened out. It wasn't a conscious decision—I wasn't thinking clearly enough beyond MAKE HER SHUT UP to say it was a true decision. I shoved her, short, open-handed jabs to her shoulder every few seconds. I had learned this from a pro.

She braced one foot behind her and rocked backwards every time I struck. "Enough! Don't push me like that!"

"You need to back the fuck off! I told you—I'm not gonna talk to you!"

"Don't talk to me like that!"

Again, it wasn't a conscious decision. I shoved her with both hands, hitting her shoulders repeatedly. She was jolted by each strike, but then righted herself like some irritating, inflatable punching bag that won't stay down.

"Come on!" I shouted, daring her. "Ask me something now!" Another shove. Then another.

"Stop!" She pushed my hands away, and kind of a shove-slap, shove-slap cycle progressed as she tried to avoid contact.

"Fuck you!"

She reached for me. What little conscious thought I was still capable of ended. My knees bent, my fists clenched, and I brought one fist up between us.

Nanoseconds before the punch landed, she caught a handful of the shoulder of my sweatshirt. When I hit her, she already had a grip on me. The punch knocked her off balance and she took some steps backward to regain it. She half-stumbled past the coffee table—did she catch her ankle on it? I couldn't be sure. The couch was directly behind her now, and when she couldn't take one more step back, momentum carried her anyway and she sat down fast.

I was closer than I wanted to be and things were moving very quickly. She dragged me with her those few steps while I tried twisting her hand loose. When she fell backward onto the couch, she yanked on my shirt. Accident? Intentional? I didn't know. I lost my balance. She pulled me over her knee. Accident? Intentional? I didn't know that either. I dropped with an audible *ooof*. She grabbed my sleeve and had an elbow ...resting???.. .jammed???...between my shoulder blades. I was stuck.

"Let go! You better fucking let me go right now!" I yelled.

"You are in too precarious a position to talk to me like that," she said.

"Fuck you! Let go!"

She didn't say anything more. Maybe it shouldn't have been so much a surprise when she started to smack me.

When she did finally let go, I couldn't look at her. I jerked upright, snatched up my jacket and ran. She took a few steps after me, calling for me to stop. *No way*. I didn't know where I was going—just away. I slammed the car door and squealed out of the parking space while Viv called me from her front door.

My thoughts raced, more images than words or ideas. She had **hit** me. The irony of being panic-struck over this didn't occur to me for many years. I spent ten years being punched, kicked, stomped on, spit on, knocked down stairs. I went to school with black eyes, blue ears, handprints on me, patches of hair ripped out, and more recently shown up at Eustace's house sporting part of a footprint. But she had hit me.

I picked up speed on the expressway, nudging the rattling Pinto to over seventy. It shuddered but tried to comply, and the slideshow in my head sped up along with the car. The father. The house. The dog. The blood on my hand. Mono. The dog. The father. ("It'll be okay. Just don't cry.") I wasn't crying. The dog. The father. The house. Pat. Chick. The dog. The father.

How much would it hurt?

I didn't plan it. I paced a pickup truck almost twice the size of my car for a few seconds. Would it be fast? Would I flip? Go airborne? Break my neck? Crush my skull? I revved the Pinto a little harder and pulled forward of the pickup. Holding my breath, I jerked the wheel and swerved in front of the truck, stepping on the brake.

Tires screeched. The pickup shot into the left lane where I had just been, overtaking me as the Pinto slowed. The driver shouted something at me and gestured wildly. Other cars were now pulling around me too, dodging me, horns blaring.

"HIT ME!" I screamed at his taillights. "HIT ME!"

Was There Ever Really a Frying Pan?

The adrenaline surge was incredible. My vision seemed sharper, my hearing more acute, my heart pounded and except for the fact that I was also nauseated, I thought I could tuck the Pinto under one arm and jog back to Maureen's from New Jersey. I punched the dashboard, then the passenger seat, emitting a loud guttural growl that wasn't really language. I was still here. The pickup truck had missed me. Maybe it would have worked differently in heavier traffic. Did I cut in close enough to the pickup's front end?

I was still edgy when I arrived at Maureen's and thankfully she didn't ask how my day went. I might sound a little on the hysterical side if I told her, "Well, it was good up until I punched my teacher in the face and then she kicked my ass and when I left her house I drove into the path of a speeding pickup truck, but hey, other than that, same old, same old." I kept my mouth shut and closed up in my room at the first opportunity.

How was I going to face Viv at school tomorrow? I had **told** her repeatedly that I didn't want to talk about the things she was asking about. I should have left sooner. She had hit me. Well, why not? I reasoned. I hit her first. Twice. This was all my fault. I should have cleared out at the first question.

To go where?

I stopped, mid-self-criticism. What exactly were the options?

I got...crickets.

***

I had to make Viv understand. She didn't get to know about this. While it was very tempting to consider cutting any contact with her outside of school, I was drawn, even though I didn't want to be and didn't trust it, to the fact that she was asking me about something that everyone else avoided. Part of me was relieved to be recognized. But what she recognized was limited. She knew only that the father had died. It wasn't just that he had died. It was everything that led up to it, and the mess that was created when he died.

What would people think of me if I told them what living with the father and Michael had been like? How could I explain to anyone what it was like to have hammers thrown at your face? Or to jump on your brother's back when he has the father by the hair and he's hitting him in the face over and over, and the father is drunk, crying, bleeding, and begging to be left alone? Or to have the father go missing for days at a time, leaving you alone in the house with someone like Michael? Could I ever tell anyone about the pigeon? Or what it was like to wake up to the father pacing the living room, stopping to load a handgun, because drug dealers were outside our house with baseball bats, waiting for Michael to return and talking about just breaking in? What it was like to be dragged out of sleep by Michael rampaging through the house, looking for drugs he thought he had, punching and slapping me awake, overturning my bed with me in it, emptying my dresser drawers and closet—as if I would touch that shit? What it was like to have Michael on top of you, holding handfuls of your hair, beating your head against the floor, your hair coming out in clumps and the world spinning out of focus? What it was like to have Michael on top of you, holding a pillow over your face, his knees on your arms, rubbing against your chest while you go limp under him and everything starts to grey out? Wordless shame burned.

Don't look.

(It'll be okay. Just don't cry.)

("It's okay, he didn't mean it." "He didn't **mean** it? He didn't **mean** that he would rape me? What else could he have **meant** when he said, 'I'll rape you so you can see how you like it' after he punched the shit out of me and has me pinned to a wall? How many meanings does that have, Dad?" No answer.)

At least I wasn't crying.

Don't look.

That's what Vlv wanted to hear about? This whole "Tell me how you feel" thing...how **did** it make me feel? *Well, like I* *want to drive in front of a pickup truck. Let's not dig any deeper than that.*

Anger and embarrassment accompanied self-blame and me to school the next morning. In homeroom, I didn't speak to anyone and cleared out as soon as the bell rang. I had to make her understand. I returned to Viv's classroom later, intent on my mission.

"Look, I just don't want to talk about that stuff at all. With anyone."

"Mmm hmm." She was getting ready to go home.

"So don't ask me anything else. Just leave it alone, okay?"

"Don't tell me what I can ask."

I ran one hand over the top of my head and tried a different angle. "I'm really okay, and I really don't need you to ask me about that stuff."

"Mmm hmmm." Very non-committal. She wasn't looking at me.

"And don't touch me again, alright? And don't hit me."

Before I could add that I wouldn't hit her again either, she said, "I did hit you."

The one hand that I had run over the top of my head clutched hair on the back of my skull, and I pulled as my frustration built. Her acknowledgment of what happened felt so...trivial. "Don't do it again," I said, louder than before.

"If you hit me again, I'll do it again. Somebody has to take you in hand."

I released my grip on my hair and stuffed my fist in my uniform pocket. I wanted to hit her right then. What did I need to say to make her understand? "No!" I searched for the right words. "NO! No questions! And you don't hit me!"

There. That seemed clear.

"You're a kid. You don't get all the choices, sorry."

"What is wrong with you? I'm fine, if you'd just leave it alone. Why can't you just back off?"

"There's nothing wrong with me. And you are not fine."

Fleetingly, I considered slamming her head against the blackboard. I clenched my teeth, frustration now fully entwined with my anger and embarrassment. "Fuck this!"

***

After a few hours at work, I calmed down enough to try thinking it through one more time. Clearly, she hadn't understood me. Before I went to bed, I wrote down what I wanted to say.

> *I know you think you're helping, but you can't. It will be better if you*
> *just don't ask me lots of questions. Please don't touch me anymore.*
> *I don't like to be touched. And don't hit me.*
> *Nobody gets to hit me.*

I thought that was pretty straight forward. I wondered if I should say something about being sorry that I had hit her and opted against it. I could apologize later. I read it again. It was short, rational, and polite. How could she object? How could she miss my point?

***

I set the note on Viv's desk. "Please read that. That's all I want to say."

She agreed she would read it. I told her I would talk to her about it before I left for work. She agreed to that too. When I returned that afternoon, she handed me the piece of paper. "I wrote some comments in the margins."

I unfolded it, expecting to see that she finally understood what I was asking. Her responses to my comments inked in red around the edges were something like:

Don't tell me what to do.
I know you think you're helping but you can't. It will be better if you just don't ask me lots of questions. Please don't touch me anymore. *You don't decide.*
I don't like to be touched. And don't hit me. Nobody gets to hit me.

I will touch you. *If you do that, I'll spank you.*

Merely a repeat of everything we'd already argued over.

Heat built up in my ears. I was too embarrassed to speak and knew nothing socially acceptable would come out right now anyway. I had to be done. I walked out.

After work, I pulled the paper out again and reread it. Nope, I wasn't misunderstanding it. I couldn't tell if she was ignoring what I tried to tell her or if somehow I wasn't clear. Not that it mattered; it didn't change the outcome. I shoved a pile of books aside. Fuck this. I couldn't deal with her right now. I folded the paper in half and jammed it in a drawer. Fuck it all. If she couldn't get what I was asking, I'd just stay away from her.

***

The day that senior prom was originally scheduled brought us the worst snowstorm Philadelphia had had in decades with more than two feet of snow. Tux shops were in a tailspin trying to reschedule everyone's tux reservations. Prom seemed like a formality...a rite I had to get through, however mechanically, to make this year hurry up and get over. I liked Joey, the guy going to prom with me, a lot, and we always had fun when we worked together, but I had no energy for dating anyone. I couldn't have cared less. It was kind of like the question about college. Having a job and a place to live were more pressing.

I thought for a long time that dating would become more important when life felt manageable. It had never felt manageable living with the father and Michael. I looked forward to the time when I'd feel about a guy the way I knew some of my friends felt about their boyfriends. But I didn't, at least not yet. I didn't feel that way about anybody. Prom was rescheduled for the first weekend in March.

***

For those last couple of weeks of February, I did a good job of dodging Viv. I saw her in homeroom, but I avoided her classroom otherwise and I cleared out as fast as I could at the end of each homeroom. Maureen said nothing new about the time I had spent with her, so I tried to focus on the next hurdle, graduation. Winter hadn't loosened its grip yet and wouldn't for a few more weeks when I arrived home one early March afternoon to find Maureen looking and sounding very upset.

"I called your sister and she's coming here to talk to you."

"About what? What's wrong?"

"There's something we need to talk about and I think she should be here."

Shit! What had I done now? Was she freaked because I was out all night after prom? I thought she had understood that was my plan. I thought back over the past few weeks. Had I done laundry too late? Taken a shower at the wrong time? Left dishes in the sink? I came up blank.

When Pat got there, she looked equally upset. We sat around the kitchen table. Maureen started.

"You know I've been worried…"

I waited.

"It's not right. I think it's weird," she continued.

What the hell was she talking about? What did I do that was so awful she had called my sister to get in the middle of it?

"I went through your desk. I found your note."

It didn't immediately register what she was referring to, but the fact that she had gone through my desk put me on high alert right away.

"I called Pat and I read the note to her. Nance, are you sleeping with her—that teacher?"

"What?!"

"The note you wrote that she wrote on too—she touched you. And she says she will again. Are you..." Maureen's voice lowered to a conspiratorial tone. "Are you having an affair with her?"

This could not be happening. Stunned at first, I didn't know what to say.

"Are you gay?"

"WHAT?!" I repeated. I was having trouble taking it in. "You called Pat here because you think I'm sleeping with my teacher?"

"Are you?"

"NO!"

"But she touched you—you said so in the note. Did she make a pass at you?"

"I'm not sleeping with her. And she would never make a pass at me."

I was not about to go into the story that she had beaten me after I punched her. And neither one of them asked about it, but Maureen was completely hung up on the fact that I had told Viv not to touch me again, and she was not taking it as I had meant it.

"How do you know?"

"Because she wouldn't. Have you ever talked to her? You don't know anything about her."

Two weeks ago, I had been ready to slam Viv's head against her own blackboard. Now I felt strangely protective of her and completely betrayed.

"I know it's weird that you spend so much time with her."

Pat put a hand on my arm to interrupt. "Babe, has she done something to you?"

I shook her hand off. "NO! And I haven't seen her outside of school since before the prom."

"But before that you were going over to her house." Back to Maureen's concerns.

"Yeah, I've been to her house and I told you what I did while I was there. What are you doing going through my desk?"

"I don't trust her."

"**She** doesn't live here. That's my desk. Just say it—you don't trust **me**."

Why hadn't I thrown that goddamn piece of paper away?

"No, I don't trust you."

I stood up. Pat held onto my arm again. "Nance, wait—"

"Let's just say it then. This isn't working!"

"No, it's not working!" Maureen yelled. "You exposed both my kids to mono! You don't know how to live with other people! How many times did you keep me up all night with your laundry? You let my poor dog out and he got run over by a car! Do you know how much money that cost us?"

"**Let** him out? He charged the door! I didn't even know he was there!"

"Were you watching him? You know if boxers hurt their shoulders, they have to be put to sleep. You almost killed him. It's your fault he got hurt. If it hadn't been for you..."

I knew this was going to come up. She'd been so angry with me since Champ ran out that day. At least she was finally being honest with me. If it hadn't been for me, what? Their home wouldn't be invaded by strangers...strangers with dead parents and junkie brothers. If it hadn't been for me, the Epstein-Barr virus would not have been introduced into their home at Christmas time, even though I did everything I could think of not be a nuisance to her. The thoughts were gone in an instant, taking only enough time to scrape the top layer off barely healed wounds before they vanished.

"So you think I'm sleeping with my teacher, you think I'm gay, you think I wanted to make your kids sick, and you think I tried to kill your dog. Anything else?" My voice started to break. She was being honest, but wow, was it hard to hear. She did hate me. I hadn't been wrong about that. But it was still hard to hear. (It'll be okay. Just don't cry.)

"What do you want from me, Nance? Haven't we done enough?"

Did that question take into consideration making Christmas happen for us the year the mother died? The times she and Joe had tried to help when Michael hurt me? Or were we considering just this year?

What was that expression on her face? Frustration? Impatience? God...no. It was revulsion.

I didn't know how to answer and wasn't even sure if she expected me to. Had they? What else could I ask for? They couldn't bring my parents back. They couldn't give me my home back. This was not going to become my home. They couldn't do anything to alleviate my guilt or my fear that I should have been home to help the father that day in October, and then we wouldn't even be having this conversation. They would never be able to explain to me why the father looked as if he'd been posed when I found him. They really had done enough. This--I--was not their problem. I pulled loose from Pat's hand. I started to speak, my voice cracked again, and I refused to go any further. I turned away and went upstairs, leaving them at the table.

Pat followed me after a couple of minutes. I was in the bathroom, holding handfuls of water to my face. She squeezed in with me and rubbed small circles between my shoulder blades as I bent over the sink.

"Babe..." she said softly. "What do you want to do?"

I stood up, reaching for a towel. Taking a deep breath, I said, "She doesn't trust me and she doesn't want me here. I can't live somewhere where I'm not trusted, and she's always looking for the things I'm doing wrong whether I'm doing things wrong or not. Jesus Christ, she thinks I tried to kill Champ. I have to go."

After a moment, Pat nodded. "I think you do, too." She hugged me, kissing me on the head. "I'm sorry, babe."

"Me too." (Just don't cry.) "I'll talk to Marie and see if I can stay there for a little while."

"I'll talk to Roger about getting your stuff out of here. We'll take it to my house. After graduation, come with me. It'll be easier that way for me to help you get ready for college."

Oh yeah, that's right. We were all still deluding ourselves thinking I could go to college.

***

Nothing about it felt good, but nothing about it surprised me either. Being asked to leave when I got sick was a clue. Even before that, it had never been her idea to have me move in. I remembered being in Pat's kitchen in October, wondering when she agreed to the plan if she had tried to talk Joe out of it or if he had talked her into it. Sitting on the bed after being told I was unfit to live with, my knees drawn up and my back against the wall, I tried to make myself as small a target as possible.

Pat had left. I hadn't gone back downstairs. My presence was definitely not requested. I didn't know if Pat and Maureen had had words before Pat left; if so, they had been exchanged in whispers.

Arms around my legs, I squeezed harder and chewed on the inside of my cheek. What had I done wrong? This couldn't be just because of Viv. Could it? How did anyone get from Point A where Viv wanted me to talk about the father dying to Point B where Maureen thought Viv was trying to hurt me? I thought I was reading Viv correctly: she didn't understand why I wouldn't just talk to her. For that, I had punched her in the face—twice. How could anyone misinterpret that for her hurting me?

I wished I could call Marie right then, but the phone was in the kitchen. In those small row homes, the kitchen-bone was connected directly to the living room-bone, often without the advantage of a divider wall. I had no privacy. I couldn't very well go stand in the kitchen with Maureen and the kids eight feet away in the living room and call the father's girlfriend to tell her I was being displaced.

My thoughts circled to the house down the street. My house. Or what was supposed to be my house. The father's house. Now Michael's house. Where my dog lived. I hoped.

I bit harder and tasted blood. My shoulders felt uncomfortably tight, and I could tell the tendons were standing out on my neck again. My house.

Nope, I don't have a house. I don't have a place to be.

Joe's voice: *You don't talk to us, Nance. Sometimes you could talk to us.*

Maureen's voice: *It's all your fault he got hurt...if it hadn't been for you...*

Michael's voice: *This is MY house, you stupid whore.*

Pat's voice: *Is this what he's like with you?*

The memories swirled into one another. I clamped my hands around my head, pulling my hair, trying to channel some of it out. It didn't help much.

What would I say to Marie? Maureen doesn't want me here? I can't be here? Maureen thinks I'm having an affair with a teacher from my school? She thinks I want to hurt her family? She thinks I'm gay?

For that matter, what would I say to Aunt Connie and the rest of the family? That sent a chill through me, and I recalled clearly the feeling I had when Maureen told me not to come back at Christmas time. You are not family. Don't get comfortable. The magnitude of this situation came sharply into focus. This wasn't just about Maureen and me. Aunt Connie, Doreen, Rick, David...they were Maureen's family. I wasn't family. I didn't belong.

That knife-like pain I recognized from the father's funeral went through my chest. I shifted my arms from around my legs to around my middle and hunched over into a tight ball. This was supposed to have been my best option. Now what?

Chick's voice: *You can't stay here.*

Maureen's voice: *No, this is not working!*

Michael's voice: *Don't you fucking come back here!*

When I squeezed my eyes shut, I could see the sky the way I saw it the afternoon Michael kicked me out of the front door of the father's house, a long, skinny sky between stretches of row home roofs, jarring in and out of focus as I whacked my head against each concrete step. I opened my eyes quickly. I didn't want to see that. But I also didn't really want to look around at this room. I didn't belong here. I never had.

It was a blue pickup truck, I remembered, more in images than in words, and it was big. I could still feel the sideways lurch and the drag of the brakes when I swerved in front of the truck. I hadn't cut it close enough.

I glanced at my desk, then at the dresser. For all I cared, Pat didn't need to ask Roger to come move this stuff to their house. Give it back to Michael. He had everything else. Put it on the curb on trash day. What difference would it make?

("It'll be okay. Just don't cry.")

If I'd been closer, that truck would have hit me. I wouldn't make the same mistake again.

***

"Heya, baby! How you doin'?" Marie was glad to see me. Since the dog situation, I had visited only sporadically, finding it awkward and even painful to spend time there.

I pulled out the chair where the father usually sat at Marie's kitchen table. She always sat at the far end near the back door and he always sat at the end closer to the doorway to the dining room. I could picture him, feet out to the sides almost straddling the chair, elbows on the table, leaning forward, a stream of blue smoke rising from the Winston in the ashtray in front of him. This was one of the other reasons being here felt awkward and painful.

"What can I getcha? Want some Coke?" she asked.

I nodded. She poured.

"I know this isn't the greatest timing, with your mother staying with you and all," I started. "It's just that things aren't working out at my cousin's."

I hesitated, unsure of how much to tell her. Marie didn't know my cousins well. She had met David many times, but in seven years, she had never met any of the others. She'd met David because he was the only one willing (*Brave enough? Patient enough?*) to step foot in our house after the mother was gone. My connection to David, Ricky and Doreen was all that tied our families together.

It dawned on me that the night the father died, Marie had opted not to come to see me, even though she had said she would. ("*We'll come. I'll find a ride.*") Her daughter and her son and his wife had come to see me. Was that because she just couldn't pull it together? Or was that because she knew she might not have been welcome at Maureen's house? When they arrived that night, we stood on the porch. No one invited them in or offered them a drink, as Marie had just done for me. God, what did I need—an anvil to the head? Of course they were left on the porch. They weren't family.

Well, what do you know? I wasn't family either. We were all going to be out on that porch together.

"You ain't gettin' along?"

"More than that. I need to leave. It's…it's just…I can't…she doesn't…" So far, I was doing a bang-up job of expressing myself. I took a deep breath. "I can't stay there anymore. I was wondering…Pat and I talked…would it be okay for me to be here for a while?"

Marie started nodding even before I finished speaking. "Sure, Nance. You can be here. It's crowded, but you can be here."

Marie lived in a small two-bedroom house that her sons had bought for her a couple of years before. She and her daughter shared one room. One grown son had the second room. Her other son, the one who'd come to Maureen's that night in October, lived in New Jersey. Recently, her mother had come to stay as well, and she slept on the couch every night. One more person was living with her now than in October when I had decided not to move in because it had been too crowded. Marie would open her home to me, but she'd have to put me on the floor somewhere.

I shifted in the chair that the father had sat in for hundreds of evening visits over the years he and Marie were together. I wondered if he'd been sitting in this very chair when he asked her to marry him, or if she was sitting in that chair when she declined because she wouldn't live in the same house with Michael. Or if my dog had rested under this table, waiting patiently and listening for the front door to open on those days I couldn't get here to see her. The pain in the room was almost tangible.

Being Fine

I slept on the floor in Marie's room. Or rather, I rested there. I wasn't sure you could call what I was able to do "sleeping." I dozed, waking frequently. I didn't have a place to put my clothes, so I piled them around the room and hoped they wouldn't be in the way. If they were, Marie never mentioned it. I realized quickly, though, that a benefit to not sleeping well or much was that at least I had stopped crying during the night.

My work schedule made things even more challenging. Still working the closing shift as many evenings as I could, I felt guilty about coming in at one a.m. and waking Marie when I put my blankets together on the floor. Not working was not a consideration. Marie never complained about the early morning wake ups. To the contrary, she usually asked how work had been and then wished me a good night's sleep. I'd been there only a few days when Pat asked if I would come see her, and I agreed I would visit that weekend.

Pat and Roger lived in rural Chester County, southwest of the city, close to the Delaware state line in one direction and to the Amish farming community in the other. I couldn't imagine a place I would less like to live. The area was undeveloped. I was a city kid. I looked around and wondered how they managed to survive without a corner store. Not only wasn't there a corner store, there weren't sidewalks, so technically there wasn't a corner! Accustomed to everything being within walking distance or, at the farthest, a bus ride away, I hated being cut off and surrounded only by trees for company. Pat loved it. I teased her that she had a screw loose.

Once off US Route 1, Pennsylvania State Routes 796 and 896 cut twisted paths with only sporadic directional striping through farmland. On the way to Pat's house, most of it was narrow, two lane roadways with no shoulder and the occasional blind curve. Street lights were unheard of. The roads had been carved through hillsides and long stretches were flanked by steep embankments lined with generations-old trees. In the flatter areas close to the Amish farms, the woods came directly to the edges of the road, branches forming a canopy over the asphalt. It couldn't have been more perfect.

It was almost dark when I exited Route 1 and headed south. I trailed another car, paying little attention to make or model. Numb to what I was about to do, I stayed close to that car, running the route in my head. I knew the road well enough. I had figured out a different approach than what I had done the day I'd taken off from Viv's.

There were few passing zones on 896 due to the obstructed views caused by curves in the road and the rolling inclines of Pennsylvania farm country. The road could not have been called congested by any stretch of the imagination, but it was regularly traveled in both directions. I counted on that. I stayed on the bumper of the other car until we hit the stretch just north of New London where I gauged visibility was at its lowest. Clenching my teeth, I pulled into the left lane in the no-passing zone and floored it.

Well, "floored it" might be something of a misnomer as related to a ten-year-old Pinto. It chugged happily along, drawing on all the engine power of its sixteen asthmatic gerbils, inching up parallel with the other car. I could see nothing ahead of me. If a car came around a curve or over an incline, I would have three choices: head on collision, take the shoulder and wrap the Pinto around a tree, or hit the car in the right lane. Which one I ended up with would be determined by how fast my reflexes were and how much of a coward I turned out to be.

Sweat jumped up to the surface of my skin. I could hear my own heartbeat and I strained against the steering wheel, not sure if I should push or pull. I may have done both at the same time. The car beside me blasted its horn. I held the accelerator to the floor, leaning into the steering column like a jockey urging on his horse. *Headlights—give me headlights!* Unexpectedly, the car in the right lane slowed, dropping back to give me a wide berth.

Game over.

No oncoming headlights. No choice to make.

At Pat's, I pulled up outside the house and parked at the edge of the front yard. I took a few seconds to slow my breathing, pressing the sleeve of my sweatshirt against my face. I felt a little wild-eyed. When I thought I was sufficiently pulled together, I went in.

Pat turned away from making dinner to hug me hello. "Hi, babe. How are you?"

What else could I say?

"Fine."

***

I found a broken chaise lounge in the basement at Marie's. When I asked, she indicated that she didn't mind if I brought it upstairs. It didn't recline fully, so I slept partly sitting up, but at least I was off the floor. Roaches were a common problem in those row houses. If your neighbors had them, so did you. Marie kept her house sprayed to repel them, but they were still around. I had no interest in sharing my blankets with them. I wanted off the floor. Let them get their own blankets.

Pat and I had spent much of the weekend talking about getting me ready for college. She could help with financial aid forms since she had just finished filing the father's taxes. She had all of the information she needed. What she didn't have, though, was my interest or even my belief that I would still be here in August to go away to school. All it would take were headlights of an oncoming car, and the whole college discussion was out the window.

A year ago, I had entertained the idea of applying to the Air Force Academy in Colorado. Chick was career Air Force, twenty years, expecting to retire as a Lt. Colonel, and he thought he would be able to help me secure my Congressional letter of recommendation. The risk was that it might take some time (the first women at the academy started only two years earlier, so there was some question about how well received the request would be by the people from whom we sought that letter), meaning I'd need to take a year off between high school and college if things didn't go smoothly. He didn't say it, but I understood the implied, "A year...or more." He advised me it would be better to go through the academy and enter active duty as an officer, not to just enlist as he had done. From the vantage point of living with Michael, entering the military appealed. It meant routine. It meant understood roles and jobs. The part that didn't appeal was the wait. Wait where? At home with the father and Michael? No thanks.

A year prior with that Air Force Academy question laid to rest, Mrs. Eustace helped me pursue information about early admission to college. Any college. This followed an ugly situation with Michael that ended with him coming at me and the father getting between us. In his effort to control the situation, the father grabbed me—being smaller and probably easier to hang onto. He backed me against a wall and held me there, his fingers digging into my triceps, preventing me from swinging at Michael or shielding myself. He tried to block Michael, but Michael repeatedly reached around and over him to punch me. Unable to shake the father off or defend myself, all I could do was to keep Michael from hitting me in the face and take the brunt of the blows on my head while the father shouted his ever-useful, "Hey, Mike! Hey, Mike!"

A year prior, I would have done anything to get out of that house. Eustace advocated on my behalf, looking for a loophole, but the answer did not change. "The Archdiocese does not support students leaving high school after junior year to go to college." My teachers would not be permitted to write letters of recommendation for me and the school would not supply my needed paperwork for an application. I guessed in junior year that it was because they were too cheap to give up a year's worth of tuition. Well...I certainly showed them. The father was dead and my tuition had been waived for the year. How do you like them apples?

So they wanted to keep me for the last year of high school. Here I was, minus both parents, having bombed out of living with my cousin and having assaulted a teacher, now dozing nightly in a broken chaise lounge and looking for headlights of oncoming vehicles so I could make my suicide look like an accident. Going to the moon felt more realistic than going away to college.

But I was fine.

***

"You look awfully tired. Is there something going on? Did something happen?"

I had cooled off about my arguments with Viv and we were in her classroom at the end of the day. It had been over a month since the day I'd walked away from her. I hated to admit it but I missed her. I also missed the memory-free space that came with her....that is, until she attempted to drag memories into it.

"I had to leave Maureen's."

"Why?"

"It just wasn't working out."

Oh, and by the way, she thinks we were having an affair.

No way. That was one sentence that was never going to come out of me.

Viv focused on the more practical matter. "Where are you living?"

I shrugged. "I'm staying with my father's girlfriend."

"I didn't know your father had a girlfriend."

"They were together for seven years."

"She has a spare room for you?"

No, but she isn't accusing me of being gay, either, so I'm staying.

"Uhhh...she has room for me."

Viv caught the evasion. "What does that mean?"

I tried to play it down. "There's space."

"Let me guess. You sleep on the couch."

"Mmm...I could."

"But you don't?"

I shook my head. She motioned at me with one hand to talk to her. "Well, no. Her mother sleeps on the couch."

"So where do you sleep?"

"Kinda...on the floor."

"On the floor," she repeated.

"Well, I have a chair."

"Oh, a chair! Terrific! How does that help?"

"Then I'm not directly on the floor. I didn't like sleeping on the floor." I was not about to tell her that the chair was broken.

Viv sighed. "What's your father's girlfriend's name? She does have one, right?"

"Marie."

"Is this okay until graduation?"

How the hell would I know? I thought the last place was supposed to be okay! For all I knew, it would be just a few more days until Marie found something inherently lacking in my character or accused me of some unthinkable act of malice and deemed me unfit to live with too.

"I think so."

Viv invited me over for dinner later that week. She asked me no questions. Marie apparently thought nothing of it, other than to wish me a pleasant time and ask what time I thought I'd be back.

***

Closing crew had left and the overnight custodian was mopping the lobby. I watched the clock's second hand creep past midnight with my homework spread out on top of the completed day-end paperwork. I'd punched out a while ago. I should go. I would inevitably wake Marie when I got in. And as much as I knew I should, I didn't want to.

I hadn't anticipated that being at Marie's would be so hard. Not hard like being at Maureen's had been hard, because I had felt so much like an intruder and I was worried that Maureen never wanted me there. I knew I was welcome at Marie's. But there were no memories of the father at Maureen's and Marie's house was filled with them.

I wondered how crazy I was becoming. I also wondered how crazy I would get before I found the right car on whatever road, so this mess would just be done. How many times would it take before the Pinto upended or got crunched like a ball of paper?

I also wondered why I wasn't able to make this feel enough okay at Marie's that getting crunched up like a ball of paper was less appealing. Just one more thing I was failing at miserably. Add it to the list: leaving the father alone to die, agreeing to kill my own dog and then abandoning her, being deemed substandard and invited to leave Maureen's house…not just substandard, but deviant, perverted (*don't forget malicious*) and certainly not someone to be around little kids, and now not finding a way to settle at Marie's when she was all but offering me the shirt off her back.

The custodian rattled past with his wheeled mop bucket. "You goin' home tonight or what?"

Or what sounded like the right answer.

***

"Bowling?" I laughed. "You're joking, right?"

Debbi laughed too. "No, I'm serious. I'm on the bowling team."

I looked at Robyn quickly. "You in?"

We were gathered at our usual table in the cafeteria, where we had sat every day since the beginning of the year. I'd been friends with Robyn since freshman year, but being friends with Debbi felt newer. She was one of those Naval Base people, a title that immediately made her something of an outsider and something she occasionally commented on.

South Philadelphia was a very territorial place. To insiders, we identified ourselves by intersections, defined by the corner where people spent their time. Every neighborhood had **that** corner. The hub of our neighborhood was 29th and Tasker, where Dean's Bar operated, closely followed by 30th and Tasker, referred to in our shorthand and on jackets as 3T0. As young kids, we were discouraged from crossing into neighborhoods where people of different ethnicities lived. The Irish didn't hang around in the Italian neighborhoods, nor the Italians in the Polish neighborhoods.

Even before I started driving, it was impressed upon me often that the only reason to enter other neighborhoods was because they stood between where you were and where you needed to go. Michael referred to the Asian refugees who appeared in adjacent neighborhoods in the mid- to late- 70s with ethnic slurs and once demonstrated to me the correct way to stab someone using a butcher knife and an old 3TO jacket he'd outgrown as a target. My skin crawled as the knife slashed through the gold windbreaker with green lettering and he intoned about the proper angle so the knife couldn't be taken away from you. When the first African-American family moved onto our street in the early 80s, the entire front of their house, windows and all, was painted white one Saturday night. The message was clear and they moved out within a few days. Neighborhood was as much our identity as our ethnicity and great effort was put into maintaining both.

 The Philadelphia Naval Base where Debbi's father was stationed eluded all of us. It was filled with people who had lived all over the world so we didn't understand how they defined their allegiances. Some of my friends had never lived anywhere else and had been only as far as New Jersey on vacations with their families, and then usually to the same hotel or rental house year after year. When Debbi told us she had moved here from Alaska, some people reacted as if she'd said Outer Mongolia or behind the Berlin Wall. In some families, ethnicity and intersections drove decisions in South Philly from where kids went to school to choosing a spouse to buying a home, but the Naval Base had no clear markers that anyone could understand. And a bigger mystery, not everyone there was Catholic, and we'd been indoctrinated from the time we entered school to believe that all non-Catholics were going to hell. They were not us.

 My indoctrination failed. Believing organized religion, especially Catholicism, to be nothing more than a corporation selling fear and guilt (espousing this theory in Catholic school had not won me any friends among the nuns and prompted more than one of them to say, "Thank you, Anne, that's very enlightening, we need to move on."), I dismissed the whole outcast idea. I found the "other-ing" limiting. Who should tell me which friends I could have, Catholic or otherwise? I could think for myself, thanks.

Debbi and I had been friendly through the first three years of school, sharing several classes. Since the beginning of senior year, though, we had eaten lunch together every day, and it felt safe to say we were friends. But, unlike Robyn, I hadn't spent time with Debbi outside of school. Not that it should matter too much. For the last year and a half, I hadn't spent much time with any of my friends including Robyn, because I was usually working.

I considered Debbi's suggestion that I meet her and another friend at the bowling alley to watch their match. I had the evening off. Evenings at Marie's meant something decidedly different now anyway, without the father. (*Don't look.*) "Yeah, okay, I'll come."

"You want to stay at my house tonight? We can hang out after."

I hesitated again. What if I cried in my sleep? How the hell would I explain that? I was starting to think of it as a version of wetting the bed and something definitely not up for public disclosure.

"Uhhhh..."

"Come on. It'll be fun."

I was sure Marie wouldn't mind. But still...

Broken chaise lounge?

"Your parents won't care?"

What if they asked me something I couldn't answer? What if they asked me **anything**? How could I explain my living situation?

"No, they won't care."

"Uhhh...okay."

I was super nervous that night, waiting for the dreaded questions, but they never came. I met Debbi's parents, Jim and Pat, and her grandmother, her brother Chris, and their dogs. No one seemed to find my presence weird. Quite the opposite, people talked to me as if it were just another day. I marveled at that.

I crashed that night in Debbi's room on an air mattress. It was the ultimate luxury. Jim and Pat said good night to her—and then to me—as if it was the most normal thing in the world. I marveled at that, too. I fell asleep thinking it would be best to keep my mouth shut so they wouldn't realize that I, personally, was not the most normal thing in the world.

***

Another mid-week closing shift ended with my homework piled up on the manager's desk after the crew left for the night. The custodian greeted me with his customary grunted, "Hullo," before he wheeled out a trash can piled high with filled garbage bags. The six-month anniversary of finding the father approached. I'd been at Marie's about a month. That meant it was five months since I'd seen my dog, five months since the last time I'd been inside the house where I'd grown up. It felt like an eternity and yet so much of this still felt alien and unreal. A month since leaving Maureen's equaled a month of no contact with my Aunt Connie or any of the rest of my cousins. The ache of missing them on top of missing the father and my dog was physical. If I gave it much thought, it could stop me in my tracks, so most of the time, I tried hard not to. I tried not to think about anything important.

Sitting alone except for the custodian wrestling with trash in the corral out back, my wish to feel settled at Marie's collided violently with my dread of going back to her house. My wish to see my dog collided with my terror of Michael. My wish to reach out to Aunt Connie collided with my apprehension that she wouldn't want anything to do with me. My wish to climb right out of my skin and not BE any more collided with images of pickup trucks and flashing ambulance lights, and that was the only combination that felt remotely tolerable.

I collected my belongings from the break room. I had washed my school uniform shirt with a load of towels. I hoped it would be dry by morning. I dozed in my car that night, parked under the street light in the parking lot. It was still cold in April. My feet didn't go numb completely but I did have to stir around and turn on the engine from time to time to run the heater. In the morning, I let myself back in to wash up while the custodian cleaned windows in the lobby. Opening crew would arrive soon. I needed to get dressed and scram. When Marie asked later, I told her I'd spent the night at a friend's. I didn't want her to know how hard it was for me to be there.

***

Marie didn't ask a lot of questions, but Viv did. She called me back after homeroom ended.

"You look like you've had a rough night. Have you slept?"

I shrugged.

"What does that mean?"

I looked away.

"Should I take that as a no? Is everything okay at Marie's?"

"Well...yeah."

"That's not very convincing."

I shrugged again.

"What's going on?"

I realized I couldn't lie, looking directly at her. "Yeah, everything is fine at Marie's." That was true enough.

"But...?"

"I didn't go to Marie's last night." I looked out the window past her.

"Oh. Where did you go? Debbi's?"

"No."

"Where?"

I glanced toward the door.

"Oh no, you don't," she said, hooking a finger into the cuff of my rolled-up shirt sleeve. "Don't duck out. Come on. Where were you?" She perched on the edge of her desk.

"I just...stayed in my car."

"All night?"

"No, I was inside at work part of the night."

"So where did you sleep?" She let go of my sleeve.

"Well, kind of in my car."

"Why?"

I looked at the floor.

"Okay, never mind why." She flapped a hand. "Where are you going to be tonight?"

"I don't know. I have to work. And I gotta go. I'm gonna be late for my class." Other students piled up in the doorway.

"Alright, here's the deal," she said, her voice lowering. "If you have a problem, you call me. Call me collect. I don't care what time it is." She pulled on my sleeve again. "Promise me no more sleeping in your car?"

I shrugged, unwilling to commit to that, now looking at a different place on the floor.

"Come on. No more sleeping in your car. It's still cold out."

Slowly, I nodded. I had no intention of calling her, collect or otherwise, on the nights I didn't want to go to Marie's. But I did need to get to my next class.

***

The first visit at Debbi's must have gone well because she invited me back the following weekend. Evidently, I hadn't frightened her parents or done anything that made me suspect in their eyes. Several overnights in, Jim and Pat still had not asked me any questions about where I was from or why I was spending so much time at their house all of a sudden. Their household boundary seemed more flexible than other families. Come as you are, crazy or not! When the weekend visits went so well, Debbi invited me to stay over during the week. If I wasn't working, I accepted. I even reduced my hours at work a little so we could go with our friends to watch our softball team play during home games.

One afternoon before the end of April, Debbi invited me to have dinner and stay over. I walked in to find that Jim had put up an army cot, set the air mattress on top of it and made it like a bed. I had a bed.

At dinner, Jim asked, "So will you be staying home tonight or going back to Marie's?"

They had never asked a single question.

***

I couldn't find a parking spot on Aunt Connie's street, so I parked at the end of my old street. (*My house. Nope. I don't have a house.*) I needed to see Aunt Connie. I needed to find out if I was still welcome. Or welcome again...maybe any hard feelings about the falling out with Maureen had blown over.

My aunt was home alone, which was unusual. It was the middle of the afternoon, early enough that my younger cousins were still at school and the older ones were working or at their own homes. I entered tentatively and when I closed the door behind me, she looked up.

"Well..." she said. "Look who it is." She didn't use the nickname she'd called me as long as I could remember.

"Hi."

"Hi."

I had no idea where to go with this conversation and was suddenly very sorry I had come.

"Uhh...how's everybody?" I asked.

"Fine," she said, non-committal. She didn't ask how I was.

I couldn't tell if she was angry at me, disappointed, disgusted or something else entirely. I couldn't tell from her expression what she knew—or thought she knew—about what had prompted my blow up with Maureen. Did she miss me? Was she glad I was gone? From her lack of expression, I wasn't ready to put it all on the line that I missed her and the rest of the family. I was afraid of what she might say to all that. Why was I doing this? I wasn't family. This wasn't going to get me anywhere.

"Aunt Connie, I didn't...do you...I'm not..." My chest ached and a lump formed in my throat. So far, this was falling flat. My communication skills still left something to be desired.

She lit a cigarette and held up her hand toward me. "Don't. I can't get into this." Her tone wasn't unkind, just resigned and tired. Tired of me? Was that my fault? Guilt flooded me, replacing trepidation. How many times had I run to Aunt Connie's after Michael had beaten me, or to prevent him from beating me, dragging my family drama into her house? I had worn her out.

I wasn't sure, though, that I understood her correctly. Did she think I'd come to ask her to take sides? That was never going to happen. I didn't want her in the middle. I didn't want a middle because I didn't want sides. I just wanted to come home. I wanted it to matter that I missed her and my cousins and thought about them every day. I wanted it to matter that when I stayed at Marie's, I slept sitting up on a broken chaise lounge and that it hurt so much to be there, I would sleep in my car to avoid it. I wanted it to matter that I wasn't having an affair, would never hurt Maureen's dog, was as asexual as a person could possibly be. She couldn't do anything about any of it. I wasn't going to be moving back into Maureen's house but I wanted it to matter. I couldn't say any of that.

"Okay." My voice broke. "Okay." I thought I might throw up on her kitchen floor.

"I can't," she repeated.

Still unsure what she thought I was asking her to do, I had my answer. Aunt Connie didn't say goodbye as I turned around to leave. I couldn't speak. Maybe she couldn't either.

When I reached my parked car, my breathing had gone ragged and shallow. My hands trembled and I dropped my keys in the gutter. That was all it took. I punched the car window as hard as I could, an enormous purple lump erupting between my last two knuckles.

She didn't say goodbye to me. She didn't say anything, except that she couldn't get involved.

(*Just don't cry.*)

I tried to make a fist to punch the car again, needing to vent this. My fingers didn't bend the way they had a few minutes ago. I wondered how much damage I'd do if I hit the car again. I grabbed the keys up out of the gutter and pain shot up my forearm when my fingers closed around the ring. Don't bother. I had a full tank of gas and the Schuylkill Expressway was just ten minutes away.

The adrenaline rush was phenomenal.

***

"Come on, we'll take my car," Debbi said.

"No, it's okay, we can take my car."

"I'm not getting in that thing."

"What's wrong with my car?"

"It's a wreck! What do you do—tie your seatbelts in a knot and hope you don't get in an accident?"

"Uhhh...I'm not sure it **has** seatbelts."

"How can you not be sure if it has seatbelts, for crying out loud?"

"I don't ever use them."

"What?! Don't tell me that!"

I hesitated. If she was this freaked out by me not using seatbelts, she'd run screaming if I told her what I'd done after I'd left my aunt's house yesterday. What was the point of seatbelts when the whole plan was to go headfirst through the windshield? How many times had I heard her criticize drivers of cars with unrestrained little kids in them? "The first time they have to stop fast, those kids are going through the windshield!" she always said. To which I usually sat there thinking, *well, yeah...*

I played dumb. "Don't tell you what?"

"That you don't use your seatbelts. You mean never?"

"No. Never."

"I am not getting in that car with you. Do you know how dangerous that is?"

"Didn't really think about it." Didn't really care, either. I didn't know anyone else who used seatbelts. Seatbelt laws wouldn't go into effect for years. Debbi was ahead of her time.

"Well, don't think about it some more—while we're in my car. Let's go."

When I got in her car, I thought about offering to tie her seatbelt in a knot, but I didn't think she'd find it funny. I opened the window as Debbi picked up speed. "Hey, you know when I went to my sister's last time?"

"Yeah. You weren't home all weekend," she said, borrowing Jim's joke.

I poked a foot out the open window and scrunched down in the seat to get more comfortable. "We went to a movie and on the way back to Pat's house, she asked me if Viv was gay."

"Why?"

"I dunno. It's been a theme since Maureen made it up in her head."

"What did you go see?"

"*Tootsie.*"

Debbi let that sink in for a moment. "No way! She took you to see a movie about a man dressing up as a woman to find out if you think Viv is gay?"

I hadn't thought of it like that and the idea made me laugh. "Yeah, she did. But I don't think she knew what it was about."

"So you gonna tell Viv-o?"

I groaned. "Wasn't planning on it."

"She'll think it's funny. Then she'll say something like, 'But if you met Jimmy, you'd like him—he's a nice guy,'" she said, quoting Viv's standard line whenever we asked questions about her ex-husband.

"It feels like one of those things that you just want to say I won't dignify this with an answer, you know what I mean?"

"I think you should tell her."

"Huh-uh. Because it's not just that. It's the whole 'What does she want from you' line of questioning."

Debbi pondered that. "I don't think she wants anything from us."

"Me neither."

"Wanna go see *Sophie's Choice*? It's still playing at the base theater."

"We've seen it four times."

"I love that movie."
"Okay."

                        ***

I changed my mind later and told Viv about the question. I cringed, waiting for her to get angry and demand that I leave right now. Why would she continue to spend time with me when I was surrounded by people who constantly questioned her character and now her orientation?

"Oh, for God's sake…" Viv began. "Would you please give me your sister's phone number? I'll call her myself and she can ask me whatever she wants."

That surprised me.

Viv went on, seeming to think out loud, now rummaging in the kitchen. "What do I want from you? What **would** I want from you? The only goal here is to get you to graduation. It's no big mystery. I ran into Gerri from the science department at lunch the other day, and we're both looking at each other going, 'We've got a depressed kid on our hands, what do we do?' It's only ever been about graduation and it's only ever going to **be** about graduation."

It never occurred to me that I might be depressed. I thought she could be exaggerating.

She tossed a pen on the table in front of me and slapped a piece of paper down. "Your sister's phone number, please?"

I started to scribble.

Her tone softened. "Have you eaten today?"

Home Stretch to Graduation

The request to come to the Guidance Office was a first and I couldn't imagine why the Director of Guidance wanted to speak to me. This could only mean a problem. If Sister Clarence from the Activities Office was stirring up trouble around my tuition, I wondered if I'd be able to reach my sister in the middle of the day to field questions. I held the hall pass out to the person closest to the entrance, mumbled my name and pointed to the direction on the paper to *See Jo Canning*. She waved me toward a chair to wait.

Above me on the door hung the list of the college acceptances that were announced now almost daily. Mine was up there, accepted by the only college I had applied to. All of my friends were up there too, many with multiple schools listed after their names. My application to a single school was as much an indicator of my disbelief that I was going to get that far as it was about how much I was willing to give up out of a paycheck making $3.65 an hour. I didn't see the point in blowing a lot of money on applications for other schools, not for some place I never planned to attend. When asked, I consistently stuck to the story that I wanted to go where my nephew Bob was; I had visited and liked it and that was enough.

An interior office door opened, and Sister Emily emerged with a student. She nodded and smiled. "Anne."

I nodded back. "S'ter."

At the same time, Jo Canning came through the main door. She picked up the hall pass I'd left on the desk and looked at me, probably matching my ID pin with the name on the pass. She invited me into the office that Sister Emily had just vacated. Apparently this was Canning's office.

"Anne, I wanted to talk to you about your college plans," she said, sitting down at her desk. She offered me a seat with a gesture, pulling a file folder out of a pile. I remained on my feet.

Why? My eyes narrowed and I said nothing.

"You've applied to just one school, is that correct?"

"Yes."

"And been accepted?" She flipped pages on her desk.

"Yes."

"You haven't applied to others?"

"No." I thought we had covered that in the "you've applied to just one school" question.

"Why is that?" She stopped flipping pages.

"That's where I want to go."

"Anne, with your grades, I think it would be a good move for you to consider other schools."

That was almost amusing. When I didn't say anything, she continued.

"I know there are some unusual circumstances that you're dealing with."

Unusual? I wondered which of my teachers had bent her ear and gotten this discussion scheduled. It seemed unlikely that she'd have zeroed in on me out of almost five hundred graduating seniors for a personal meeting when she had never had a reason to even know my name before today.

"Has anyone talked to you about other schools?"

"Not really."

"Has anyone talked to you about applying elsewhere?"

"No."

Oh for crying out loud, what do you want?

"How about scholarships? Anyone talk to you about that?"

"No. Well, not a lot. Mrs. Eustace has mentioned it a couple of times."

"Good. What do you think of Rosemont?"

Not sure where she was heading with this sudden turn, I leaned against the doorframe with my arms crossed. "I don't know Rosemont."

"Rosemont is a great school."

I said nothing. She mistook it for interest.

"Anne, I've got a full scholarship available to Rosemont. Yours if you want it."

"Oh. Uhh...well...no, if I go-"

"You don't need to answer me now. Think about this. It's a full scholarship to a Catholic college—you'll get a great education."

Was she even going to ask me if I was interested in a Catholic college after twelve years of Catholic school? Did this imply it was a women's school? After four years of an all-girls high school? "As I said, given your grades and what we know you're capable of, this is a much better choice for you than a state school."

What did she know about what I was capable of? These days, I was most capable of flipping burgers and bouts of insanity while driving.

"I don't think—" I started.

"Please don't answer now. I want you to take some time with this."

"I really don't need time. I don't want to go to a Catholic college." *Or any other college, for that matter.*

"Of course you do—it's a great opportunity."

"No, really, I don't."

"It's a full scholarship. It's not a good idea to turn this down."

Should I just tell her I wasn't going to be here long enough to start college? No, she didn't need to know that. I hadn't even told Eustace that much. That was mine.

"Maybe you should take a couple of days and talk to your family."

You mean my brother and sister that no longer want anything to do with the Catholic Church? Or the brother that holds me down and gropes me? Oh yeah, that would help. I reframed the sarcasm into, "No. I don't want it."

"Anne—"

I reached for the hall pass. "Can you sign me out, please?"

She didn't move right away. I thought for a moment that I might have to leave without her signature, which was going to raise questions when I got to my next class. Slowly, she signed the form. I tried to take it and she held onto it, prompting me to look at her again.

"Just think about it," she said.

"I really would like a different experience," I replied, hoping that would be adequate. I left the 'like being dead' part unspoken.

She sighed and nodded, again very slowly. "Please come back and see me if you change your mind." She let go of the hall pass.

When donkeys fly, I thought.

***

Staying with Debbi's family was getting easier. They seemed to have no expectations that I do or say anything special to explain myself. I just had to show up if I had an evening off and dinner happened. Debbi and I had gotten into a pattern of her inviting me over on any evenings when I was off, so by the beginning of May, I was spending more time there than as not.

I assumed by now that Jim and Pat had just gotten used to having me there so much. My army cot was a permanent fixture in Debbi's room. This wasn't really home, but it was as homelike as I could tolerate, and I started to settle in. So when Jim said it the first time during dinner, I almost dropped the bowl I was holding.

"Now, when they pack us up for the move…"

I didn't hear what he said after that opening. They were moving? My stomach filled suddenly with ice and I turned to Debbi, trying to keep the panic out of my voice. "You're moving?"

"Dad's being shipped to Panama."

Panama! Not even just a couple of states away! They were being sent out of the whole country! She appeared very calm about the whole thing. Either that or I was having a stroke and my perception was distorted.

"When?" I squeaked.

"Right after graduation. Mom and Dad'll go to Panama, but I'm just going to California a little early." Debbi had been accepted to Cal State Fullerton.

We graduated in little more than a month. I lowered my head over my plate thinking, just breathe. Just breathe. This'll pass. Keep breathing. The conversation carried on around me, just another typical night for them. I didn't realize it, but a Navy family being relocated to some distant place **was** just another typical night for them.

("It'll be okay. Just don't cry.")

My sister was insistent that I leave Philadelphia right after graduation. Our last conversation about this had gotten a little heated. Through our argument, I had hung onto the idea of finding a real job and a place to live in Philadelphia, putting those out there as my goals. I knew Debbi had to leave, but I had been thinking August. I bit down hard on the inside of my cheek to focus myself. She had to go. I wasn't family. They had to go without me. In a month.

***

I thought I should give it one more try, but my courage flagged at the last minute. Parked at the end of my old street with a month left until graduation and facing a departure with no idea when I might return, my nerve failed halfway to my aunt's house. I stopped at the corner, outside the store where our families had bought bread and milk for my whole life. I couldn't go through with this. When I left last time, she hadn't said goodbye, hadn't asked me to stay. I had been fighting tears so hard I hadn't been able to say goodbye to her, either. What if we just had a repeat of that? What if she thought I had come to try to get her to take sides again?

It might have taken thirty seconds to realize I couldn't carry this plan to its end. It felt like an eternity hovering there, looking toward my aunt's house, feeling like a stranger with his nose pressed against someone's living room window. I missed Aunt Connie, David, Rick, and Doreen beyond words. But I couldn't do it. I turned around and retraced my steps to my car.

As I rounded the corner of the father's street, I came face to face with my brother Michael. I went cold, fists clenching reflexively around handfuls of sweat. I angled to one side to get around him, avoiding eye contact.

"Hey..." he started in a snide tone.

After years of having to deduce if I was in danger from the subtleties of body language and tone of voice, I knew I was not at risk. We were outside. He never hit me when the neighbors might see. This was simply sport. Maybe if he hadn't spoken...but he did.

He had my house. He had my dog. He had everything the father had worked for. My family wanted nothing to do with me. I was army cot surfing in someone else's house and that family was leaving in a month. My anger—at him, at this all—surged to the surface and boiled over.

"FUCK YOU!" I screamed, cutting off what he was starting to say, the force behind my words scraping my throat. "FUCK YOU!"

I couldn't have said it enough times. I couldn't have screamed it loudly enough. It brought me onto my tiptoes, my whole body a drawn bow. I wished him dead. I wanted to kill him myself right there. I wanted his blood in a pool on the concrete.

He laughed as if I were the best joke he'd ever heard and then waved and kept walking.

How convenient that the expressway was so close.

***

Viv distributed notices in homeroom regarding who could participate in senior week activities and what the expectations upon us were. Our school dedicated a week of activities for the seniors shortly before graduation: a trip to the zoo, a costume party, the mother-daughter luncheon and the father-daughter dance. I was surprised we were being allowed to go to the zoo. Rumor had it that someone in last year's graduating class fed speed to the monkeys. For a while, it looked like our school would be barred from ever going there again. I wasn't interested in the costume party and was short a few parents to participate in the mother-daughter luncheon or father-daughter dance. I read to the bottom of the page. Only students who had paid the activities fee that had been due the third week in October would be able to take part in the senior week plans.

During the third week of October, I had just buried the father and was at Pat's house puzzling through where I'd live in the coming months. I hadn't paid any activity fee. I didn't even know a fee had to be paid until now. I crunched the paper up, tossed it in the garbage and hoped no one in **my** graduating class would feed speed to the poor monkeys.

***

Debbi and I were sitting on the floor in Viv's living room later that week when Viv asked about senior week activities, interrupting my MTV hypnosis. "I recommend no speed for the monkeys," I joked, trying to elude the question.

"Are you going to the luncheon?" she asked.

Debbi said yes. I said nothing and hoped no one would notice.

"You." From the couch above and behind me, Viv nudged me. "Are you going?"

So much for that dodge. "Nope."

"How about the zoo?"

Debbi said yes and again, I said nothing.

"This is the last big thing before graduation." Viv poked my shoulder once more. "Why don't you want to go?"

"I can't," I said.

"Why not? You make the schedule—just don't schedule yourself."

I inclined my head so I could see them both. "No, not that, but I probably will work. You know that notice you gave us about the fee that was due in October? That was the week after. I wasn't in school to pay it."

Recognition dawned and Viv started to shake her head. "No, that's taken care of."

"No, it's not. I wasn't here."

Her gaze slid sideways and she spoke in a neutral tone. "The girls in homeroom took up a collection. They wouldn't leave you out. Mrs. Diamond and I put in the rest to bring it to the total. Your fee is paid. You can go to anything you want."

It didn't seem like her to make a joke about this. My neighbor contributed? Viv put up her own money? I had a sense of what Catholic high school teachers earned and it wasn't enough to start footing bills for their students. Why hadn't she said something? I would have paid them back, all of them.

"So," she continued, looking back at me, "what do you want to do?"

"Well, I'm not going to the father-daughter thing, let's start with that, but the zoo could be okay."

"Dad said he would take both of us," Debbi offered.

"I'd rather skip that one."

"Mother-daughter luncheon?" Viv asked again.

"I dunno. I could ask Marie to go, I guess."

"You sure? Dad's serious about wanting to take us both." Back to Debbi.

"I'm sure. I don't want to go to that one."

Debbi got up to get a drink. From the kitchen, she said, "Hey, did you tell Viv-o you ran into your brother?"

Viv jumped on that. "You ran into Michael?"

"Yeah."

"What happened?"

"Nothing."

She "tsked" at me impatiently. "Did he speak to you?"

I wondered if she was holding out hope that Michael and I were going to have some magical reunion, the two orphans who realize suddenly that they're all alone in the world and that they really do love each other and go running at each other in slow motion across a field of daisies, with arms outstretched. Man, was she barking up the wrong family tree. If she really believed that, I was surprised she hadn't started barking at the moon, too. "He started to."

"Did you say anything to him?"

In the kitchen, Debbi snorted. "Boy, did she."

"Yeah. He said hey and I yelled fuck you. He kept walking and I got in the car and drove away."

Viv squinted just the tiniest bit. If I hadn't been looking directly at her, I probably wouldn't have even noticed. "You know talking to me like that is going to land you over my knee."

Oh. My. God. I froze.

Coming around the kitchen wall, Debbi stopped in mid-stride and burst out laughing, trying to keep a full glass of water from ending up down the front of her clothes or all over the floor. It felt like Viv had just clubbed me between the eyes. She had not just said that. In front of Debbi? Who was, by the way, still doubled over laughing. I wished the floor would open up and swallow me. I ducked my head, blood rushing up my neck and into my face, my ears burning, and I reminded myself that she had no context for what I had said to Michael. I wasn't about to tell her. Debbi sat back down, still snickering. My ears burned hotter.

***

Marie accepted my invitation to attend the mother-daughter lunch. I felt like a fraud, given the absence of a mother and being acutely aware that I wasn't anyone's daughter anymore. I continued to politely decline Debbi's offer to crash the father-daughter dance as Jim's second date. I had enough distance that I could squeak by with a substitute mother but the father wound was still bleeding.

I worked the night of the father-daughter dance, preferring to sweep floors and drop fry baskets to probing the father's absence. I kept reminding myself that I didn't care about this, that going would have been a waste of the evening, then I'd wonder why I had to keep reminding myself. As with Christmas, I wished it away.

Shortly after ten p.m., Debbi and Jim came in. The dance was over and father-daughter combinations were scattering across South Philly to have a late dinner. She didn't say so and neither did he, but I knew why they were there when they could have been in any other restaurant in the city. Senior week was finished. Next stop, graduation, and no one had fed speed to the monkeys.

We would graduate on June 9th. On the afternoon of the 8th, a special mass was held for the seniors at Saints Peter and Paul Basilica in Center City, the mother church of the Archdiocese of Philadelphia. By early in that week, all finals had to be completed, books returned, and caps and gowns distributed to get us ready for the two days of events.

I saw a bittersweet week coming at me. I didn't care about the mass, but graduation was the turning point I'd been kicking and clawing to reach. Arching over the reason to stay in Philadelphia all of these months was Debbi's departure, scheduled for the day after we graduated.

Her family mapped out their plans over dinners with and without me. Our class graduated on Friday. Jim and Pat would finish packing Debbi up for California, put her on a plane on Saturday, and then they would leave on Monday. The rest of my friends were spending the week following graduation in Wildwood for senior week down the shore. I had agreed to go months ago and had put a deposit on a place to stay with a few of them. I no longer cared about going but now I was financially committed to it.

As expected, early in the week, a large box occupied Viv's desktop. "When I call your name," she projected over the background noise, "please come up and get your cap and gown!" She went through the list of names, handing out assigned caps and gowns with associated instructions for returning them after graduation.

I held the stiff, plastic wrapped square in both hands, turning it over, marveling at the size and shape—so small for what it represented! I hugged it. I wanted to climb on my desk and dance like Snoopy on top of the piano in the Charlie Brown Christmas special.

Someone rapped on the door and opened it, approaching Viv's desk with a note. It was a runner from one of the offices.   She stopped at the desk and instead of giving the note to Viv, which would have been typical, she faced us and said loudly, "I've come to get Anne Mullen's cap and gown back. She has not paid her tuition, and she will not be allowed to participate in the mass or in commencement!"

Suddenly, there was silence. My face burned. This could only be a runner from the Activities Office. My bet was, while the blood pounded in my ears, that she had been told to say that out loud.

A few eyes must have started to shift slowly in my direction. The runner deduced who I was and turned to me. "I'll take that back to the Activities Office now," she said, holding out her hands.

Like hell she would. I pivoted away from her and headed for the door.

"Anne! Wait! Don't!" Viv dropped the bundle she held and came after me. "Do not leave this room!"

I flung the door open, the runner on my heels, and Viv right behind her.

"Anne! Get back here!"

I broke into a run in the hallway.

"Anne!"

I hit the doorway at the top of the stairwell at full speed, clutching the package under my arm like a football. The door slammed backwards, bouncing off the tiled wall. The messenger wasn't chasing me but she was close behind. What could she do if she caught up with me? She'd been instructed to bring my cap and gown to the Activities Office. That's exactly what I intended to do. I charged into the office and Sister Clarence looked up from the counter, startled. She was probably expecting her flying monkeys to return, but she got me instead.

As it had the afternoon with Michael, the anger that simmered just under the surface on a good day found its boiling point and spilled over the edges of my brain. It pooled into waiting humiliation, swirling together until I couldn't tell one from the other.

"You cannot-" Sister Clarence began.

I gripped the plastic-wrapped square like a Frisbee, whipped it forward and let it fly. "Keep it, you bitch!" I shouted.

The package sailed across the room and over the counter and struck Sister Clarence in the face.

"You!" she yelled, putting a hand to the bridge of her nose. "You!"

I wheeled around. The messenger reached the doorway, her eyes wide. Whatever she'd just seen was not something one saw every day in this school. As I pushed past her, Sister Clarence shouted after me. "Keep it? **I will** keep it! You will be barred from graduation! You will not do this and walk away from me!"

She was right. Technically, I wasn't walking. I was running again and I had already been excluded from graduation because she was so sure I had cheated the school out of my tuition. Well, now she had a real reason to bar me. Her voice followed me down the hall until I came to the stairs, and the stairwell door closed behind me, shutting her out. Having sealed the deal that I couldn't walk with my class at commencement, I debated just leaving the building. What was the point in staying? Finals were over. They could collect whatever remaining textbooks I still had from my locker, or Viv's classroom, where I had just left some.

The buzzer ended homeroom and the stairwell filled with hundreds of students like a Catholic ant farm. I could leave but where would I go? Debbi was somewhere else in the building. I couldn't go to her house, where I'd left my car. I couldn't get on to the Naval base without her, and if anyone was home, it was likely to be viewed as very odd that I'd be looking for a place to hang out at this hour. I couldn't picture myself explaining myself to Debbi's mom that I'd just assaulted a nun. I was already worried that they thought I was odd. I didn't want to go to Marie's. I worked later but it was too early to go in now. I decided to retrieve my books from Viv's room and go through the motions of the rest of the day. If they called me from class later to confront me, there was nothing else they could do to me. They had already taken the only thing that mattered. I paused, fingertips squeezing between my eyes. Let them send for me. Let them confront me. What difference would it make?

***

By the time I crossed paths with Viv, she already knew what had transpired in the Activities Office. She never told me who told her. No one had called for me through the rest of the day, so I didn't even see Viv until the following day during my last official homeroom. I could tell she was angry at me. Every time she looked at me, her eyes narrowed or her eyebrows lowered. As I was leaving, she said, "I have an appointment to speak to Father Slane this afternoon."

"Why?" *Someone thinking about having me arrested?* I didn't say that part out loud.

"Because I'd like to speak with him."

That wasn't much of an answer. It was all she gave me.

We ran on a shortened schedule that day. Without books and with no tests left, there was really nothing for us to do. The rest of the school was about to go into finals. I would have placed money on the fact that the school administrators would be happy to see me gone; I had morphed into the only discipline problem on the honor roll.

At the end of the last school day, I was unlocking the Pinto when a single honk sounded behind me. I turned. Viv's blue Century idled at the curb on the other side of the street about two car lengths down. She opened the window.

"Come here." She pointed at the ground beside her car.

I retracted my key from the Pinto's lock and jogged across the street.

Viv didn't waste words on a greeting. "**This** is why somebody needs to take you in hand. Did I tell you not to leave yesterday? Did I tell you not to leave my room?"

"Yeah..."

"Do you think you could have listened? Do you have to try to handle everything yourself? Are you just **driven** to make this more difficult?"

"Well, I—"

"I just came from meeting with Father Slane."

I hesitated. "About what?"

"What do you think?" She thumped the steering wheel in her frustration. "You **hit** Sister Clarence in the face!"

The sarcastic part of my brain wanted to point out to her that the concept shouldn't really be all that foreign to her, since I had also hit her in the face a couple of times. Given her expression, I opted to ask, "What happened?"

She reached across the passenger seat and shoved her briefcase aside with an angry jab. The plastic-wrapped square of my cap and gown rested under it. She picked it up and pushed it toward me through the window. Across the plastic, someone had scrawled KEEP IT in what looked like grease pencil.

The thought that the quote wasn't completely accurate came and went quickly. I bit my tongue on that and took the square from Viv. "What did you say to Father Slane?"

"Never mind what I said to him!" she snapped. "All you need to know is that you should feel very lucky that you have to work tonight and that you're not coming over to my house!"

I backed up a step involuntarily. That didn't even qualify as thinly veiled.

"And for the next two days," she continued, "do not do **anything** to get yourself in trouble! Do you understand me?"

"Yeah, okay. I won't." I couldn't tell if she was angrier that I had hit Sister Clarence or because I had left her room while she was telling me not to, but I nodded, one palm outward to indicate I wouldn't argue with her. I got the point. She said nothing else. She glared at me for a few more seconds, put her car in drive and pulled away.

I hugged my cap and gown to my chest and watched her go.

***

With Debbi packing to move, I stayed at Marie's the night before graduation, again not sleeping well. My sister planned to pick me up there to take me into Center City and Chick would meet us there. On the steps outside the cathedral, families gathered in various configurations to take pictures. *Whatever you said to Father Slane, thank you, Viv!* Chick and

Pat flanked me in our photo. He looked drawn and washed out, dealing with some unknown health issue that he didn't want to talk about, and she put on her best game face for my big day. My picture with Debbi's family looked more relaxed. My sister reminded me a couple of times that day that they weren't really my family, and she didn't understand why I was so attached to them. I didn't know how she could look back at this past year and not understand.

Chick and Pat took me out for lunch after the many goodbyes were said, walking to the restaurant along the historic cobblestone streets of Center City. Under other circumstances, this very likely would have been a nice day. I'm sure my friends had graduation parties that night but I didn't go to any. When we finished lunch, I returned to Marie's and waited for Saturday, dreading it. Viv called and asked if I wanted to come over to her house the next day, and she would take me to the airport to say goodbye to everyone before Debbi's flight. She no longer sounded angry at me. I didn't care if she was. Graduation was over. We had reached the goal. On Saturday afternoon, I left the Pinto at Viv's house and she drove us to the airport.

Debbi, her brother Chris and their Gram were flying to California. Jim and Pat needed to stay a couple more days to finalize packing, shipping and base housing clean-up details, and then they would leave Philadelphia on Monday on their way to Jim's next station in Panama. Chris and Gram said good-bye to me first and then Jim and Pat, each of them hugging me tightly. When it was time to say good-bye to Debbi, my eyes hit the ground and everything became puddles and prisms. We made some stupid comments to each other, awkward jokes to try to relieve the strain. She fidgeted and bounced one leg, her discomfort clear. Our hug was short, then she needed to board. Jim and Pat stayed to see her plane off the ground. I couldn't.

In the parking garage, I slammed Viv's car door and huddled against it, bent forward with my arms crossed, rogue tears sliding from the corners of my closed eyes. *(It'll be okay. Just don't cry. Just don't cry.)*

Vlv shut the driver's door quietly and turned the engine over to get the air conditioner running. She put a hand on my shoulder.

I shook it off.

"Come here," she said quietly.

"No." I brushed the rogue tears away viciously with one fist.

"Come on. Don't tell me no." She put her hand on the back of my neck. I cringed. "Come here." She pulled me toward her.

"Don't." I pulled in the opposite direction.

"Ssshhhh. Come here."

It crossed my mind that I should just get out of the car. I'd be okay in a minute. Then my head pressed against her shoulder and the puddles spilled out of their own accord. She covered the other side of my head with her free hand, cradling it against her collarbone.

Don't look.

("It'll be okay. Just don't cry.")

"No!"

"Ssshhhhh."

I wrestled with the immediacy of losing Debbi and her family and the all-encompassing loss of the father, the mother, the dog, the home, Aunt Connie, and all of my cousins. My vocabulary gutted yet again, I kept telling her no, even as puddles splashed on her polo shirt and made little circles.

Now I don't think I was ever talking to her.

The Tipping Point

Pat took me shopping for things I'd need for a dorm room. I pretended excitement, especially on the days I drove 896 too fast or on the wrong side of the road, with Journey's "Don't Stop Believin'" blaring from the car speakers. Fine. I'd go away to school. I could create an accident there just as easily as anywhere else.

Occasionally, Pat asked why I wasn't spending time with people socially. Why was I not making friends? I didn't know how to explain that I didn't care about making friends with people I'd never see again after this summer. I didn't care about anything. Lacking what felt like the appropriate words, I opted to say nothing.

On the afternoon before Bob and I left for the semester, I sat at the kitchen table with Pat, trying to present myself as buoyed over the idea of leaving. She flicked ashes into the ashtray and said, "Why don't you go ahead and bring down the stuff you want packed in the car, pile it behind the couch and then we'll see where we stand."

I looked at her with what I hoped was a serious expression. "Pat, if I go ahead and bring down the stuff I want packed in the car and pile it behind the couch, chances are…" I paused to make sure she was listening… "I'll be standing behind the couch."

I couldn't do buoyed but I could manage sarcasm. She laughed and waved me away from the table to go pack for my Big, New Start.

***

It took all of about a week and a half to realize I hated having a roommate. Whose idea was it to put people who had never met—or had met only briefly during freshman orientation—alone in the same room? Was I supposed to be able to close my eyes and sleep? With a total stranger right there? That made no sense. I had no clue who this person was or what she was capable of. Feeling too awkward to get up and leave when she'd come staggering in, not to mention having nowhere else to go, I pulled the pillow over my head and tried to mentally transport myself elsewhere.

Similar to living in the father's house, it was simply easier to be absent. As a freshman, my car was parked in the farthest, darkest lot across campus, but still available. It didn't occur to me to ask for a roommate change. I didn't even realize that could be done. So on those nights when I knew she was drinking at one of the off-campus houses, I made a bee line for my car in that remote parking lot before I expected her to return and went for a drive.

Had there been an inkling of hope that I would feel more pulled together once I started freshman year, it didn't last long. Before Labor Day weekend, I was already missing my morning classes, apathetic about notes, quizzes, and assignments. When my roommate wasn't around, all I wanted to do was sleep. And forget. Everything.

I declared a major in psych, which I thought oddly amusing at best and probably just my sarcastic streak showing through. I couldn't fathom how I might use such a degree. I had no burning desire to help anyone. I simply wanted to understand what had happened for the last ten years and what the effect might be on me as I tried to shake free of it—if I even could.

During the second week of classes, I went by the psych lab to get a signature on a form and found myself surrounded by pigeons in cages lined with newspapers. I stopped in my tracks and when I finally located my voice, I asked the student lab assistant why the pigeons were there.

"That's a project for junior year," she said, barely glancing up.

A project? With pigeons?

The image of my little blue-grey buddy on the pavement outside the father's house invaded the room. *WHOMPH!* Just as quickly, the image morphed into my little blue-grey buddy, medium well done, in unimaginable agony, bloody white foam swelling from his throat.

I squeaked.

"What?" the lab assistant asked irritably.

I backed out of the room, closing the door quietly. When I turned toward the stairs, my feet broke out in a run without any instructions from my brain. All three of us, my feet, my brain and the rest of me, stopped about two blocks away when the side door of my dorm came into view. I dropped the psych major the following day and let them categorize me as undeclared. Undeclared was good for now.

I wasn't surprised when wanting **to forget** shifted into the territory of wanting **to be gone**, then meandered into needing it to look like an accident and considering how and where that best might happen. On the contrary, it felt really familiar, just in a new place with different options for doing it and less risk of anybody I knew finding me when it was done. Cutting through the first floor of the cafeteria on a day I had managed to get out of bed and actually make it to a class, snuffling some unidentifiable smell from some unrecognizable food they'd feed us later, I saw a poster for the counseling center.

What a ridiculous concept.

I didn't need that. We don't talk to people.

I stared at it, shifting my *History of the English Language* textbook from hand to hand. I didn't care about the history of the English language but was conscious of my time. If I didn't get moving, I'd be late for ROTC—the class I had registered for so I could jump off the dorm roof when they taught rappelling to the cadets toward the end of first semester.

The pressure is on when one is expected to jump off a six-story building. You can't make mistakes when you rappel off the roof into a pit surrounded by a four-foot concrete retaining wall outside the maintenance storage area, but you know...accidents happen. Six stories was a long way down.

In my cousin Joe's voice: *You don't talk to us, Nance. Sometimes you could talk to us.*

In Eustace's voice: *Okay, you.* **What** *is going on?*

In Viv's voice: *We've got a depressed kid on our hands—what do we do?*

I am not depressed!

Viv's voice again: *At some point, you're gonna need to talk to someone.*

I pivoted away from the pillar and headed for the double glass doors to the street that led to my dorm. *Oh no. No, I don't. I am fine.*

One last word from Viv: *You're working too many hours, you just failed a class, you look exhausted all the time! You're not fine! I tried to hug you and you hit me. That's not fine!*

She always did like to get the last word.

Shut up, I thought in the general direction of Viv's memory. And to myself I thought, *deal with this. Whatever this is. Just fucking deal with it!*

While my roommate showered and got ready for whatever party she was going to that evening, I stewed. Finally, the words "counseling center, my ass" crossed my mind, and I grabbed my car keys and left the dorm.

It wasn't quite cold enough to snow, but it was misting, a low cloud blanketing the mountaintop, dampening everything and reducing visibility. I pulled out of the parking lot and the tires spun just a bit on the slick asphalt, kind of a whirr-whirr-SCRITCH as the rubber threw small stones and then caught. I headed north toward Tioga Dam and the New York border. The roads were eerily quiet when I reached the town line. I had no idea where I was going.

Small, red tail lights ahead of me enlarged as I got closer to the loaded flatbed hauling logs toward the paper mill just over the state line. I fell in behind it for a stretch of unlit road, mindlessly following the two red dots. More impulse than plan, I revved the Dodge's eight-cylinder engine, an upgrade from the Pinto I'd sold for fifty bucks for parts over the summer, and inched closer to the truck's back end. Would he feel it if I got close enough to touch him? Would I? Maybe I wouldn't have to wait several weeks for rappelling off the roof. I was driving on a mountaintop. In the dark. In the rain.

I didn't know this road well enough to predict it but a gold No Passing sign tipped me off. When the dotted line solidified to two clear yellow lines, I floored the accelerator and pulled into the southbound lane. The Dodge's engine was much bigger than the Pinto's and I picked up speed without the car feeling as if it would shake itself apart. I wondered if the mist would cover headlights until the last possible second or if I would know when someone was coming.

We approached a curve, the silhouettes of huge spruce and pine trees blocking any sign of oncoming cars. My heart thumped and just like on 896, I could hear my pulse everywhere. Despite the cool weather, sweat ran into one of my eyes, and my palms slid on the vinyl steering wheel cover, bumping over the indentations where the lanyard was tightly wrapped. The truck driver laid on his horn. We were moving too fast for him to slam on his brakes. He would jackknife.

We went into the curve, me blind to whatever was headed southbound and straddling the line demarcating the shoulder, and him shouting at me through his closed window. Sweat broke out all over me to match the sweat running down my forehead. I thought if I tried, I could see it on the backs of my hands, locked around the steering wheel, but it was too dark. The tiny hairs on my neck hummed as my pulse demanded they stand at attention.

Could I pass and get back in my own lane before another car came? Should I? I could. I would try. We'd see if I made it. I clenched the wheel and stamped on the accelerator, neck and neck with the cab of the truck. In my lower vision, now acute, the speedometer needle hovered at the far right of the high beam indicator, the only gauge for my speed in the dark with the dashboard light burned out. I estimated that we were both going about seventy miles an hour, maybe eighty. There was no way that truck was stopping for me.

As we exited the curve, I squeezed the Dodge back onto the northbound lane, the truck's horn protesting. Unaware that I'd been holding my breath, the exhalation exploded out of my chest, growing into a scream that I pulled out of my socks. My scream drowned out the truck's horn, and I surfed the adrenaline rush for several dark miles, the steering wheel in a white-knuckled choke hold.

Counseling center, my ass.

***

    I yanked myself awake, flailing in my nightmare and trying to push Michael off me for the third time this week. If not Michael, cold dads with black tongues presented themselves in snappy boxer shorts in the back room in my old house. Take your pick. We had two recurring themes here at my Big, New Start at college, neither one of them conducive to restful sleep.

    The strip of light shining under the door showed me one lump on my roommate's side of the room. I curled up on my side, facing her, so I would be aware if she moved. I had no reason to think she would hurt me. In the daylight, she was harmless—scattered and a little flaky, and she needed to stop eating the Pop Tarts I kept on my shelf, but she was harmless. In the dim lighting, when I was supposed to turn my back on her and close my eyes, her proximity scared the hell out of me.

    I didn't think that was so normal. I doubted that the roommate combinations up and down the hall were made up of one person in every duo who had trouble dropping off to sleep because they felt an overpowering urge to keep watch on the person who used the other bed. I had to find some way to stop this.

    The woman who met me for my first appointment at the Counseling Center (counseling center, my ass!) was pleasant to the point of being bland. Unable to sleep and tempted to go out on the back roads and find a logging truck every night to recapture that exquisite adrenaline rush, I decided to give this a shot. I didn't know if it could help since you can't fix dead, but I didn't think it could hurt. Sitting on the couch in her too cute and overly warm office, eying cross-stitched pillows and strategically placed teddy bears, now I wasn't so sure.

    She sat opposite me in a rocker, her legs crossed, pen poised above the form on her clipboard. She was wearing a long skirt and leggings and she looked like Holly Hobby. "Tell me about your family?" she asked, almost apologetically.

    Am I not supposed to notice that you're asking me personal questions? Or forgive you for asking them?

"My sister lives outside Philadelphia. My brother is in New Jersey."

"Your parents?"

"Gone."

She glanced up from her form. "Gone?"

"Dead."

She nodded. "Yes, I figured that was what gone meant. Can you tell me how? When?"

"She died of cancer in 1973. He died last year. Heart attack."

Don't look.

"Who did you live with before the semester started?"

Well….how to explain this? I opted for the short version. "I stayed at my sister's."

She scribbled something on her form. "You were very young when your mom died."

I nodded and said nothing.

"Eight?" she guessed.

"Seven," I confirmed.

Scribble scribble.

She asked a few more questions that produced scribbling and then she set the form aside. "So what brings you in today?"

Good god, was I supposed to be able to answer that? Is THAT how these things worked?

"I...well...I..."

Where the hell could I start? Yes, the mother is indeed dead, and the father was really cold when I found him, but if I had gone home sooner he might still be alive and I still dream about it? I just passed a logging truck in a no passing zone and I liked it? And I'm going to do it again? I also can't close my eyes and fall asleep when my roommate is in the room? Oh by the way, I dream about my brother groping me and rubbing himself against me until he got off on it, but our parish priest told me when I was twelve that if I just prayed hard enough he would stop that, except he didn't? And just one more quick thing—I'm planning to cut the rappelling ropes when I drop off the dorm roof with Sgt. Z. next month?

She waited patiently for me to stop stammering. I briefly considered smacking her in the head with one of her teddy bears or maybe that clipboard. What brought me in today? What the hell kind of question was that? When I quit sputtering, a few seconds of silence passed, then she asked, "How about if we start with your sister? How are things with your sister?"

"Hard."

"What makes it hard?"

"I have a hard time talking to her."

There! I had put together a complete and accurate sentence!

She nodded. "Okay." She shifted in her rocker. "Well, what do you know about assertive communication?"

I stared at her blankly. I punched people in the head. Wasn't that assertive enough? Forget passive aggressive communication; I went straight for aggressive-aggressive communication. If I had smacked her with her own teddy bear a minute and a half ago, I wondered if she would have changed her question.

She started to explain and I tried to follow along, speculating how learning about "I" statements was going to make any difference in my disturbed sleep or in my willingness to drive headfirst into another car. Maybe I should have known about this last year. I could picture using this skill, faced off with Viv. "I am getting very angry with your incessant questions and any second now, I am going to punch you directly in the face!" Those seemed like two pretty clear "I" statements to me. Or maybe even clearer, "Excuse me, Sergeant, I am going to cut through these ropes just enough so that when I drop off the building, they will snap, and I will fall six stories and probably land on that concrete retaining wall."

Confused and uncertain even how to phrase the question about how this would help, I played along until the end of the appointment. Had she just latched onto the challenge of talking to Pat because it was convenient? Of all the things we could have been talking about, my communication with Pat wasn't on the list, and Pat was hardly the only person to whom I had a hard time talking. I made a second appointment and cancelled it a couple of days later. Assertive communication, my ass.

***

By the end of September, I had already missed several ROTC classes and time was dragging to get to the part where rappelling was taught. I dropped the class. By the middle of October, I wasn't doing so well with any of my other classes, either. I made it to about every third History of the English Language and about every other Philosophy. I saw no point in debating whether or not a chair really existed or if I simply manifested it with my mind because I wanted to see a chair. Perhaps if we'd posed a question about whether those headlights coming at me really existed or if my car would make any noise when it went over an embankment if no one was around to hear the crash. . . Now **those** were useful questions! With midterms approaching, I was already failing Chemistry, so I just stopped going. The weather had started to turn, and the sky was a consistent slate color. It would snow here much earlier than it ever snowed at home, making it even less appealing to get up and go to class.

I limped through the first anniversary of the father's death with no acknowledgment from what was left of my family that the day meant anything. I didn't know what I was expecting. My being several hundred miles away was quite possibly just a big relief.

"Want to walk downtown with me? I have to go to the store."

It was my new friend Kate, from the chemistry class I was failing.

"Yeah. Okay."

Cold drizzle turned to freezing rain on our way back up the hill as it got dark. Standing at the corner of Main St. and Route 6, the trucking route through to Wellsboro, another one of those unplanned-but-why-not opportunities popped up. Kate crossed the road ahead of me. Eastbound, a tractor trailer bore down on us, probably going fifty-five in the forty mile per hour zone. Westbound, a school bus approached. They would pass each other in the slippery intersection just feet from where I was standing.

I shot out into the middle of the road, stationing myself on the yellow line. As expected, they passed me at the same moment, the wind a cyclone around me, the sound of both engines and both horns deafening. I breathed diesel exhaust, wondering if it would be the last thing I'd ever smell. I could have reached out in either direction and touched them both at the same time. The ground rumbled with their combined weight. All it would take was one of the drivers to hit the brake, not knowing where I was, and the tires would slide on the wet leaves and slick blacktop. Swallowed by the sound, I waited for the skid that would lead to being smashed between the two vehicles, perhaps dismembered and tossed in different places on the road. It would be fast. I would never know what happened.

("GET THE FUCK OUT! I WILL FUCKING KILL YOU!")

("He didn't **mean** it? He didn't mean that he would rape me? What else could he have meant when he said, 'I'll rape you so you can see how you like it' after he punched the shit out of me and has me pinned to a wall? How many meanings does that have, Dad?")

("It'll be okay. Just don't cry.")

Come on! Do it! Brake!

And then they were past me.

I remained on the yellow line, pumping adrenaline bringing me up on my tiptoes. Kate waited on the curb, the blood drained from her face, the bag she carried hanging limply at her side. Her eyes were huge. I started in her direction, appreciating the wild rush coursing through me.

When I got to the curb, she punched me in the shoulder and then hit me with the bag. "You fucking idiot! What is WRONG with you?"

I wanted to tell her I had a reason to do that, but tears welled up in her eyes and I stopped. What **was** wrong with me? Again, good god, was I supposed to be able to answer that?

Maybe I should have stayed a psych major so I'd have some chance of being able to explain myself. (*WHOMPH!*) Okay, never mind that. Maybe if I'd gone back to the Counseling Center for some more tips on assertive communication, I'd be able to reply. I could own this and just tell her bluntly, "Look, I want to die," remembering, of course, to put the correct amount of emphasis on my "I" statements. Without speaking, I fell into step beside her and we climbed the rest of the way up the hill to the dorms.

***

By the end of October, I stopped trying to sleep in my assigned room. My ongoing discomfort with my roommate made the idea of sleeping in the Pinto more appealing. Kate's roommate had left at the beginning of the semester and had never been replaced, so I started staying in her room. I went back to my dorm to shower and get clean clothes. My roommate was more disappointed that the Pop Tart stash was diminishing than the fact that I really just did not care to be in her company.

In November, when the ROTC cadets were finally getting their rappelling lessons, I got sick. I shrugged off the first sign of sore throat, thinking I was getting a cold. When it got worse and my temperature spiked, I half wondered if I'd picked up mono again.

"You should go down to the clinic," Kate observed, several days into my not feeling well. "But be careful about the pervy doctor. He makes all the girls take their shirts off no matter what they go in for."

Well THAT certainly sounded appealing. I made a mental note to avoid the clinic at all costs. Besides, this would eventually go away on its own.

Or not.

"Didn't you go to the clinic yet? " Kate asked for the third time that week.

"I'm fine," I pointed out.

"You're an idiot. Go see the damn doctor!"

You could use some "I" statements in there, I thought, but said nothing.

After a couple more days of my fever not dropping and aching in body joints I didn't even know I had, I finally went to the clinic. When the pervy doctor asked me to take my sweatshirt off, I did, having put on an additional tee shirt under it which I refused to remove. He cleared his throat and looked at me over the top of his glasses. I stared back and waited. He gave me antibiotics and sent me on my way. Having seen the damn doctor, I stuffed the pills in my jacket pocket, went to Kate's room and fell asleep on her spare bed.

"Did you go?" she asked, flying in between classes.

"Yeah."

"Did the perv make you take your shirt off?"

"No, I wouldn't do that. I wore a tee shirt under everything."

"What did he give you?"

"I think it's tetracycline." I didn't mention that I hadn't taken any yet. That was categorized need-to-know only.

"Good. You'll feel better soon."

The following day, she asked if I felt better yet. I told her I was fine and skipped telling her that I was actually hoping it would become pneumonia and make me even sicker. People die from pneumonia.

"What did you say he gave you?"

"Tetracycline."

"Where is it?" she asked, looking around at the few things scattered on the top of the spare dresser that I had claimed as my own.

"In my jacket."

She poked a hand in my jacket pocket and extracted the envelope of pills.

"Well, you haven't opened them yet."

"I know that."

"They don't help if you don't take them. You do know that, right?"

I nodded.

"So….what…you're just gonna stay sick?"

"I'm fine."

"You're an idiot. Take one of these. I'll get you some water."

I looked at the outstretched envelope of pills and shook my head. "No, really, I'm fine."

"Come on, don't joke. Take this." She wagged it at me.

"I'm okay."

She opened the little envelope and shook one of the pills out in her hand. She held that out to me next. "Here."

"I'll be fine."

"Jesus! Would you just take the fucking thing?" she snapped.

I kind of shrugged at her, non-committal.

Before I could blink, she put her hand on my head. "Quit screwing around! Tell me you'll take this!"

I wrenched sideways and fought panic. Don't slam my head...don't slam my head... I could almost feel the sickening motion of my skull being driven toward the wall. I had no idea why I thought she'd slam my head. Other folks would take such a gesture as a gesture of caring.

"Ok! Get off!"

"Take the pill! God, you're burning up!"

It seemed kind of pointless to insist that I was fine, since she was touching me and could tell how high my fever was. "Okay, okay, I'll take the fucking pill."

She wouldn't move from in front of me until she saw me swallow the pill. I just wanted to fall down and go back to sleep. The last thing she said on her way out the door was, "Jesus. What. A. Maroon."

It was one of my favorite Bugs Bunny quotes but only when I was directing it at someone else. It bothered me that someone thought I was a moron, and I decided all of this messiness could have been avoided had I just stayed in ROTC and jumped off the roof. She would never have known. No one would have known. I crawled under the covers and pulled them up to my ears, wondering why it mattered so much to her that I was sick.

It sure as hell didn't matter to me.

How's this for an "I" statement? **I** am okay with the idea of dying.

Assertive communication, my ass. I should have punched that counselor.

* * *

I couldn't go back to Pat's after my first year of college. I couldn't stand the thought of being that close to Philadelphia and cut off from my friends and my cousins. That just hurt too much. I took Kate up on her offer to come home with her for the summer. Her hometown had a factory where all the returning college students got jobs; I would be able to find work without a problem.

My decision was not well received. Pat expected I would spend my breaks at her house; she thought of her house as my home. I didn't know how to tell her without hurting her feelings that when I'd come back for the winter break between semesters, the break seemed interminable. Not because of anything she did or didn't do. I didn't know how to explain it, but I needed to stay far away from the city and the memories of all that had happened. It was the only way I found peace. I was never sure that Pat understood that.

The factory work, in its stifling, un-air conditioned building, was back breaking and boring. A trained chimp could have done the jobs I was assigned. It wasn't even as interesting as working fast food had been and paid just as poorly, but the second shift schedule was consistent. That meant a reliable paycheck to get me through my next year, then my third year. Even in the middle of heat waves, when temperatures around the tube-sealing machines probably topped one hundred twenty degrees and I fainted when I stood up from my station, I tried not to miss time from work.

With a settled place to stay during breaks, distance from the city and its memories, and a small group of new friends, my compulsion to outpace tractor trailers slowly ebbed away. I didn't give any more consideration to the Counseling Center experience, assuming that what remained of the nightmares and the occasional trouble sleeping would also disappear eventually. I waited, figuring that I hadn't gotten to the place of having such terrible dreams in a short time or simple manner. Having them go away was going to take some time.

Halfway through my sophomore year, I dismissed any major in the math or science field. Psychology was still out of the question but social work appealed. Clinical social work dealt with some of the same questions I wanted answered without involving any pigeon projects. I declared myself a social work major with the same caveat in mind that I'd had when I started to major in psych. I had no burning desire to help people; I just wanted to understand. In the cultural background rumble, the Centers for Disease Control in Atlanta had already invested several years in its research on AIDS, the issue on which much of my career would later hinge. At the time, HIV and AIDS were insignificant to me, and all that mattered was that no pigeons were involved in my education.

I kicked and clawed to bring up my grades. I'd finished my first semester with two Cs, two Ds and an F, and spent the next three semesters feeling as though I were running behind and needed desperately to catch up. I heard other students discussing the option of Year Five and could not picture myself prolonging this experience. I wanted out. I wanted a job. I wanted to feel rooted somewhere.

When I learned that social work students could complete their internship during the summer between junior and senior year, I knew that was the path I wanted to take. I could graduate college in three and a half years instead of four, despite my slow start out of the gate freshman year. I took a creative writing course credit by exam and replaced the F on my transcript. I tested out of French to list three more credits to my favor. With those credits, I was on track to graduate in December instead of June, as long as all went well in my internship.

I drove to New York on a grey afternoon, mid-week in the spring of junior year, to interview with the clinical director of a residential treatment facility for mentally ill kids. The director, a tall, angular woman in her late fifties, greeted me with an admirable handshake and offered me a chair in her office. She was quirky, earth-mother-y, and laughed easily. I liked her right away.

She offered me the internship I wanted, starting as soon as spring semester ended. I'd work forty hours a week with her as my supervisor of record, but in cooperation with and under the guidance of several other certified social workers with whom I'd share cases. My placement was an experiment for the agency, situating a full-time position in the emergency shelter building, where I was assigned to work with kids who would move to the next level of care on campus.

During my second week, while I was still getting to know kids and social workers, one of the team members asked me to join her when she took one of her assigned kids to court for a family hearing. She didn't speak to me much, but I was just the intern, after all. I figured she just wasn't as outgoing as some of the other social workers I'd met. By the end of May, the first kid of my assigned kids was accepted into her building and she was going to be his social worker. I braced myself for a quiet summer and hoped the other team members talked enough to make up for it.

"Do you know how to fill this form out?" she asked, showing me a blank form in the client chart. "You'll find this information here…" she flipped to a different section, "…and then you'll find the family stuff here…"

I leaned on the edge of her desk and nodded. "Okay. This gets done by when?"

From memory, she ran through the list of which forms were completed by which deadlines according to the child's intake date and handed me the binder. She leaned back in her chair. "Have you talked to Daryl's teacher about what happened in her class?"

Without looking up from the chart, I nodded again.

"What did you think?"

Absorbed in my reading, I neglected to click on my out-loud filter. "Hmm. Personally, I didn't think she had both oars in the water." I immediately regretted being so sarcastic. This social worker didn't know me. I didn't know if she had unspoken alliances with her colleagues. What the hell was I thinking?

I dared a peek upwards. Kathy had tipped her chair forward again, folded her arms on her desk and sat there. Laughing.

"I...uhhhhh..." I started.

She waved it off. "That was my take too."

When I left her office that afternoon to go back to my own, I thought maybe I'd judged her a little too quickly. Maybe it wouldn't be a quiet summer.

***

"My housemate and I belong to a softball team that plays Monday nights. You want to come watch a game?" Kathy asked.

"Oh. Yeah. I guess."

A month into my field placement, I was in and out of Kathy's office daily, as well as the offices of two other social workers on campus. I tended to think of them more as my supervisors than I thought of my official supervisor, whom I saw once a week during our allotted time. Questions about the kids and their treatment plans and family interactions came up routinely. It made more sense to ask the questions of the people who would take over the case when the kids moved into their buildings. Kathy's invitation was unexpected but appreciated.

I met the first housemate at the game. She had two other housemates. One was out of state for the summer working as a camp counselor, and the other worked multiple jobs and was hardly ever in the house. Sitting on their front porch after the game, Kathy propped her feet on the railing.

"So how's it going so far?" she asked.

I understood she meant my field placement. Her question was benign enough and I would ask it of my interns many times in future years. I never expected to react to it. It irritated me that she would ask and I wasn't sure why. Worse, it unnerved me that I wanted to confide in her that I was horrified to read some of the client charts and realize that I could have easily been one of the kids with whom we were working. I could never tell her that and I was angry at myself for wanting to share that. *("For Chrissake, nobody needs to know!")* I snapped at her, more forcefully than I needed to and we changed the topic.

A few days later, standing in her office, another unsettling topic popped up.

"Social workers have to deal with their own stuff—their own baggage. To be good at this, you don't have a choice."

All of the little hairs stood up on the back of my neck. Was she implying that she knew something of my history? I had said nothing. I **would** say nothing. It was already the middle of June. Placement ended in eight weeks. As with Viv, it would not be smart to confide in someone who would be out of my life in such a short period of time. I did what I knew: I played the question down.

Kathy didn't seem to pay much attention to the dodge and changed the topic smoothly as she reached for a client file on the corner of her desk. "Kill that animal on the wall behind you, would you?"

I turned and crushed the spider making its way up the wall beside her filing cabinet after thanking it silently for creating a diversion. *Deal with their own stuff? I might as well quit now!*

***

"I'm going home over the holiday weekend. Want to drive out and join me? You can meet my family."

I hesitated. "Where's home?"

"Buffalo. Where are your parents?" Kathy poured coffee from the tiny coffee maker on the small side table into the mug on the institutional steel desk.

I hated that everyone assumed I had parents. I mumbled something and we moved on to the next question. It was an innocent enough question. She wasn't trying to pump me for information, it just happened to come up. But I detested the strained silence and that look people gave me upon finding out that my parents had died before I got out of high school. I could do without it now.

"You'll find, if you stay in the field," Kathy said, "that most social workers have really strong nurturance needs."

"I would hate that."

"Yeah. Maybe you should go to law school." She grinned.

Disarmed, I started to laugh.

***

"There's no point in talking about this!" My voice grew sharper. "My internship is over in seven weeks. I'm not going to open up a bunch of stuff that I can't do anything with."

Kathy nodded and shifted on the porch swing so it rocked back and forth slowly. "Remember what I said, though. You're an excellent diagnostician. To be a good clinician, you really need to deal with your own stuff."

"I'm fine. And besides," I said, a note of sarcasm creeping into my tone, "why would I want to open up this stuff with you? You're …terribly average."

She laughed and put a hand on the back of my head in a half-smack, half-push gesture. "It'll make you good at what you do. Do you think about this stuff I tell you?"

"Not if I can help it!"

"Come on, think about it." She waited for me to answer her original question. When I didn't, she finally said, "Uhhh…can you think out loud?"

"Probably not."

She rolled her eyes. "Okay. Don't think out loud." She glanced at her watch. "I've got a racquetball game early tomorrow so I need to go to bed. See you tomorrow?"

As I got in the Dodge to head home, I was surprised by the wave of anger that overtook me. I didn't want **to want** to talk about anything. It infuriated me that I did. I wanted to tell her what had happened—not just that the parents were dead but how they died and how I found him and how horrendous that last year of high school had been. I pictured trying to tell her about Michael, about the beatings. My stomach sank. I could not possibly share that information with her. She was my boss. And now she was my friend. Even if I told her, what good would it do? She couldn't do anything about it. She couldn't fix dead either, no matter how good her clinical skills were. It was best to leave it alone.

By the time I got back to the apartment I shared with Kate, another impulse tugged insistently on my shirttail. I pulled out a blank pad of legal paper and sat down. I couldn't tell her...not in person. I started to write. It wasn't ideal. But it was more than I'd done before.

***

"Look, you've got six weeks of your placement left," Kathy said. "You can get some of this out now or not—and try to figure it out later when you get a job."

We were at her house after work on a rainy Monday. The softball game had been cancelled.

"So I've got six weeks of placement left. Why would I do this now?" I countered.

Kathy threw her hands up in the air. "You've got such potential, and all I see is you throwing it away because you won't deal with whatever the stuff is you're carrying!"

That was frustration. I recognized it and met it with my own. "Everything is fine! You need to back off!"

"Talk to me!" she coaxed.

Don't push me!

We faced each other, a few feet apart. Sweat broke out on my forehead. She was too close. When she took a step toward me, panic surged along with my determination to keep her at arm's length. On her next step, I clenched a fist and hit her with a right uppercut, catching her on the chin.

SHIT! I just hit my boss!

This startling realization didn't quell the panic, and the punch didn't stop Kathy. She grabbed one of my wrists and wrapped her arms around me in a bear hug. I froze. Jesus Christ, she was **touching** me! I tried to pull away. She tightened the bear hug. She leaned against the closest wall and slid into a sitting position. I had no choice but to go with her, until we were on the floor.

"Is that how he hit you?" she said quietly.

I couldn't speak. I wanted to ask, "Which time?"

For the longest time, neither of us said anything. Finally, she loosened the bear hug and put a hand on my head, pressing it against her shoulder. "It's okay. You're okay."

The jury was still out on that.

***

It never came up again that I hit her. We continued through the next weeks with me taking two steps forward and one step back in terms of confiding in her and confronting my history. I wanted to tell her and I continued not to want to want it. I shared in bits and broken pieces as much as I could find words for but often, when the opportunity to tell her about something came up, I found myself overwhelmed and angry—at her and at myself. More often than not, I would slam my car door and drive way too fast, furious at whatever she had asked, even if I had indicated a willingness to sit there while she asked that question. But I was even more furious at my own inability to express anything.

My placement ended in the middle of August. I had one more semester left before graduation. I had made it through my internship without spilling any major family secrets and I was almost done. Part of me (the father's influence?) was proud of having made it through the summer without having spilled anything. Another part of me felt the cynical "I told you so" kick in that I had not dealt with any of the history I was dragging around with me like an albatross. I **could** do this work without divulging anything. We didn't need that. We didn't talk about such things.

When Kathy invited me to go with her at the end of August to visit her family again, I accepted, figuring we were playing the superficial game of "we'll pretend we'll still be friends now that we no longer work together." I left my car at her house and drove with her to Buffalo. Watching her with her family, I went into a slow burn that lasted the entire weekend. Bitter questions kept popping into my head. How could I ever explain my history to somebody who had had such a drastically different family experience? Her family actually liked her. Her parents and her brother were genuinely kind, funny people. She thought she could understand if I decided to share my background with her?

When we returned at the end of the weekend, I went into the house to retrieve my keys. Kathy followed me in, carrying her overnight bag. I made it to the kitchen before my rage started to boil over. She had said nothing. I'm sure my verbal assault felt like it was coming right out of nowhere.

She didn't respond as quickly as I thought she should—as quickly as my anger seemed to warrant. I grabbed two fistfuls of the front of her shirt and slammed her against the kitchen wall. Again. She wasn't my boss anymore. Why not?

"You think you know? You think I'm gonna talk to you? Go ahead, ask me something now! I'll take your fucking head off!"

God, I sounded just like Michael. That was alarming but it didn't stop me. I slammed her against the wall a third time.

She wrapped her hands over mine, attempting to dislodge them. "Enough!" she snapped at me.

"You think you're gonna tell me what's enough?"

WHAM! I bounced her off the wall again.

"What the hell?" At least indignant and possibly starting to get angry herself, she brought both arms up sharply underneath my forearms and broke my grip on her shirt. "You really want to do this?" She sidestepped so her back was no longer against the wall.

I shoved her, catching her in the collarbone with the base of my palm.

I never saw it coming. She brushed my hand aside, using my own momentum against me and taking a step behind me. Like when I'd hit her before, she wrapped her arms around me in a bear hug again, pinning my arms to my sides.

"You want to act like a brat? Okay. Fine. I'll treat you like a brat." She turned sideways so she was holding me against her side and dropped to her knees. I went down with her, trying to pull my arms loose. Once on the floor, she leaned against a low cabinet door, holding me in front of her with both my arms crossed in front of my body and a tight grip on my wrists, fixing them to my ribs. She was doing to me what I had seen done to the kids at work.

In seconds, I realized I could not free my arms. I threw myself backwards against her, then pitched forward. She followed every move I made.

"Let go!" I demanded. "Let go right now!"

"No. I'm not letting go."

I pulled. I squirmed. I jerked from side to side, my frustration building.

"Let GO!"

"No. Why don't you talk to me now about what happened? Why don't you tell me about everybody you've lost? About being homeless?"

("I'll rape you and we'll see how you like that.")

("GET THE FUCK OUT! I WILL FUCKING KILL YOU!")

I hadn't really understood why the kids at work had gotten so agitated when they ended up in a hold like this. Now I had a very clear idea why. This was maddening. I couldn't shut her up. I pulled harder, swearing at her. She ignored me and held on. I wanted to hurt her. Badly. I would do great damage to her when I got loose.

("It'll be okay. Just don't cry.")

"Why don't you tell me how much it hurts that nobody was there for you when you were seven? And nobody was there for you when you were seventeen? Why don't you tell me how angry you are that you were alone?"

He looked posed. What happened that day? And why didn't I go home?

I was rattled by the sense of something approaching, something I couldn't see. I fought wildly to break her grip. I had to get away from her, from what she was saying, before something horrible happened, although I had no idea what horrible thing was possible in the middle of her kitchen.

That first towering wave of grief and rage was a physical sensation that pulled me under and took my breath away. I would drown in it. I no longer felt Kathy sitting behind me, no longer felt the kitchen floor beneath me. I could get no air in and no sound out and all I wanted to do was scream.

I lost track of time. I lost track of Kathy. When the waves tossed me back up on shore like a stranded starfish, I became aware of her again. She still had my arms locked immobile across the front of my body and she was praying out loud. I caught the first few words and then another wave sucked me under.

The next time I surfaced, Kathy was holding me and rocking. I had wrapped my arms around one of hers as tightly as I could, and I was sobbing, deep, choking sobs that made it feel as if my spine were being wrenched out through the top of my head. The sun had been shining the first time I bounced her off the wall. It was now fully dark beyond the kitchen window. I wasn't sure how many hours we'd been sitting there.

Above me, I heard Kathy say quietly, "**This** is what should have happened when you were seven. And seventeen. **This**."

I wasn't sure which one of those I was. Or if I was neither. Maybe I was both. At the time, it didn't matter.

Epilogue

1997

Michael died first.

Philadelphia, my aunt, my cousins, Marie, and especially Michael were fifteen years behind me. I hadn't seen or spoken to him that entire time, although Chick and Jedda occasionally mentioned him. I had sporadic contact with Marie, my aunt, and a couple of cousins. Every contact left me wondering if anyone really knew why I had left, if anyone had thought it odd that I disappeared and never came back, if anyone had missed me. And if they knew, how much did they know? And when did they know it?

"Michael hasn't been able to hold a job. We don't know how long he's been without heat."

I hope the bastard freezes.

"Michael lost his job again. We aren't sure he's eating."

Please, god, don't let that sick son of a bitch eat my dog.

"Michael was attacked by some guys from the neighborhood. They pushed their way into the house and beat him with a bat. They broke his arm in something like eleven places."

Too bad they missed his head...

"Michael's been clean for two years. He'd really like to talk to you."

No. Not just no. Hell no!

"Michael's getting married. He'd really like if he could talk to you and invite you to the wedding."

Not in this lifetime.

"Michael and his wife are having a baby."

The content never mattered. I liked my Michael-free life and I was not inclined to open the door to communicate with him. If I had learned anything working in the HIV field, it was that relapse was part of recovery and I did not want to be in contact with him when he relapsed.

"I told him," Jedda said, "that if he **really** wants to make amends, he should just leave you alone."

"You know," I replied, staring into my coffee cup, "I used to wish horrible things on him. I don't do that anymore. Now I even wish him well, but I wish him well far away from me. I don't need to be part of his amends. So he wants to take care of himself. Great. But it doesn't preempt my taking care of myself and that includes being left alone."

She nodded. "You decide. You don't owe him contact. He can do his steps without talking to you. Lots of people do."

Chick was a bit more obtuse. Having survived lung cancer and now dealing actively with congestive heart failure, Chick's jovial perspective implied we could all be one big happy family. I suspected he was making some amends of his own by trying to bring his siblings together before he got any sicker. He suggested a few times that I should be "over all of that stuff" and I should now be at a point where I could shake hands and start new. I wasn't tempted.

***

I got up earlier than normal to allow for the half hour drive time to my agency's satellite office where our managers' meeting was scheduled. I let the dogs out and made enough coffee to take a cup with me when I left. Bebo, my Chow mix who bordered on doggy brilliance, "yarked" at the back door, her signature "Come 'n' git me" when she wanted back inside. Zach, my Golden Retriever, let her signal for him as well. I wondered if they ever disagreed about when to come in. Beeb would win. That's just the kind of guy Zach was. Very sweet, but smart like a box of rocks. I left their kibble down and kissed them both as I headed for the door, juggling briefcase, keys, and full travel cup.

"Oh, Nance, DePalmer House is looking for you. Paul wants you to call him before you go into the meeting." The office assistant handed me a pink While You Were Out note as I rounded the corner of her desk.

I refilled my coffee and found an empty office to perch in to return Paul's call. Just beyond the office door, the conference room was filling up. I rushed Paul a little, hoping he didn't mind.

Our executive director called the meeting to order and began working his way through the agenda, focused mostly on the insurance changes about to be dropped on the mental health field. I liked Carl, but if he said "economies of scale" one more time, I might poke myself in the eye with a spork.

Carl always reminded me of Wile E. Coyote, Super Genius. He had a photographic memory and there was no topic the man hadn't read about and couldn't discuss. He would become my measure of a great executive director when I took that step in my career. In his enthusiasm to grow our agency, though, I was usually running to keep pace with him. Not the kind of running you see in the park on a sunny afternoon, running more like a toddler whose legs don't quite connect to their brain and who is going to have a spectacular crash at any minute. I waited for two years for something to blow up in my face and leave me covered in soot with just my eyes showing…or blow all my hair off…or something.

In my office back in Syracuse, the phone on my credenza rang. My outgoing message kicked on, as always, recommending that the caller press my office assistant's number and speak directly to her in case of an emergency. The light blinked and the call rolled over to my assistant's office.

"…leaving us in competition for step down beds…" Carl was saying, seated at the head of the conference table in Oneida, oblivious to the phone ringing in Syracuse half an hour away.

Someone knocked lightly on the conference room door. Carl glanced up, puzzled and slightly annoyed. The office assistant poked her head in, searching the room. "Liz, can you step out here?"

My immediate supervisor, Liz, spun away from the long table and closed the door behind her. This must be big. The office assistant wouldn't interrupt a managers' meeting unless it was an emergency. Carl continued.

In less than a minute, Liz reopened the door, approached me and tapped me on the shoulder. "Nance, can you come out in the hallway?"

This interruption brought a quizzical look from Carl. I didn't have time to say anything. Liz plucked at my sleeve, meaning to hurry me up. I had just talked to Paul, so I doubted anything was wrong in our HIV programs. Had a client gotten hurt in one of the other services in my department? In our group home for chemical dependency? In the other house for people living with chronic mental illness? In our day program?

Liz took a few steps away from the door to give me clearance to close it behind me. We were standing in the alcove that led to one of the conference room entrances. I expected we would go to the front office, where I figured one of my staff people was either standing or waiting on hold for me to pick up the phone but we stopped. Liz turned with a pained expression on her face. "Nance, I'm sorry to have to tell you. Your brother died."

My breathing went shallow. "Which one?" I whispered.

"Michael."

I leaned against the wall. Thank god, thank god, thank god—not that he was dead, but that it wasn't Chick.

Liz put a hand on my arm. "Your other brother is going to call you. He tried your office and he got your message to roll over to another line. They called here looking for you. Why don't you wait in my office for his call?"

"But the meeting..." I said, numb.

She gave me an odd look. "I'll tell Carl. I don't expect you to come back in."

***

I debated for only a short time about whether or not I'd go to the funeral. It wouldn't be for Michael. I had already made my peace with the absence of contact. It would be for Chick, who had somehow managed to maintain a semblance of a relationship with him and who was now going to be called upon to bury his little brother. Grimly, I wondered if he knew how close he'd been to burying his little sister. Or, as I sometimes joked, his "other little brother." I bought a new black suit for the funeral and drove to Philadelphia.

I stayed with Pat and Roger, using Bob's old room. This would be unnerving. Knots formed in my stomach at the thought of driving through our neighborhood and stepping inside the funeral home where viewing services for both parents had been held. I would likely run into relatives that I hadn't seen since I left. How awkward could this get?

I buttoned my shirt and went downstairs with my jacket over my arm. Pat waited for me in the kitchen. "Ready when you are," I said.

Pat drove us the hour into South Philly in her new BMW. Roger drove in with Bob in Bob's car so the two of us could have some time to talk, but we drove mostly in silence. She cut through our old neighborhood. I was grateful she spared me the drive down our old street. I didn't want to see that house, not even from a distance in a moving vehicle. The knots in my stomach coiled tighter as she pulled up alongside the church and elementary school that had formed so many years of our lives. It looked the same. I bet it still smelled the same.

She interrupted my musing. "I have to ask you something."

I turned from the church. "What?"

She dropped the gearshift into first and set the hand brake before she looked back at me. When she did, her eyes had filled with tears. "Why didn't you come back?"

"Come back?" I repeated, feeling a bit dense. "I'm here. I am back."

"No. I mean then. You left and you never came back." Tears trailed quickly down her face. She pawed through her bag for a tissue. "Why didn't you ever come back? Did you have any idea how hurt I was?"

Stymied, I opened my mouth to answer then closed it again. What the hell should I say to that? How could I explain this? And why did I have to? Of all of the people I had wondered about asking me why I left, she was not on the list. Did she really not know?

"I couldn't," I finally choked out.

"What does that mean? Why couldn't you?" She was mopping tears as fast as they overflowed.

"It's too hard to be here," I said flatly.

"What's too hard?!"

I shifted in the seat. Did we really need to do this now? "I don't expect you to understand but being here...everything about being here reminds me of everybody I lost. Of everything I lost. Of being lost. It's too hard to come back here and feel it. Being here makes it too close."

"But I miss you."

I nodded. "I'm sorry." I didn't know what else to say.

She dried her eyes and checked her makeup in the visor mirror. She sighed. "Okay. Let's go do this."

As we approached the entrance, my heart raced and a wave of nausea brushed close enough that it left my muscles a little quivery and my hands sweaty. The funeral home director, the same man who had carried out services for the parents, greeted us by the door. I knew from experience that the casket would be ahead of us to the right, and two smaller rooms beyond that for family and friends to gather. The smallest room in the far back was the room where I had climbed up in Pat's lap at the mother's funeral and sat with her while she cried. My chest was uncomfortably tight and my teeth clenched. Was it too late to leave?

The casket lid was closed, a framed photo of Michael set in the center of it. I recoiled at the image, remembering the smell of sour milk when he would get on top of me, that uniquely Michael-smell that pervaded his room along with an undertone of urine from him wetting the bed well into high school. I wrenched my head around so I didn't have to look at the photo.

Chick had told us the casket would be closed. Michael's official cause of death was accidental overdose but just prior to his death, he had also sustained a blow to the head that fractured his skull. The police surmised he had fallen and struck his head on an old floor model TV. Judging from the trail of blood around the first floor that Chick described, he had crawled through several rooms before finally collapsing on top of a heat grate where he died.

His estranged wife found him three days later when he failed to show up to pick up their daughter for a visit and she'd been unable to raise him by phone. Lying for three days on top of that heat grate had caused his head to swell so much larger than the size of a normal head, the funeral home director had not been able to correct it enough to hold an open casket service.

That was okay with me. The photo was hard enough to look at.

I had no sooner registered the photo than we were in the greeting line. I followed Pat without speaking as people filed up to the casket, knelt down to pray, then stood up to meet Michael's family. I remained on my feet. Chick and Jedda were already here. Next to Chick at the start of the greeting line, stood the woman Michael had married, the same woman Michael had been dating when the father died. I had not seen her since the father's funeral. Our "What did you know and when?" conversation wouldn't happen for a number of years and at Michael's funeral, I didn't believe it ever would.

Her hug was immediate and it felt genuine. "You came! I didn't know if you'd come!" she sobbed. "I didn't know...thank you for coming!"

I hugged her back, feeling clumsy and stiff. "Hello."

She squeezed me a little tighter. "I can't believe you came. Chick said he didn't know if you would be here."

"I would be here." I bit off the rest of that sentence that went something like, "But it's sure as hell not for Michael."

People crowded in behind us, done with their prayers and ready to move on. She let go of me and I went to Chick.

"How are you? You okay?" I muttered against his shoulder as he bent down to hug me.

His words were unintelligible and he hugged me hard. I squeezed him back. Pain rolled off him in waves. My heart ached for him. When he stood up, he was again Major Mullen, all stoicism, posture, and right angle turns.

("It'll be okay. Just don't cry.")

I knew he wouldn't. He wouldn't even need to be told.

Jedda kissed my cheek, pressed her head against mine and said softly, "He's so glad you're here. You are a very classy lady, do you know that?"

I shrugged. "Where else would I be?"

She gripped my hand. "It means more to him than you'll know."

I smiled. "Good, 'cause **you** know that **he's** the only reason I'm here!" I whispered.

She started to laugh and caught herself, widening her eyes as if to say—which I understood clearly—"Smartass!" She shooed me off to the side so she could greet the people behind us.

I nudged my way through the throng of visitors approaching the smallest back room where I remembered a water dispenser. I filled a small paper cone and looked around for an open seat. The couches and folding chairs were lined with people I'd never met. As I turned toward the door, a stocky man with red hair blocked my path.

"Nancy, right?" he said. He held his hand out. "Bill Dunphy. I'm so sorry for your loss."

I recognized his name and I accepted his extended hand without thinking. He had gone through school with Michael. I wasn't aware they were friends, but then again there was no reason why I should be. My loss? I didn't consider this my loss. I considered this a gain for our family.

I sidestepped around him, looking for Pat among the visitors. Chick and Jedda were still standing in the greeting line. As I neared, Jedda leaned toward me and said, "Chick needs to sit down for a while."

Yeah, he did. The posture and right angles couldn't disguise the grey tone of his skin and I knew it had nothing to do with his grief. His congestive heart failure was progressing quickly; he tired easily and looked ten years older than he really was. Jedda put her arm through his and they walked away slowly.

Michael's wife turned to me. "I'm so glad you're here."

"I'm here for Chick," I said softly.

She nodded. Before she could speak again, a visitor stood up from where he knelt in front of the casket and turned to her to give her a hug. She thanked him. He moved on.

To me.

I realized too late I was standing where Chick and Jedda had just been. As the man I'd never met reached for my hand and offered me his condolences, it occurred to me that I was now part of the greeting line. Me? Wait! How the hell did that happen? Would it be wrong to say I wasn't part of the greeting line, that I had just been standing there because Michael's wife spoke to me? Would it be wrong to try to pass myself off as a stranger who had wandered into the wrong funeral and really had no idea whose service this was? I tried to keep my expression as neutral as possible as I shook the man's hand. It crossed my mind quickly that maybe a Candid Camera was hidden somewhere in the funeral home.

Another person moved through, then another, each sharing their sympathy with me.

My sister appeared at my elbow. "What the hell are YOU doing here?"

"I dunno! It just happened!"

Beside me, Michael's wife shuddered. I slid an arm around her and, as Pat always did for me, I rubbed small circles on her back. I had no idea how she could have tolerated dating him (*sour milk*), let alone married him and reproduced with him. I had no idea how she could have believed whatever lies he'd told her about our history and why I had left. But I was standing right here and her grief was palpable. I wouldn't wish such pain on anyone. She leaned against me. I held her until she composed herself again and wondered if this fit the definition of irony. What the hell was I doing here, indeed!

Across the room, the front door opened and some of my cousins came in.

I hadn't seen my cousin Maureen in ten years. I'd returned to Philadelphia for my five year high school reunion, stopped by our neighborhood to say hi to a friend who lived on her street and decided to break the ice and say hello to Maureen while I was there. I stumbled over my words and wondered why she hugged me. She jumped into conversation with me easily, as if nothing had ever happened. Maybe for her, nothing had ever happened. My awkwardness made five minutes seem like weeks and that had been the last time I'd come into South Philly until now.

I wondered who else would come through over the evening. I'd been here less than half an hour and I already couldn't wait to get the hell out.

***

The following morning, I chugged coffee and made one last run to the bathroom before we left for the funeral. As I stepped off the bottom stair into the living room, Roger stood up to join me, and we waited by the dining room table for Pat to emerge from her bedroom. Roger stuffed both hands in his pockets.

"You know what Patti thinks, don't you?" he asked quietly.

"About what?" I picked a fuzz off my jacket sleeve.

"About Michael."

My head lifted and my eyes met his. "What does she think?"

That he was crazy? Old news. That he should never have gotten married? No joke! That he definitely should not have had a kid? Not rocket science, my friend!

"She thinks he killed Charlie."

I was stunned into momentary silence. My knees almost gave out and I reached behind me for the edge of table for support. "She thinks he killed our father?" I finally whispered.

"Yeah."

"Me too!" I could barely get the words out.

Coherent thought fled. I had isolated that fear in the most distant part of my brain for fifteen years, unable to put that entire sentence together to another person. Not to my partner, not to my best friend. Not even to myself. ("And for Chrissake, nobody needs to know what's going on in our house!")

Had she thought this the whole time? The whole time I was living at Maureen's, down the street from him, crying in my sleep and waking up covered in cold sweat? When I was living out of my car, unable to get comfortable anywhere and really settle in? When I was borrowing an air mattress at Debbi's and coming to consciousness some mornings with the outline of my own hands imprinted on my biceps from holding myself together even in my sleep?

"Why? Why does she think that?"

"Because he called your house the night Charlie died."

I nodded. "While the paramedics were there."

"To say hi," Roger continued.

"Chick told me that too. But why would he call? It's not like either one of us would have wanted to talk to him—he didn't just call home to say hi."

"Patti thinks he was checking up on things because he already knew something was wrong."

It felt like Roger had just punched me in the stomach. My blood ran cold and my skin raised up thousands of little bumps, all screaming their own tiny protests. "He knew something was wrong because he did it," I said weakly, pushing words past the sock in my esophagus.

Yes, I knew this. Like the night I found the father, I knew this as much as I had known he was already dead when I walked down the street under the pretense of getting ready to go to the hospital with him. What I had feared that year, what I had never been able to say out loud to another person, was realized out loud. He looked posed because he had been. Because Michael had hurt him.

Don't look!

No, not just that he hurt him. He...he... I cast around, floundering among old images in my brain. The father wasn't bruised. He didn't beat him the way he beat me.

The father's tongue was black. Did that mean anything at all?

Time slowed as the image crystalized in my mind's eye. Did he suffocate him? I grasped the table edge harder to keep upright, locked on Roger, speechless. If Michael put a pillow over his face like he used to do to me, that wouldn't leave bruises. For a man who'd already had three heart attacks, would that stress be enough to cause his final, fatal heart attack? Or did his heart last long enough that he asphyxiated under his own pillow? He didn't know to go limp, like I had learned. I had never told him that part.

An almost audible *click* of memory aligning reinforced the fear.

("Stupid bitch! You don't like it—don't do it! But don't fucking tell me...I'll sit here in my quarter of this house and smoke my joint and do whatever the fuck I want!")

Michael, shouting at Pat, the day after the father died. *The day after the father died.* How would he have known he would be getting a quarter of the house? At that point, Chick and Pat hadn't even started looking for the father's will. How could he possibly have known everything would end up being split four ways? Had he seen that will we never found? Had he **taken** it? I could see his smug expression from that afternoon, daring Pat to disagree with him that it was his quarter of that house.

Chick's voice rose up behind the image. "We're not going to do an autopsy. There's no need."

Oh dear god. Did Chick suspect? Had he suspected back then? Is that why we skipped the autopsy? Did Michael kill him to get the house? Did they have a fight because Michael found the will and confronted the father that he'd been left out of it? Were the two factors unrelated? Was Chick covering for what he thought Michael was capable of—what we all, apparently, thought Michael might be capable of?

The bedroom door opened and Pat clicked across the hardwood floor. "Everybody ready?"

We both stared at her.

***

I avoided the greeting line and stayed toward the back of the building, close to the room with the water dispenser. I wished for coffee. Then I wished I had stuck a flask of vodka in my jacket pocket.

"Hey, you're Nancy," the voice said.

I looked up to find a weathered man with red rimmed eyes standing in front of me. I nodded and he put his hand out to me. I accepted.

"Bobby. Mikey and I were friends all through school. You probably don't remember me."

My stomach heaved and in his grip, my hand filmed over with sweat. The voice snapped into place. Memories crowded each other and I pulled my hand back quickly.

Held on the floor, with Michael on top of me, rocking and rubbing his groin against my chest, several of his friends, drunk, stoned, or both, jammed in behind him and around us. His hands tangled in my hair, and he lifted my head off the floor and slammed it down again.

I never saw who said it first.

"Hit her again, Mikey! Harder!"

The chant was picked up by the rest of them until all I could hear was, "Hit her again, Mikey! Harder! Harder!" and their laughter, punctuated by the dull whack of my own skull against the carpeted living room floor. This man with his red rimmed eyes had been in that room.

I pushed the image away, furious. "I know who you are," I said and turned away from him. He didn't follow me. In the bathroom, I took deep breaths and tried to stretch the shakes away. You probably don't remember me? Who could forget? Did he think I was an idiot? Or was it—and this seemed more likely—that he didn't remember what had happened those days? Angry tears stung behind my eyes and I yanked my glasses off, digging my fingers into the burn.

Not here. I would **not** do this here. Michael's funeral? Hell, I wouldn't do THIS anywhere—not because of him.

DID HE REALLY THINK I WOULDN'T REMEMBER? Son of a bitch!

I pivoted and punched the wall, my fury at full boil. I didn't feel the swelling erupt between my last two knuckles, but the sight of the big blue lump reminded me immediately of standing on the corner of my old street, cut off from my family, hammering on the driver's window of the Pinto, now long gone. I crossed my arms, tucking my injured hand under the opposite arm, then pulled it out and turned the cold water faucet on, holding it under the stream.

It'll be okay. It'll be okay. It'll be okay. Just don't cry. I stayed in the bathroom until I stopped shaking. When I went back out, he was gone.

* * *

We paused at the back of the church, just inside the vestibule near the holy water font, the greyish-white marble bowl on a marble pedestal of blessed water used to cross oneself when entering and exiting the church a familiar sight. Michael's casket was covered with a layer of shiny white fabric, and Chick started to remove it before the casket was taken up the center aisle for the mass. I stood between Chick and Pat, and Chick extended the far end of the fabric to Pat to help him fold.

("Hit her again, Mikey! Harder! Harder!")

("You probably don't remember me.")

I felt my lower lip tremble. Shit. Not here.

In mid-fold, Chick happened to be looking at me when I jerked my head sideways and blinked hard to focus. "It's okay to cry for him," he said very softly.

The ridiculousness of his statement stilled the tremble. Now? Cry now? Cry for him? After twenty-five years of "It'll be okay, just don't cry"? I wished I had no idea how he thought that was even remotely possible. Chick smoothed the folded fabric and said, again very softly, "You don't have to keep all of that in."

Does "all of that" include you putting me on the street when I was seventeen, I thought, unable to meet his gaze. *Does it include you knowing that this son of a bitch suffocated our father when you decided not to have an autopsy done so we could bury him quickly?* I wanted to scream, DID YOU KNOW THIS WHOLE TIME?

Chick turned away as the pallbearers got into position and took Michael's casket to the front of the church. He gave the eulogy. I sat through his delivery, watching people's heaving shoulders all around me, watching Chick's own heaving shoulders and lowered head as he talked brokenly about the horror of burying his baby brother. He never mentioned the horror of the idea that his baby brother might have suffocated our father.

***

March, 2002

I talked to Chick Monday afternoon of Easter week, right before I left my office for a meeting. He was living on the transplant unit at Temple University Hospital, waiting for a new heart, and we'd spoken more by phone in the last nine months than we had probably spoken my entire life. If I still lived on the East coast, it would have been so much easier to spend time with him. The year after Michael died, I had accepted an executive director position in a small agency working with LGBT youth in the Midwest. I was half a day away and left with phone calls and occasional emails as our primary means of communication.

"They're still trying to figure out what this infection in my lung is," he said.

"So what are they doing?" I asked, piling the materials I needed for the upcoming meeting on top of my day planner.

"Well, they're worried about doing a biopsy. With the one lung, that's always a big risk. All the blood work is showing that it's something, but they don't know what."

He and Jedda had fought hard for this transplant option. Since he had lost his other lung to lung cancer, he was considered very high risk for the procedure. Other transplant programs had turned him down. Temple had been his last chance. He was so sick now, he had moved onto the "heart floor" because their home was far enough away that if anything happened with his heart, he would not survive the trip to the hospital. After Michael's death, he had been repeatedly hospitalized. We had had some close calls, but they'd always managed to stabilize him and send him home again. Prior to coming to Temple, the message seemed to be that they were sending him home to wait it out and be kept comfortable, but the message at Temple was of hope of living for years post-surgery.

We had spent many evenings during this nine month stretch planning the fishing trip we would take when his surgery was complete. He wanted to charter a boat off the Carolina coast, and I wanted to land something as big as myself that took all day to get inside the boat. He had explained the whole process to me: how many weeks he'd remain inpatient after the new heart was put in, how many weeks after being released he had to remain within a certain geographic area to the hospital in case his body rejected the heart and he had to be med-evac'ed back, how long before he'd be cleared to go out on a fishing charter. I hoped that he'd be cleared within six months to a year. The only wild card was when he'd have the new heart put in. We were nine months into a wait that averaged three hundred sixty-four days. The most fun part was teasing him about how those poor doctors were ever going to find a way to transplant something into him that he'd never had in the first place.

"I'll find out more from the cardiologist tomorrow."

I checked my time. I needed to leave for my meeting. "I'm going to Syracuse tomorrow for a few days. I'll call you tomorrow night when I get in to see what you found out."

"Sounds good. Drive safe."
"Yeah, I will. Love you."
"Love you, too, babe."

***

I slept in a little the next morning and got started on my drive later than I really wanted. Zach occupied the back seat, asleep with his big head on his giant golden paws for most of the twelve hour trip. We were approaching the second anniversary of losing Beeb, whom I'd had for fifteen years. Zach was still beside himself without her and he went everywhere with me. It was after ten when I arrived in the Syracuse area. It was too late to call Chick. The man needed his beauty sleep. I unloaded my car into the guest bedroom at my friends' house and Zach and I went to bed.

The following morning, I called Chick's hospital room for my update. "Ours" answered.

"You need to come now," he said, his speech pressured.

I was suddenly wide awake. "What happened?"

"He crashed Monday night. They don't know what's wrong. They induced a coma and they've got him on a ventilator. It's bad. If you're coming, come now," he repeated.

It was always bad. Last year, he'd had a reaction to one of his medications and had hiccups for nine days. If his blood thinner medication was the slightest bit out of whack, he got a nosebleed just sitting up in bed. He'd had two strokes since Michael died; we worried about every headache. Nothing was simple, and it seemed some days that every function of his body was controlled by the medical field.

I was nodding against the phone as if Ours would be able to feel it and know I was agreeing. "Yes, I'll come. I'll be there this afternoon."

When I hung up, the friends whose home I was visiting were both waiting expectantly. "I have to go. It's bad and if I'm going, I have to go now."

We'd done this before. This was the third time in the last two years that I'd gotten the "if you're coming, come now" call. Each time, I dropped what I was doing and took off for Pennsylvania from wherever I was. Each time rocked me. Each time, we had no idea if he would survive.

I gathered up my belongings, jamming everything back into my overnight bag. When I dragged it downstairs with Zach lumbering after me, my friends were in the living room, car keys in hand.

"We'll drive you," Ronnie said.

"You don't need to do that-"

"You're tired and you're upset. You were on the road all day yesterday. We don't want you on the road alone today. I called Ma and she's coming to stay with Zach, so you can leave him here," Holly informed me.

"No, I can't ask-"

"You didn't ask. Let's go." Holly opened the door and gestured me out.

***

It was overcast most of the drive and raining lightly in a few places as we drove through the Poconos on the northeast extension of the Pennsylvania turnpike. For late March, this was fortunate. We could easily have been driving through a blizzard. The trees lining the roads were still bare, struggling to bring up their first spring buds. There wasn't much to look at, so I slouched in the back of Ronnie's car, with my head against the window, staring at the back of the driver's seat.

A couple of hours into the five hour drive, I mumbled, "I don't know where I'm staying when we get there."

Holly turned. "Ronnie called her cousin just outside the city. We're all going to stay there tonight."

"Are you coming to the hospital with me?"

Ronnie responded this time. "Yeah. Why don't we take you there, and we'll find something to do until you want to leave. Or until they throw you out. And then we can go to my cousin's for the night. We'll bring you back in the morning."

I couldn't think through the logistics. I hadn't contacted Pat to tell her I'd be in the area. I was hesitant to assume it would be okay for me to crash there, let alone me with two strangers. Beyond that, I'd have to return to Syracuse some time later. My car was in Holly's driveway and Zach was in her living room, probably asleep on the couch beside Holly's mom at this very moment. I decided to go with Ronnie's logic and perch with her at this alleged cousin's house in the suburbs.

They dropped me at the hospital entrance. I walked in alone. Approaching the information desk, I heard the echo of Ours' words: "If you're coming, come now." Immediately behind them, bathed in hospital-scent disinfectant: "It'll be okay. Just don't cry."

Over the rumble of both, I asked for Chick's room.

"Only immediate family may visit."

"I'm his sister."

Jedda jumped to her feet when I walked in. She said nothing, but put her arms around me and rested her head on my shoulder. I hugged her tight. Her face was gaunt, her eyes red, the lids raw looking. I was sure she hadn't slept. I took her hands and prodded her back to the chair where she'd been sitting.

"What have I missed?" I asked. I squeezed past her legs and along the side of the bed so I could get closer to Chick. I kissed him on the forehead.

("How you doin', Chuckles?")

It sprang out of nowhere, that image of the father in his dinner-napkin-nightgown and his pale grey skin, my sister just finishing his shave that Saturday morning when he'd had his first and second heart attacks. Chick was that ghastly colorless color now, under a stubble of beard. Our father had been exactly three months past his fifty-seventh birthday when he died. Chick was just six weeks past his.

She cleared her throat. "He crashed not long after he talked to you. He was having trouble breathing and then he stopped altogether. They keep him sedated so he doesn't fight the vent tube."

I eyed the white tube taped to his mouth and run down his throat. The machine across the bed breathed for him. The dialysis machine next to me filtered his blood. Everywhere I looked, machines beeped and pinged and measured and dispensed and maintained. Everywhere except when I looked at Jedda. Science didn't have a machine that could measure what was going on for her.

"He said they were still doing tests about the infection in his lung?" It came out as a question.

"We don't have the results yet."

"Have you spoken to the cardiologist?"

"Yes, and he'll be back first thing in the morning."

We sat silently after that, listening to the machines live for him. On a stretch break, I stepped out long enough to call my sister and gave her the same message Ours gave me. If you're coming, come now.

"I'll be there," she promised.

Holly and Ronnie appeared from nowhere at the end of visiting hours. I had no idea where they'd been for the last few hours.

"Babe, where are you going to stay tonight?" Jedda asked. She didn't need to worry about that. She had lived at the hospital with Chick for the last nine months, sleeping on a cot beside his bed or in the lone chair.

"With my friends. I'll be back first thing in the morning, okay?" I kissed her on the cheek and squeezed her hand.

At Ronnie's cousin's house, we piled into the living room. I dozed twisted sideways in a chair and a half with an ottoman. My back ached. My neck ached. My soul ached. I didn't want to do this again, this loss. I didn't want my family to have to absorb it again. There weren't many of us left.

The unit director was on the floor when I arrived the next morning and she told us that for the next few days until Chick's test results returned, we had round the clock access to him. He would be moved to a different room so we didn't disturb anyone and we could come and go as we needed to. That didn't feel like a good sign.

Pat and I rotated with Jedda, two of us sitting bedside at a time, giving the third one a break to walk around, make a trip to the restroom, or go on a coffee run which was how all three of us remained coherent. I knew what we were doing, even if the doctors weren't saying it. I knew death watch when I was sitting it.

We switched seats with Jedda so she could make some phone calls. Pat took her chair.

"Oh brother dear, the sisty-uglers are here to visit!" she called out, sing-song.

"The hospice nurses have told us when our guys are in comas, the last thing they lose is their hearing, so he can probably hear you," I pointed out.

"Yeah? Good!" She started to sing "Chickery Chick" to him, a song from 1945 that she said the mother had sung to him when he was a little boy and where his nickname had originated. I wondered what it was like to have a mom who sang to you. Before I could get too far into my contemplation, Pat stopped singing and began hunting through her bag for Kleenex. She couldn't finish the song. I put a hand on her shoulder and she covered it with her own.

"Did I ever tell you about the time I called his hospital room and told him I knew how I wanted to die?" It seemed as good a time for this story as any.

She shook her head, still dabbing at her eyes.

"I call him every few days to tell him some stupid joke just to make sure he laughs once in a while. So I called him this one day and said, 'Hey, you know how everybody in our family dies early?' And he said yes. And I said, 'I've decided how I want to go!' He said, 'Whaddya mean? How the hell do you want to go?' So I told him. 'I want to die of a broken neck. With Tina Turner's legs wrapped around my head.'"

Pat gasped. "You did NOT!"

"Oh yes I did! Then I hung up on him. Jedda told me later he sat there with the phone in his hand for about eight seconds and he just started to roar. She said he laughed until he cried. When I visited him the next time, every damn nurse on the floor greeted me with, 'So yoooouuu're Nancy!'"

Pat was dabbing at her eyes again but it wasn't sadness this time. Two feet in front of us, Chickery Chick's machines continued to live for him.

***

I slipped out to use the restroom and when I returned to Chick's room, Pat and Jedda were both gone. As I crossed the threshold, one of his machines started to beep loudly and the signal changed on the screen. Startled, I turned around to call for a nurse but before I could say anything, blue scrubs passed me and poked at the machine.

"Is he okay?" I asked, knowing it was a relative term.

"Everything's fine," he said. That was also relative. He angled around me and Chick and I were alone.

I pulled the chair closer to the bedside. "Did you hear all of that?" I asked. "It was like you were a game show contestant, all those machines beeping and pinging. I'm almost certain you just won a goat on a razor scooter."

I knew it was just a reflex but his left eyebrow raised and then lowered. Did he know I was here? I sighed and scooted to the edge of the chair so I could reach his hand. I picked it up, limp and warm, and wrapped both of my own around it. For a moment, it was silent. Then remembering that he could probably hear me, I decided to talk to him.

"You've been doing this for a long time. I know you're tired." I rubbed his forearm. "If you're staying because you're worried about Jedda, I'll be here for her. I won't let anything happen to her. If you need to go so you can rest, you should go. I got it."

I didn't expect an answer. I pressed the back of his hand to my cheek, our hands palm to palm. My chest ached. *Did you know? Did you know Michael suffocated our father? Did you know when you decided to put me out on the street and make me homeless? Did you know what happened in that house? Did Michael ever tell you the truth? Do you know I don't want to lose you? My family is almost gone. I don't want to do this with you too. But if you need to go, it's okay, and we're okay, and I got this.*

When Pat returned a few minutes later, I gave her some time alone with him.

***

I spent Thursday night at Pat's house, borrowing Bob's old room again as I had when I came back for Michael's funeral. We returned to the hospital Good Friday morning. Jedda was in a huddle with the cardiologist and a couple of other doctors including the unit director when we arrived.

"...and you said we would have access to my husband round the clock!"

"Yes, Mrs. Mullen. Those are the orders."

"Well, I'm telling you, if I buzz to be let onto the floor one more time and get told to come back in ten or fifteen minutes, there's going to be a problem!"

"Which nurse is telling you to wait? They're all aware of the plan."

"The Indian nurse. She has sent me away several times telling me they're in the middle of something or now is not a good time—now is the ONLY time I have! If she tells me one more time to go away and come back, I'm going to slap that goddamned dot off her head!"

"Mrs. Mullen, I will speak with the nurses and this will not be a problem again. I will be back to see you this afternoon to go over Major Mullen's test results."

Glancing between Pat and me, Jedda burst out laughing. She sounded close to hysteria. I stepped closer and put an arm around her. "You okay? I think you got your point across!"

"I'm okay. They can't keep sending me away!"

"No, I think you've made that really clear. Can I get you some coffee?"

She shook her head. "Maybe later." She turned in the direction of Chick's room and we started our new day of watch.

When the director returned later, we gathered in one of the family lounges reserved for private conversations.

"Unfortunately, at this time, we are unable to identify the masses in the Major's lung."

"What does that mean?" Jedda asked. "It's not cancer?"

"We cannot ascertain that it is cancer."

A collective sigh sounded in the room.

"However, we are also unable to ascertain that it is not cancer and that is just as troubling."

"Then you think it could be?"

"We don't know."

Confused and restless rustling came next.

"What are our next steps?" Jedda asked quietly.

The cardiologist glanced around: Jedda, Ours, Pat, me, back to Jedda. "With any kind of lung infection that we cannot identify, we cannot pursue the Major's transplant." A pause. "We have to remove the Major from the transplant list."

In case any of us had not understood that.

Jedda flinched as if she'd been slapped.

"The Major did not wish to be kept alive by artificial means."

"Oh, my poor baby," Jedda whispered.

"It's time for you to review the Major's advance directives. You may want to think about calling the family together."

No one spoke.

"I'll make sure the chart is available to you. There's no rush, Mrs. Mullen. We can do this anytime this weekend."

"What will happen when we turn off those machines?"

"He may live a few hours. Or a few days. Or a few minutes."

I swallowed hard against the coffee rising up my esophagus. Guess we'd find out if he was tired enough to stop fighting.

***

I was surprised when Jedda took my arm and walked me toward the nurse's station. "There's something you need to be aware of."

The nurse handed us the binder open to Chick's living will. Chick had designated Jedda the primary person to make his end of life decisions, with me listed as his secondary. Me?! My heart sank through the floor.

"He knew you would do what he asked for," she said.

I flipped through the pages. No artificial means of support. No heroic measures. Do not resuscitate. This was clear. If it came to being kept alive on life support machines, Chick wanted to die.

Chilled, I handed the chart back to Jedda. "Who do you need to call? And how long will you give them?"

She gave them until Sunday. On Saturday, I returned to Syracuse to get my own vehicle. On Sunday morning, Jedda called while I was having breakfast with Holly's mother to thank her for caring for Zach.

"Everyone will be here by this afternoon. Do you think we should do this today?"

"Yes. If everyone's had their chance to say good-bye, we have to."

After breakfast, I went back to the hospital, leaving Zach with Holly. Pat was already there. Michael's wife, whom I hadn't seen since his funeral, had come. All three of Chick and Jedda's kids, His, Hers and Ours, were there.

At a few minutes after eight p.m., Jedda, His, Hers, and Ours, Pat, and I crowded into the tiny room. The doctor and nurse didn't speak to us as they worked to disconnect all of the beeping and pinging machines that had given us extra days with Chickery Chick. They dimmed the lights on the way out and left us alone. Ours worked his way through Psalm 23.

In the absolute silence that followed the last machine shutting down and the reading ending, Pat reached across the bed and we joined hands above Chick's legs.

At the top of the bed, Jedda put her hand on Chick's chest, rubbing gently, her nail beds bloody. "Breathe, baby. Please breathe."

Silence.

"Send him home with something he's familiar with," Pat whispered, squeezing my hand. "Hail Mary..."

I put my free hand on his thigh, and she put her other hand on his opposite thigh and I joined her in a prayer I hadn't said in two decades to a god I no longer believed in.

What did you know?

Doesn't matter. Go ahead. I got this.
And we sent Chickery Chick home.

Three weeks later, I stood in front of a room of a hundred and fifty people and gave my first presentation on the developmental needs of LGBT youth, wearing the suit I wore to Chick's funeral. It was an historic moment, the coming together of one hundred and fifty allies for LGBT high school students in a county where professionals routinely denied that any gay students attended suburban high schools. Cringing at every loud bang from the workmen on the adjacent roof, evoking memories of the twenty-one gun salute at Chick's military funeral, the work of my agency took a new turn as it became apparent that in 2002, unlike 1983, people would talk about kids who were homeless, about kids who were struggling to stay in school until graduation, and about kids who were fighting to stay alive. We could talk about runaway kids and throwaway kids, all while I was standing in the training room of the most prominent psychiatric hospital in the suburbs, where—by all rights—I might well have spent some time in 1983, had anybody been watching closely.

Did you know?

Each time I looked around the room, the same thought came back.

Go ahead. I got this.

Part 3
Paying It Forward, Creating Community

1998

    I started meeting them in late in August, when I was hired as the executive director of a new not-for-profit agency working with LGBT youth in Illinois. My official start date wasn't for another six weeks, but I was visiting friends, and the board members who interviewed me invited me to stop in to the Monday night drop-in center and meet some of the youth group members and the volunteers who would become my team.

    Walking in the door from a job in HIV housing at a time in the epidemic when cocktails of drugs were just getting launched, I was burned out on social work. In my first year in my last job, many of my clients, staff and friends died, some of AIDS related illnesses, some of overdoses when they relapsed or miscalculated their dose. It felt like I attended funerals and memorial services practically every week. There were times when our clients had no family contact and our staff team were the only attendees at the funeral, or we had to make arrangements for them to be buried in the Potter's Field, because no one claimed their bodies or cared that they had died. Over the following three years, the drug cocktails improved the situation and the residents recovered more quickly and went into independent housing again, but the losses took a toll on all of us. I came to my new agency thinking I could give this two years, then I was going to chiropractic school or massage school. **Anything** but social work.

    When group started that first Monday night, I realized immediately that this job would have a different tone than what I was accustomed to. This job had the potential to be...what was that concept? Oh yes! This job had the potential to be fun!

    "So I'm Geo, I'm sixteen and my week was...like...really good," one group member with a shaggy hair cut said. "I met this guy online. He's like forty. And I'm gonna meet him in person this weekend."

My eyebrows went up and I shot a glance at the volunteer facilitating the check-in. Was this typical? If it was, what was the prescribed response?

Before she or I could speak, another youth leaned forward, hands in front of him, fingers splayed for emphasis. "That is **so** illegal!" he said loudly.

Geo laughed. "I know, right?"

Having the ground broken for objections, other participants started pointing out flaws in his logic. He alternated between laughing and assuring them he would be fine. It took only a couple of minutes of the participants telling him he wasn't being smart before his plans changed and he agreed not to meet the man. The kids resumed check-in, moving past Geo's announcement.

"I'm Amy, I'm sixteen. My week was okay," the next girl continued. "I got my nose pierced and my mother…like…flipped out. She still won't, like, speak to me. I don't know why." She giggled.

Your mother probably thinks you mutilated your face and you don't understand why she would be upset, I thought wryly. Interesting. Oh yes. This job had the potential to be fun.

***

My official start date rolled around and I returned to Illinois. I planned to spend lots of evenings in the drop-in centers to hear more from the kids and to learn who my volunteers were. I wasn't thrilled with evening hours but considering I expected to give this job only two years, I could tolerate it.

My first Thursday group turned into something vastly different than the two Monday groups I had observed. Monday group had been upbeat, funny. We walked away clueless about what would become national news in less than forty-eight hours. Sometime Tuesday night, a young college student in Laramie, Wyoming made friends with two men in a bar and they offered him a ride home. He was robbed, pistol-whipped, beaten and hung on a fence post to die. Discovered Wednesday by a passing cyclist, he was at first mistaken for a scarecrow because he'd been so disfigured. By Thursday, it was the topic of group discussion. Was he gay? Was he attacked because he was out?

The following Monday evening, I waited for the volunteer to arrive and unlock the church door. I stood on the curb at the end of the parking lot with a few group members who arrived early. In the deepening twilight, Geo inclined his head and looked up at me from his seat on the curb.

"Did you hear?" he asked. "That boy died."

The chill that had crept over me on Thursday night returned. Standing on the curb with three of the kids, I was horrified at the thought of any of them enduring an attack like Matthew Shepard endured. Who was he? Did he laugh about the chance to meet a guy online like Geo had? Was he battling with his mom over tattoos and piercings like Amy was? Was he comfortable in his own skin and confident that all would be right in his world until two guys shattered his skull? The idea that someone might hurt one of them took my breath away.

The volunteer we were waiting for turned into the parking lot and I followed her inside, relieved that I didn't have to speak or be expected to even know what to say for another few minutes. I was two weeks into my new job, intending to leave in short order, and clueless what I'd learn about the kids I came to consider "my kids" and what they'd teach me about myself and my story.

***

Creating Community with Ryan: Parallels On Brothers

2013

"My brother is my best friend." With that declaration, Ryan gave me a quizzical look, as though I would only ask such a question if I were an alien. "He is always there for me, no matter what time of day, night, whatever." She laughed. "Even when I don't necessarily want him there, he's still there."

"Did you guys fight as kids?" I asked.

She nodded. "Sure. But we would fight for five minutes and then be over it."

"No one ever really got hurt then?"

She shook her head no. "He punched me once, when we were fighting over keeping a door open or closing it. Five minutes later, we were both in trouble with our mom. I don't even remember if the door got shut or left open."

"Was Aaron a resource for you back then too or is that more a recent thing?"

"Then too. I went to a Catholic junior high and they were the worst three years of my life. Aaron went all twelve years. We called the school OLGC (Our Lady of Garbage Cans). Aaron was going to go into first grade, and our mother asked if there was room to place me. I had to go through testing and got put in the "B" group. Taking a class at the public school during the day, plus being overweight and the new kid at school, I was told 'Go home, don't come back, we don't want you here.' I tried to play sports to fit in, but the coaches wouldn't play me."

"That could get lonely even with Aaron. Did you feel isolated?"

"Yeah," she agreed. "I made two attempts to hurt myself, one in sixth and one in eighth grade. I confessed later to our priest. He did nothing. He didn't even offer me a phone number. He was no help. It drove me away from the church."

I nodded. I could totally see how **that** might happen. "How did you handle coming out to Aaron?"

"It was about the time that Ellen came out on TV—remember that? I told Aaron before telling anyone else. He's always been someone who will keep his word about not telling anything I've asked him not to repeat."

"How did he handle it?"

"He's always been fine with it. He says, 'I don't care who you love, as long as you're happy.'"

"How was it bringing Aaron into your social circle at the Thursday night drop-in center?"

She held her hands out, palms up. "It was just like bringing another friend along. He's been along with me for so much else."

"Was there anything about the Thursday night group that made your coming out easier?"

"Having resources and having access to other people like me that I could talk to about it. I was young when I started to wonder about it. I was in grade school. My mom still thinks this is a phase and I've been out for sixteen years. Dad doesn't talk about it much but he just wants me to be happy."

Ryan visited the drop-in centers at the time when I was still able to attend every group. Sitting with her fourteen years later, I could still remember her sign-in number from having counted it so many times for state reports. "Do you remember us meeting?"

"You did my intake. You were the first face I saw when I came. I knew you were the person I could go to if something was wrong. You and Brian were running group a lot in those days. It was a bummer when you couldn't come anymore."

I flinched. Brian was the first intern I worked with when I came to Illinois, a bright and extremely personable man working toward his master's degree in social work. He died in 2011. It was startling to have the connection to those days of running groups with him, lounging on the floor of the church youth room, brought so clearly into focus through one of the old "kids." In my mind's eye, I could see his long legs and big boots stretched out as I stepped over him to go answer the door or take a turn at doing an intake. I hadn't considered the possibility that Ryan would hold some of my history as much as I might hold some of hers.

"What about now?" I asked, wanting very much to change the subject.

"It's not like it was when I was a kid and you were the adult. Now I see what you've done with Youth Outlook, and I think it would be really cool to have the chance to build something like this."

You have no idea!

Creating Community with Tony: Parallels On Evolving Spirituality

2001

It takes our agency a good year to build a core group of attendees at any new drop-in center. The Tuesday night group was heading into its third year when Tony found us in the summer of 2001. Attendance was increasing steadily. Of our four drop-in centers, this was our biggest and busiest site and would peak at fifty-five kids per night that summer. I often visited for the first hour of group to lend a hand with new intakes and support the staff to get the evening up and running.

On a warm Tuesday night in late spring, I did my usual "git 'em started" visit and said goodbye to the volunteers and the kids within earshot. As I headed toward the parking lot, I realized one of the staff members was finishing an intake in the hallway at the bottom of the stairs. She was laughing, as was the young person she sat with.

He was a big guy, easily already six feet tall, with a brilliant grin. He smiled at me. I smiled back. The volunteer and I exchanged a few words, and then I was out the door, leaving them to their evening. The next time I saw him, we had grown out of the upstairs room with the fireplace and moved to the basement, which was somewhat less youth-friendly but had much more space.

The kids started to gather in their check-in circle. I dropped my backpack on the table and grabbed a plastic chair close to the new guy and his fun smile.

"Does anyone have a check-in question we can use tonight?" one of the volunteers asked.

"Yeah! How about where do you get your best clothes for doing drag?"

When the check-in question reached the new guy, he said, "Hi, my name is Tony. I'm nineteen. And you know...clothes for drag..." He giggled. "Well," he whispered loudly, sharing an important secret, "she's a big girl...she has to shop at Lane Bryant."

I laughed out loud. He went on to make several other comments about dressing in drag and where he got his clothes, gesturing emphatically with his hands. By the time he was done, I had tears in my eyes from laughing. That night I stayed for the whole group just for fun.

***

2013

We were skewering my Catholic background over pizza.

"I was raised Catholic, too," Tony said, "but I started exploring Wicca and Native American beliefs at about fifteen. I was drawn to the 'older' beliefs. For a while I also explored Buddhism. By the middle of high school, I rejected Catholicism completely and went with Wicca. I started keeping more ceremonial objects related to Wiccan practices and engaging in more meditative practices."

"Did it make a difference to your family?" I asked.

He shrugged. "My mother remained active in the church. She's more your typical older Mexican woman with Our Lady of Guadalupe candles, a bust of Jesus with a crown of thorns and angel figurines in her room. She belongs to a prayer group. She does an activity with her group at Christmas time where they walk from house to house and ask to be invited in, to mimic the story of finding no room in the inn. Sometimes I have to tell her, "Mom! A group of Mexicans just can't go from house to house asking to be let in! You'll get arrested!"

I almost snorted Diet Coke out my nose. "So what caused the shift?"

"Well, around fifteen, I started to understand who I was. I always knew I was different, but at fifteen, I started to understand what the difference was. When I started listening to the messages that Catholics were giving about who I was, I got angry and disappointed. I wanted to leave before they rejected me. I kept thinking, so those are the people of my faith and that's how they feel about me. Nobody knew I was having these thoughts and feelings, so there wasn't even a chance for people to counterbalance them with positive messages.

"In college, I took a world religions class and started learning more about other religions. I went to a Jewish temple and met with a rabbi. I asked about ceremonies and beliefs, ideas about abortions, gay marriage. For a while I considered converting. It was more structured than being Wiccan, which kind of felt like this: "Hey, I'm Wiccan, I'm going to burn some candles!" To convert to Judaism, you're adopting a history of an entire people.

"Then I started going to Episcopal services. I had a positive experience with them. It made me start to wonder if I'd left too soon, that maybe all Christians aren't bad. My anger started to lift a little bit. I attended Methodist, Episcopal, UCC...saw lots of gay people at church and saw how they were treated well. It confirmed I may have been too harsh in my judgment of Catholicism. I felt like I was born again but not in the sense of preaching—in the sense of connection and my own actions.

"God was in my head but never quite in my heart. There was no emotional connection although I understood the teachings. While God wasn't in my heart, there was still something good in there.
I was in therapy and the therapist was helping me with the rejection from my mother when I was seventeen and abandoning me when I was ten when they got divorced. My father's health started to decline, and I wanted to reconcile some other family relationships, especially my brother. But it was a lot of frustration. I was drinking heavily and doing cocaine and pot to relax, anything to alter, to get me out. I would get high, start drinking, take a Vicodin, then pass out about four a.m, get up around noon, go to work and start all over again.

"I was twenty four when I tried to hurt myself. I was in the hospital about a week. This was a huge turning point in my spiritual exploration. It was the lowest point in my life. I did a lot of thinking about what got me there in the hospital. I was so used to being the strong one that I just did it in all my relationships because it was familiar. But I needed help. And I deserved help. I can't remember who said it, but I always liked the statement, 'Suffering is inevitable. Suffering alone is optional.' It wasn't someone else making me take on this role. It was me doing it. There was no voice, no guiding hand, no light...there were people, real people, relationships that I had built over time. I didn't have to imagine it in my head. I just had to reach out and they were right there. All those times I had prayed, asked for God's help, he never showed up. When I asked my friends for help, they showed up. Some people would argue that's just God working through my friends, but that cheapens what they did for me. To say that God got me through it cheapens my strength. I was the one in those sessions. I cried. I did the work. I redefined relationships. I built better relationships."

He leaned on one elbow, his head propped in his hand. "No one prays to Zeus anymore. Why not? Why did this religion win the lottery? We have to look deeper. What is religion? It's man's attempt to understand his world. Religion is not bad—it is part of our history. Everyone should take world religions. It's world history. But there has to be an understanding that we know it's not Zeus throwing down thunderbolts. We can't understand all the phenomena right now, but the gaps in our understanding of our world shrink as our understanding grows.

"Spirituality is a completely different thing for me. People can get it from religions but you don't need religion to get it. It's a way to connect. It humbles you and helps you grow. It's not just about our species. It's about interconnectedness."

"Did Youth Outlook have any impact on your spiritual explorations?"

"Yeah, sure. We had guest speakers who came in and I would quietly listen. Sometimes ministers came in to talk to us. Just the fact that we were meeting in a church created some dissonance for me in my beliefs about religious institutions. Not everyone is bad."

I remembered some of those panel discussions. I had set some of them up. I wondered if he remembered me as well as I remembered him from those early days. "Do you remember when we first met?"

It was his turn to snort. "My first night at Youth Outlook, I was doing my intake with...what was her name?...oh yeah, Susan. You walked through on your way out and Susan paused to ask if you were leaving. You said, 'Yeah, they're packing in up there like queer clowns in a phone booth!'"

Apparently he remembered it even better than I did.

"I still remember that, ten years later. Susan told me who you were. I remember you being around on and off until the inception of the youth leadership project and getting the chance to do more stuff behind the scenes. I remember wanting your approval."

"Mine? Why?"

"At that stage in my life, my mom and I had no relationship. My dad and I....well, he was busy being the stoic German that he is. I didn't have a whole lot of connection with adults...parental figures...protective authority figures....between you and Carolyn it was like Mom and Dad. We even called you Mom and Dad. And just so you know, when I asked for money for college, I was only half joking!"

I recalled the months of innuendo from the kids at the Tuesday night group as they tried to determine if the program leader, Carolyn, and I were a couple. We neither confirmed nor denied and often laughed about it outside the group setting. Carolyn's favorite joke was, "How dare you bring me all these kids and leave me alone with them?"

"How did your connection to us all change over time?"

"I felt closer to you and Carolyn, Sandra and Melissa, Eldon, and Mark. I got to meet board members and go to board meetings. I felt so adult." He pounded on the table. "We had no older gay role models before...now I've become that guy! Finally having positive gay role models, people who were healthy, not crazy, not weird, not trying to diddle me in the closet...everything we've been told "we" do...this was huge. At every level of the agency, I had to renegotiate who I was to people within the agency. I went to Mark's fiftieth birthday party and I told him that day, 'I hope to be half the gay you are when I am your age!'"

"So what does that mean to all of this? How do you identify now?"

He smiled his big Tony smile. "I consider myself the most spiritual atheist you will ever meet."

Creating Community with Max: Parallels On Desperate Acts

2009

The Board of Directors' retreat kicked off with an ice breaker question to help the newer members feel connected and to introduce the attending youth leaders to the members who hadn't met them. The question, "Why are you involved in the agency?" garnered good answers, even great ones, until it came to Max, a youth leader who had grown up in the Tuesday night drop-in center and youth leadership program.

He started his reply while looking at me. "A little while ago, we took a survey at group that asked us the same thing. What do we like about group? Why do we come? Where would we go if we didn't have Tuesday group to go to? I know I'm not the only one who said it, but I think I'm the only one **here** who did, so I'll say it again."

The clink of forks on plates stopped and the whispered side comments ended. No one moved. Once while on a speaking engagement with Max at a local university, I entered the room with a young woman who identified as lesbian and later exited the room with a young transman. Anything could happen once Max started talking.

"If the Tuesday group didn't exist, I wouldn't be here anymore," he said slowly, making eye contact with each board member. "**That's** how important this is. I would be dead now."

***

2013

Max took the chair at the end of the dining room table and chuckled. "If anyone had told me five years ago that I'd be having a beer with "God" at her house, I would have thought they were crazy."

"Five years ago, you wouldn't have been having a beer with me," I pointed out, since he was now twenty four. "You were one of my kids." I settled across from him. "Speaking of which...you had some rough stretches..."

He nodded. "It started with depression. I was sad all the time and worried about disappointing my parents. Now I think it was more gender related than I was able to realize then. I thought I had already disappointed them by being sad all the time. I was heavily medicated when I was fourteen. They gave me extra stuff for the side effects of the original drugs then gave me stuff to manage the side effects of the side effects' medication."

"Must have felt like they were poisoning you."

"Yeah. I think so."

"When you say you were sad all the time..."

"I started hurting myself in sixth grade with the bent edge of a pencil. Then I moved on to using a razor. I was already using a razor by the time I told my mom I was sad. Mom used to have the attitude that I could snap out of it. She was disgusted with me—everyone else has so much going on, how can you be sad? Even though there are genetic indicators on both sides of our family, it took a long time for her to move past the idea that there was no reason to be sad. When she started to dig a little deeper and saw it in our family lines, she became more supportive."

"Then what happened about being sad all the time?"

Max rolled his eyes and snorted. "Then there were pills! Pills like they were in a Pez dispenser—and I have a Pez dispenser collection, so I know!"

"I've seen your Pez dispenser collection. That's a lot of pills."

"Yeah. That's a lot of pills. I don't remember most of junior year except for prom. I can't pull up independent images. It's like I wasn't able to process new information to be able to make new memories. I can go back and find things if someone tells me what to look for, but I can't do that on my own."

He was quiet for a moment, then resumed. "I started cutting in middle school, when my body started to change and boys were noticeably different from girls. I cut for eight years. I cut on my chest with a pencil, but then I couldn't face having breasts, so I cut on my arms and legs.

"For gym class, I changed in the bathroom stall. There was no showering except for swim class in freshman and sophomore year. I didn't want to look at anyone, didn't want anyone to see me. I used the furthest back row of lockers, closest to the bathroom. I went from being a straight A student to carrying all Ds. No one noticed. No one said anything that I remember."

I didn't want to put words in his mouth but couldn't help wondering if he had ever cringed against his locker, thinking how he was just…nothing.

"For my last attempt, I took all the leftover medication I had at once, hoping to overdose, and then I left the house so my parents wouldn't find me. That's when I crashed into another car. It was while I was in the hospital that I was hit with the realization that there had to be a reason I kept surviving. Maybe there's a reason bigger than me for why I am still here."

I was tempted to tell him about logging trucks or yellow lines with schools buses and tractor trailers passing at the same time and decided against it. Instead I asked, "What about support from your family while all of that was going on?"

He shrugged one shoulder. "Well, they weren't unsupportive of my being bi or lesbian but I felt ostracized about cutting. My parents were not supportive when I came out as trans. My grandparents were, but my younger sister was grossed out and said the same thing my parents did. I was told, 'It's disgusting and wrong and no one is going to support it. You think our family is just going to be okay with you showing up to Christmas with a moustache? They're not.' Once my sister realized that transitioning wasn't big and ugly, and I was happy, she turned around. My parents thought I didn't know what I was talking about, I was too young to understand, I was going to be spending bunches of money on surgeries."

I nodded. "What about coming out to friends?"

"I started wondering about being trans at about eighteen, when I was dating my first girlfriend. We were goofing off and dressing up one day like we were business people and I dressed up like a business man. I liked how it looked. I can't even describe how it felt. Then Stephen ran a program on trans issues and it clicked with me that I was trans. I came out when I was almost twenty, summer of 2008."

As if I could forget the night at Aurora University, when Max and I were speaking with another youth leader and another staff member! Max bowled all of us over and came out for the first time there that night, prompting me to whisper to the staff member later, "Damn! Did you know? I wish I had known when I introduced him!"

"You hurt yourself a lot during that time," I observed. I often wondered if he was aware of how concerned the staff members and I were for him.

His voice was unemotional. "I jumped off a bridge, walking past the park. I landed on the ground and only sprained my ankle. The lesson learned—I have to try harder. This was just another thing I wasn't doing right. I jumped a couple more times but then it was easier when I started driving because I could drive into things. Light posts, a tree, other cars, a dividing wall...most ended with hospitalization because of depression. My dad was really good at fixing cars and he got a whole lot better."

"Okay, so enter Youth Outlook. What changed?"

"Having something to be a part of and that people valued me as a person. There was this whole world about LGBT culture that I didn't know about that I got to meet through Youth Outlook. Tuesday was my favorite day. I would have gone to Thursday night too!"

"Do you remember us meeting?"

I can still picture Max at seventeen, an awkward German Shepherd puppy of a kid who couldn't tell where his arms and legs ended, who bumped into things and knocked them over. It had always made me think that he was not at home inside his own skin, and I often wanted to ask him, "How does this happen—don't you **live** in there?" He started testosterone shots at nineteen, and the clumsiness melted away. All of a sudden, his body fit. He stopped bumping into things, tripping over things, knocking things over. The only way

I've ever been able to describe it was that he finally came home to live inside himself.

He laughed. "I remember hearing about you and you were God. I always thought you were going to show up and pair us up and put us on your little boat!"

"Do you think we had any effect on your growing up? Not just me---the people who surround and make up Youth Outlook."

"Tony did my intake. He asked me my drug use and I told him I didn't take any and he told me I didn't have to lie. It was a joke but it set the tone for my time there. I didn't have to lie about anything anymore. I was lying to people all the time. I knew exactly what to tell the therapist to get discharged. I knew exactly what to tell the doctor to be taken off or put on medication. I made stuff up to have control of my life. I think if it hadn't been for Youth Outlook, I would still be lying all the time, just making stuff up because it's fun and I can get away with it. Now I save it for my creative writing. Now I'm proud of parts of life that I wasn't before. POL, Youth Leadership, COD leadership, pulling my grades up, academic scholarships, all the essay contests that I've entered and won…

"Stephen was hugely influential, even at a distance. Once I found out he was trans, he became my idol. I even decided that my cat was gender queer. He was a boy dog in a girl cat's body."

It was my turn to laugh. "Anyone else?"

"Mark," he said, referring to one of my original board members who liked to present on the panel discussion for "old homos' night." "Or as we called him, Papa Pistachio…he was so much fun."

I wondered out loud to Max about the difference having opportunities to create friendships across generations made to him.

"Mark is the epitome of the It Gets Better project. Look at that perfect example of how awesome our lives will be if we can get there. He was this cool old gay guy and had lived so much more than we had and probably was still living more than we ever would."

Then I wondered if Max knew that Mark sometimes cried when he heard about the struggles that our kids—that Max himself—had been through. I wondered if he knew I did. And I wondered if he knew how very, very much it meant to me that he was sitting here in my dining room and not a statistic to chalk up to despair.

Creating Community with Sydney: Parallels On Belonging

2013

I sat in the marketing committee meeting led by one of my board members, excited to have finally pulled this group of people together. Across the table, one of the volunteers was attempting to explain to me the benefit of a social media platform called Vine. I understood about a third of what came out of her mouth. I turned to Sydney, the agency webmaster, who was sitting next to me.

"She's addressing me in a language I do not understand," I said in a stage whisper with mock sadness.

Syd covered a laugh, patted me twice on the shoulder and answered me in the same stage whisper. "It's okay, Nance, I understand it. I'll explain later."

Not the first time and certainly won't be the last, I thought and sat back up to listen. Syd had worked with our website for the last two years as a volunteer who had been a youth leader in our Tuesday night drop-in center in 2003, where she also now dedicated volunteer hours. If I could offer her a job, she wanted it. In an agency that ran primarily on volunteer power, I could only wish for that.

***

Syd and I met at one of my favorite Italian restaurants after work so I could tell her about my writing. "Wine?" I asked.

"Nah. Martini!" she said, picking up the menu.

The server brought our drinks as I set up my laptop. I had already shared an excerpt from a chapter I'd written and tonight, I wanted to find out if there was an analogous experience in her background. We could start with something easy.

"Tell me about coming out to your family?" I asked.

She nodded, reflective. "I came out when I was twenty, after several years of feeling a sense of being different from my friends. I told Dad first, figuring if it didn't go well that would have been fine, but he was okay with it. I was a senior in college and already with Teresa. Even though it went okay, I waited eight more months to tell Mom. I was closer to Mom and was worried it would hurt her.

"After I decided that it was finally time to tell her, I went to Texas with Mom over my spring break. I wanted—and planned—to tell her every day and every day Mom would fall asleep watching movies. I look back on that now and I can't believe I wasted my last college spring break in a retirement condo with Mom."

I chuckled. Not where I would have wanted to spend a spring break either.

"We even watched *Under the Tuscan Sun*. There I was, trying to find a way to relate to Mom that I might be the gay character like Sandra Oh's character, right up until Mom fell asleep. I ended up waiting two more months.

"By now, Teresa was living with me but I still hadn't told Mom. You know… the same Mom who co-signed my lease," she added dryly. "Eventually she came to visit and I could only allow her to see the living room because Teresa was hiding in the bedroom closet. As we were leaving, we were standing in the parking lot downstairs and a light went on in the bedroom. Teresa walked in front of the window and Mom flipped, yelling at me, 'There's someone in your apartment!' All I could say was, 'Oh yeeeeahhh, it's just a friend,' as I rushed her into the car."

How much do you love that image of Teresa hiding in the closet?

"The whole way to the restaurant, I was second guessing myself. I didn't want to tell Mom I was gay. What if there was another guy I became interested in? I wasn't ruling it out. It felt too limiting. Why raise the concern if not necessary? Over dinner, I finally put the full sentence together. 'Mom, I'm bi.'

"She looked at me with this panicked expression and said, 'But you'll get STDs!'" Syd laughed. "It seemed like such an odd response. She already knew Teresa. It wasn't as if I was dating a bunch of strangers. Then we didn't talk about it again.

"Even when Teresa and I had our commitment ceremony, we didn't talk about it. Mom walked in saying that she needed a drink. She never acknowledged the ceremony. It has only been a recent development to have her refer to the ceremony as our wedding."

It's one thing to read about the national statistics, but it feels different when your kids tell you about their hurts, about becoming homeless, about parents who ignore or harm them, about lost friends. Syd was not a child, not even when she was a member of the drop-in center. She'd been a young adult then, and now she was my colleague. No matter. A familiar cold sadness settled in.

I cleared my throat but before I could speak, the server showed up with our dinners. When everything was placed, and the server satisfied that we had everything we needed (except maybe unconditional acknowledgment as whole, intact people, which really wasn't in her section to deal with anyway), I redirected the story.

"Tell me about fitting in as a kid before you came to the drop–in center?"

"I started hanging out with pot smokers in eighth grade. My parents didn't like it and when they found out, they made me stop. The kids got angry at me and that's when the bullying that I went through started. I can remember so clearly the day that kids in my religion class were betting on when I would kill myself. I could hear them! In religion class!"

I paused in my typing as the thought occurred to me, *I guess you don't have to switch to a public school for that experience!*

Syd continued. "I went home that night and took sixty sleeping pills and half a bottle of Tylenol. My sister came in and saw all the packaging and she had me tell her what happened. She went and got Dad. It was late and Dad drove around looking for a drug store to get Syrup of Ipecac. He didn't want to take me to the hospital because he was scared of what they would do, how this could follow me, but there were no drug stores open at that hour. I started to fall asleep and he finally took me to the hospital.

"They pumped my stomach, kept me overnight, and told my parents the next morning that I was attention seeking. The doctor told them I was not depressed. A couple of weeks before this, I had already set up a counseling appointment because I had to talk to someone. It turned out that I couldn't see that first guy because I didn't have my parents' consent, but he notified my parents and they set up another appointment. I saw that therapist for a couple of years and never tried to overdose again.

"I started my second year at college on September 10, 2001. The next day we watched airplanes fly into the World Trade Center. It hit me really hard—harder than I expected. At the same time, I was being harassed on campus by a safety officer who had a master key to my room. He kept asking me questions like, "Why don't you have dinner with me and stay over?" I hadn't started going to the Tuesday night drop-in center yet, so I was dealing with the harassment and my reaction to 9/11 alone. I was an RA, and I was afraid to sleep in my room because I didn't know if he might just show up.

"I reported him and I had to prove I hadn't encouraged the advances. He was fired. The next day, my dorm closed because of killer mold and everyone was displaced to the Holiday Inn. I was so depressed, I stopped going to class. I was no longer an RA because I didn't have a dorm. I didn't belong anywhere. I failed every class that semester and got kicked out of school. I just stayed in bed all day. I hid from my parents; I couldn't tell them I had failed out.

"The next semester, I appealed and returned, but decided after two days I couldn't do it so I told my parents everything. I withdrew from school and moved in with my aunt. Then I got own apartment and my parents helped me out so I could afford rent. I pawned jewelry to pay for electricity and food and I maxed out credit cards."

"Where in all of that did the drop-in center fit?" I asked. "How about friends?"

"It wasn't until my freshman year of college that I finally met out gay people. Two of those were lesbians that had been out since they were sixteen and had already been to the drop-in center. I wasn't ready to go with them yet. It took another year before I was comfortable.

"I met so many more people, it was amazing. For the first time, I had friends from Joliet all the way to St. Charles. The greatest thing about group was that it was the one night a week I could always count on seeing **all** of my friends. That spring, I went to the first youth leader training that I think there ever was."

She didn't have to remind me. I still have a photo from it in my office and use it in presentations. "What's one of your favorite memories of group?"

"The time we marched in the Pride Parade in 2002," she replied without hesitation. "We walked with PFLAG. It was my first pride parade, my first time on the el. We took the train into Chicago—twenty five gay kids trooping through Union Station. One kid knew how to get there, but he took us on the wrong el, and we ended up on the wrong side of the city. He got us turned back around. and we took the right el this time, but got off at the wrong stop so all twenty five of us had to walk eight blocks to meet up with leaders. We finally decided to follow a bunch of gay people off the train thinking we would end up in the right place. But there's a gazillion gay people around—I've never seen that many gay people in my life...rainbows everywhere. Some of us tried to start a fight in front of a counter demonstration and a bunch of us posed for photos with a gay cop."

I still have that photo too.

"The drop-in center introduced me to kids from different classes, races, education levels; kids like me, kids totally different from me. It gave me some friends that I was incredibly close to for several years. The people there provided me the courage to come out, people that were just there when I needed someone most. When I first attended, I was coming out of a pretty severe depression. I was also in a rough spot financially. Sometimes I would count on the snacks at group to get me through a night. Friends from group would buy me groceries or buy my dinner when we went out after group.

"Not just one, but all of my experiences with the drop-in center and the friends I made led me to be the person I am today. If I hadn't have met my friend Mike, I wouldn't have moved in with him, had a fight, gotten my own place, and met my girlfriend who became my partner whom I was with for eight and a half years. It all adds up. The drop-in center bridged the gap between childhood and adulthood. It helped me find friends that weren't through my college or at a bar. It prepared me for coming out at an older age."

"We've created an amazing place to be," I offered.

She agreed. "We are the Island of Misfit Toys. The Youth Outlook kids are in the same boat I was in—different groups of friends, but no one who knows or likes all of you. There are a lot of different kinds of love. I look at these kids who come to group on Tuesday nights and I just love them. They deserve to be loved without conditions. I appreciate them. You don't have to be a parent to love them. I care that they're there or when they come in and they're upset. They don't necessarily need me to love them but I do anyway. We can make something better for them."

We sat with an empty wine glass and an empty martini glass between us. I wondered if it was ever so intentional for the people who set out to love me against all recommendations and again, I marveled at the agency I helped to create, where "old" kids returned to run websites and offer a hand up to "new" kids, and where I am surrounded by people working to make things better for them.

Creating Community with Alex: Parallels On Turning Points

1999

The school board meeting was standing room only. Angry parents and community members lined the walls, afraid that their child would be "recruited to a gay lifestyle." They were here for the comments portion of the agenda in regard to the school including the words "sexual orientation" in its existing non-discrimination clause. We'd already been sitting for a couple of hours while they meandered through other agenda items and my back was getting stiff.

Alex approached the microphone when the comments section commenced. "I'm a senior. I'm bisexual."

The crowd buzzed, part grumble, part support. Alex continued, pointing out her reasons for believing the inclusion was necessary, describing instances of being harassed during the course of her school day. The board members gave little reaction.

A few more people spoke, then opposing comments commenced. The man who approached the microphone next looked vaguely familiar. I thought I may have spoken on a panel presentation with him a few months ago, where he made a complete ass out of himself when he answered a student who posed the question, "What makes it any different, what you say about gay people, from what the Nazis said about the Jews during the Holocaust?" When his reply started with the statement, "Young lady, everyone knows the Jews were responsible for the Holocaust...," the students physically recoiled from him, like they were doing The Wave in reverse.

He stood at an angle so he could look at both the school board members and at Alex. He addressed them for a moment, then turned his head toward her. "Young lady, has anyone told you that you and all of your promiscuous gay friends will be dead from AIDS by the time you are twenty five? That's a fact." He waved a black binder in the air. "I have the statistics right here. You are all pedophiles—you are child molesters and you will all burn in hell."

I jerked forward in my chair, wanting to lunge to my feet and make a run at him. At the end of the row of chairs, Alex's head tipped down a little and I could see the tears welling in her eyes. Why the hell weren't the school board members stopping him? Should I? Shouldn't someone?

Did he just call her a whore?

When the meeting adjourned, the reporters surged through the room. I heard one of the school board members giving a statement to a reporter that their school did not have a bullying problem, making such a policy change unnecessary.

Not a bullying problem? Watching a grown man decimate that poor girl and call her vicious names doesn't count as bullying? What the hell was wrong with these people that they couldn't see what had just happened in front of their own faces?

I elbowed my way through the milling crowd and the ignorant, apathetic board members. I had to find Alex. I had to make sure she was okay. I found her outside with a TV reporter's microphone in front of her and the light from a video camera trained on her. As I drew closer, I heard her say, "I'm a senior and I'm bisexual..." Her voice sounded strong. I backed off. She didn't need any help.

Geez, I hope she's already out to her parents 'cause she's gonna be on the ten o'clock news!

2013

"But high school was a challenging time for you, if I remember correctly," I said. "Was it just your orientation or were there other things contributing?"

She shook her head. "It wasn't just orientation. When I was about a junior, I started having problems with depression and anxiety. I was tired all the time, I couldn't get up for school. At one point, one of the school social workers showed up at my house and sat on the end of my bed. I couldn't believe she would do that—I couldn't believe my parents would let her in the house."

I smiled. *Definitely not the way you want to start your day in high school!*

"The anxiety came later. All of a sudden, I can't focus, can't concentrate, my heart races, I get nauseated. Dad and I didn't get along during this time. He doesn't know how to handle emotions other than happiness. He would scream at me, say nasty things to me. He would fight with me then both my parents would fight about him fighting with me. I was becoming more of a smartass, and he and mom went through a hard time not getting along and it all happened at the same time."

"You took a real risk by coming out at the school board meeting that year. Do you remember that night? Do you remember the things that were said to you?"

She thought for a moment. "I remember saying I was bi but that's all. I still have clippings from newspaper letters to the editor that I saved about that meeting."

"How did you find us in the middle of all of that?"

"Through the assistant principal, Pam. She gave me this trifold with a rainbow on the front to me and Meg."

Oh boy. I rolled my eyes. I had created that trifold and I was nobody's idea of a graphic artist. But in an agency in its first year of existence with no budget for promotional materials, you make do!

"Did you know we had to get permission to go to prom together? We had to think about it —about asking, and then we were all like fuck you, we're going somewhere else and we went to the alternative prom that Wheaton Warrenville put together at the drop- in center."

One of my favorite colleagues had been hounded and almost lost her job over organizing that dance so the LGBT students had a safe, friendly experience for prom. I sighed.

"What do you remember of your drop-in center visits?"

"I remember sitting in the hallway and talking to you a lot of Tuesday nights."

"What about that?"

"I had been through Linden Oaks because I overdosed on Effexor and Ibuprofen and I had my stomach pumped. I didn't write a note, but I wrote a bunch of stuff in my journal and wrote in red ink I AM NOT GAY! I went through about a day and a half of outpatient, hated it and dropped it. It was too expensive to be on Dad's insurance, Mom had catastrophic insurance, so they had to pay for it out of pocket. I still feel guilty about how much I must have cost them. I was looking for something to help me feel better—insurance **wouldn't** help, Mom and Dad **couldn't** help, you were all I had."

I lowered my eyes so she didn't feel like I was staring at her. I, too, remembered those long Tuesday evenings in the hallway with her, as the planned program unfolded on the other side of the doorway. Our agency didn't provide clinical services, which I knew she needed—and wanted—and her hands were tied with the insurance issue. We spent night upon night problem solving the lack of insurance and the discomfort around her identity. I remembered how I feared that she might be more fragile than she appeared, the adults in her life expecting her to puzzle through her questions about her sexual orientation and her depression without needing assistance that cost anything out-of-pocket.

"Having my stomach pumped was most disgusting experience I've ever had," she said. "I was wide awake, the tube's down my throat, I can't breathe and I'm choking on it. It's punishment for feeling this bad. Dad said later, 'Don't you ever do that shit again!'"

That's helpful.

"Do you think Youth Outlook had any impact on getting you through difficult times?"

She nodded. "I had someone to listen to me. I felt like a part of something. I can remember standing in the hall talking to you—you didn't have to give a shit, I'm not your kid, you're not my teacher. But you listened. I still really struggled for a long time. It also made a difference knowing there were other gay people in the world."

My thoughts flashed on Viv. Not her kid, but determined to help, seemingly regardless of the cost to personal safety. What a legacy to leave. Thank you, Viv. Thank you, Mrs. Eustace.

"One thing that really helped was Youth Leadership. I got more self-confidence, I became more comfortable. Last year, I got Support Specialist of the Year award at work—I would never have been able to step up and take charge the way I can unless I'd gone through the Youth Leadership program."

"You hit a really low point a couple of times, even with Youth Leadership. What do you think helped you turn things around so you felt more comfortable in your skin?"

"When my cousin killed himself about seven years ago, it was big. Lots of little things helped up until then, like Youth Leadership being the best thing that ever happened to me. Eric killing himself was such a shock, I never saw it coming. He never let anyone know he was hurting inside. That's what made it clear—I have to stay focused on that there are people who do care, no matter how bad I feel. He was one of the first people I came out to, at the airport, getting ready to leave CA to come home. I told him right before I got on the plane then I ran. He said, 'I know!'"

Her voice choked off, and she looked past me. I waited, my eyes averted.

"Sorry," she whispered.

"No," I said. "Please don't be. He deserves those tears."

She took her glasses off and pressed a napkin to her eyes. "When he died, I thought about all the things I could do with my life that he can't do anymore. I wanted to be here. I wanted to do those things. I read his death report every year and I am still looking for an answer. Looking for anything. He left nothing."

"What would you say to kids now who are going through a similar difficult time?"

"It's cliché to say it gets better, so find something to be a part of. Save baby whales or baby seals, it makes you feel like you're contributing. There are things missing or incomplete inside us, but they start to fill in when you get involved with projects and other people and you feel better. I'm never gonna say, 'Don't you do that shit again.'"

That made sense. "Anything else?"

She smiled. "Yeah. And remember, kids, flavored lubes are not all they're cracked up to be."

Creating Community with Michael: Parallels On Leadership and Loss

2008

I wasn't looking for a new site to set up another drop-in center. I already had enough to do without adding one more program. But when I was asked to apply for a foundation grant that would allow us to do just that **and** hire a program manager, I couldn't get the paperwork submitted fast enough.

It was when the new Geneva site opened that we all met Michael Fairbanks, a sophomore from St. Charles. One meeting with Michael was all it took to know that he would advance through our youth leadership program without breaking a sweat. Already involved with his school's Gay Straight Alliance, active in community theater and taking a list of AP classes, he shared his plan to go to law school to become a corporate lawyer to work on inclusion policies for Fortune 500 companies. Michael invited all of his friends to attend the new Geneva drop-in center, bringing new kids with him almost every week.

"Michael, there's a house party that some of our donors are holding for us, and I'd like you to join me to talk about the drop-in center and what's going on at your school. Interested?"

He nodded. "Can I tell them about the anti-bullying training I've been working on and the panel presentation?"

"That's perfect. Plan on it."

When Michael took the floor at the party, the lights glinting off his glasses, and started to describe being bullied in his locker room, silence descended on the group. It is so striking that so many adults who grew up being bullied think that our kids are not experiencing similar situations, as if bullying somehow stopped after the Stonewall movement. Then they hear stories like Michael's and realize the world hasn't changed all that much.

"I had to go to my principal and he took me out of gym," Michael explained. "It wasn't safe for me to be there. Because of that, we started planning some training with the faculty at their meetings. I did a presentation on gay students' right to have a safe environment. No one is talking to the teachers about this."

***

2009

Michael kicked off his junior year with a bang. He served as president of his GSA and president of his French club, balancing his commitments against his youth leadership role with Youth Outlook. We honored Michael at the October gala, presenting him with the first youth leadership award. As an agency, we decided to begin offering that award based on our experience since last year and Michael's performance as a youth leader. At one end of the room stood several pieces of artwork he submitted for the silent auction. At the other end of the room, a PowerPoint presentation ran, highlighting Michael's contributions to the agency and noting his semi-finalist's award for the national GLSEN award for student advocacy on behalf of LGBT high school students.

***

2010

"I wrote a letter to Oprah!" Michael announced.
I looked up, startled. "What for?" I asked.
"For Youth Outlook!" he said proudly. He pulled a folded sheet of paper from his backpack and handed it to me.
I thought he might be joking until I opened it and it started, "Dear Oprah Winfrey." I scanned the letter. It explained what Youth Outlook was, who Michael was, and why he thought it was important for Oprah to be supportive of Youth Outlook. It was polite, it was genuine, and it brought tears to my eyes. "Did you send this to her?"
"I sent it to the newspaper. It's an open letter."
"An **open** letter!"

Basically, he dared one of the most revered celebrities in the history of television to get to know us. I looked at the letter again. His reasoning was solid. He pointed out that while things were changing, things were still difficult and dangerous and places like Youth Outlook were saving the lives of gay teenagers. He was right. It seemed like something she would talk about on her show.

Michael grinned. "I thought she'd pay attention more."

09 June 2010

Oprah Winfrey

Harpo Studios, Inc.
1058 West Washington Blvd.
Chicago, IL 60607

Dear Ms.Winfrey;

My name is Michael Fairbanks. I am 16 years old and I will be a junior at St. Charles East High School in the Fall of 2010; in St. Charles, Illinois. I am the President of my school's Gay-Straight Alliance and French club; I am the Executive Director of the Gay-Straight Alliance of St. Charles, IL; I am a member of the French National Honors Society, and I am involved in my school's music department. I am in the Chorale, Vocal Jazz Ensemble and the Chamber orchestra; the most advanced choirs and orchestra in my school. I am an openly gay young man, and as you may know, anything pertaining to GLBTIQ (Gay, Lesbian, Bisexual, Transgender, Intersex and Queer/Questioning) issues does not go over well in today's society.

Ever since I have been in middle school, I have always been bullied and harassed due to my sexual orientation. Up until this current school year, the harassment was over the roof; mainly taking place during my physical education class. I have been called a "faggot," "fag," "homo," the "gay boy," "queer," and many more. Not only have I been called these very mean and offensive names, but I have also received threats, just because I am gay. This was causing me a lot of stress. It would cause me so much stress that at points I didn't even want to go to school. Over the summer of 2009, my mother and I met with my school's administration to talk about making my school a safer place for myself, and students alike. We decided that the best and most safe way for me to get away from the bullying and harassment would to get a doctors note, and have a medical excuse. Currently, I continue making my school a safer place for all students regardless of one's sexual orientation, or gender identity/expression. I worked with my school's administration to edit our districts policy on bullying and harassment, by adding "sexual orientation, and gender." Those terms will be added to the handbook for the 2010-2011 school year.I have also been working on a sign that I have created called the "St. Charles East GLBTIQ Safe Zone," and I have already spoken at a lead teachers meeting discussing how important it is that teachers are always showing support for the students, and that the students know they can trust their teachers to have a safe classroom and someone to talk to. At the Lead teachers meeting I also talked about dealing with diversity, specifically towards the GLBTIQ community. In the fall, I plan to speak to the entire administration to address the importance of the sign. I am also on the Suicide Prevention/Awareness panel that was presented March 25. I spoke about the risk factors of the GLBTIQ community and how they are four times more likely to attempt/commit suicide than the straight community. The panel was presented in front of a live audience and was also broadcasted through every TV in the school. On July 9, 2010, the Gay-Straight Alliance of St. Charles will be hosting a GLBTIQ"Unity Day,"a day that I created for the community to celebrate diversity in the GLBTIQ community.

  Outside of School, I am a youth leader, and the president of the youth advisory board for the non-profit organization, Youth Outlook. Youth Outlook is the reason I am writing you this letter. Youth Outlook is committed to providing a safe, supportive, and respectful environment for adolescents, whether they identify as gay, lesbian, bisexual, transgender, intersex, or queer/questioning (GLBTIQ). It is also the only agency in the DuPage, Kane, and DeKalb counties of Illinois dedicated to solely serving GLBTIQ youth. All drop-in centers are open between 6:30-9:00 p.m.. There is group on Monday (DeKalb), Tuesday (Naperville), and Thursday (Geneva and Aurora) of every week. The DeKalb and Geneva groups serve youth who are 14 through 18 years old, or until they graduate high school. The Naperville and Aurora groups serve young adults ages 16 through 20. Youth Outlook provides leadership development, a social space, and wellness education on a variety of different subjects. Some of the subjects include, but not limited to; GLBTIQ issues (Harassment/Assault, Bisexualty/Biphobia, Coming out, Homophobia/Heterosexism, GLBTIQ Culture and History, and Transgender Issues), Health (Anxiety or depression, Drugs/Alcohol, STI Prevention/Treatment, sexual assault, self-esteem, and sex and sexuality), Relationships (Abusive relationships, boundaries, conflict resolution, dating issues, family issues, and negotiation skills), and other miscellaneous social activities. Youth Outlook is what I look forward to every week. When I go to the drop-in centers, the volunteers and staff members are always fun to be around, and I always know I can trust them. I have attended all the drop-in centers (Geneva, DeKalb, Naperville, and Aurora) and I enjoy them all! Recently, in the end of January 2010, Youth Outlook had to let go of their program manager, who was very loved by all the youth and myself, because Youth Outlook lost the funding for his position. Youth Outlook is facing many financial problems right now, and we really need your help. All the money donated goes to the organization, which goes to the youth. Without any money Youth Outlook would not be able to afford certain programs and activities, and Youth Outlook, if it doesn't have enough money, might not be able to run anymore. I don't know what I would be able to do without my weekly Youth Outlook. And that is why we need your help. Any amount of donation would be great, and any check should be made out to "Youth Outlook." Youth Outlook is Youth Transforming the Future.

Thank you for your time, and if you have any questions and/or concerns, please don't hesitate to contact me.

Michael D. Fairbanks

***

2013

I booted up my computer and sat back to wait. The dinosaur would take at least twenty minutes before it was ready to work. I opened my calendar and punched the message button on my desk phone to retrieve the waiting messages, scribbling phone numbers down to return calls.

"Hi, Nancy, this is Ashley Rhodebeck from the *Kane County Chronicle*. I'm calling to get your input on a story I'm doing on the death of Michael Fairbanks."

What?

I snapped upright, hands flat on the desktop. Michael? No, that couldn't be right. Michael?! No! I reached for the phone, then dropped it. As soon as my computer cooperated, I logged on and immediately did a search for Michael's name. Nothing.

I opened a new tab and launched Facebook. I'd been Facebook friends with Michael's mother since 2009, when we'd honored him at Dare to Dream. On her page, I read the chilling words that confirmed the reporter's statement. Michael had died the night before.

My cell phone rang. I snatched it up with shaking hands, thinking I needed to call the Youth Leadership Coordinator before she heard this news in the heartless way I had. I didn't even say hello.

"Tony, I just got some awful news—can I call you back in a few minutes?"

Tony's voice cracked. "About Michael."

I stilled. "You know?"

"One of the kids that used to come to group with him all the time sent me a message."

He wouldn't kill himself...He wouldn't. Not Michael.

He didn't. Michael's death was ruled accidental. Talking to his mother later that morning, I learned that Michael had started self-medicating several months after his cousin committed suicide.

"He withdrew from all of us. He hasn't been the same since," she said.

He graduated last spring. He wasn't supposed to be here. He hadn't wanted us to know he was in the area. He hadn't wanted us to know he was depressed. He hadn't wanted to bother us or maybe he hadn't wanted us to think differently of him and the complicated bereavement he endured.

When I think about what we, as a staff, as an agency, as a community, have lost, I don't know if it helps at all that it was an accident. It didn't stop my tears when one of his friends approached his casket and sang "Amazing Grace" to him *a capella* at his funeral service. Michael gave everyone around him permission to be exactly who they are, and he wanted nothing more than to be loved for exactly who he was. Michael changed lives and we are all cheated by this loss. In my heart, Michael will always be sixteen, challenging his school administrators to keep LGBT kids safe and writing to Oprah to ask her to help, this superhero boy whose talents we will never fully know.

I wish Oprah had responded. I think she would have loved Michael.

Creating Community with Stephen:
Parallels On Surviving Violence

2003

Stephen twisted in his chair, pulling one foot under the opposite leg. His jeans were ragged and ripped out at both knees, his workboots scuffed. "I was wondering," he said, "if there's anything else I could do for the agency? I think I'm kind of outgrowing the drop-in centers."

"Well, we just got a grant from Starbucks for youth leadership and diversity..." I replied.

I doubt it was his intention, but that simple question opened up new avenues for involving the youth leaders in our work. A conversation over coffee one afternoon, brainstorming what else Stephen could do to further the agency's mission combined with the new Starbucks grant, culminated in my hiring him—the first youth leader to move into a paid staff position—to formalize and develop the Youth Leadership program. He was eighteen years old. I couldn't wait for him to start.

2013

"I was out of class in the hall. These kids surrounded me...this mixed group of five, both girls and boys... insulting me, shouting homophobic slurs. I told them I was just trying to go to the bathroom and to leave me alone. Usually for LGBT kids, using the bathroom during class time tends to be safer, rather than between classes. They pushed me into the lockers. I tried to walk away and one tripped me as another pushed me, and my head slammed against the locker. Blood started dripping down my face, and I was trying to figure out how to stand up and walk away and how to cover it up. I was shocked that they were laughing as if this were nothing. A couple of them kicked me while I was on the ground, so I stayed there. When they finally walked away, I got up and went to the bathroom. Got cleaned up, tried to cover the cut on my head. It was partially under my hairline, so it didn't show much. I didn't want to talk to anyone about it. I got in trouble for not showing up to class—think I got detention or Saturday school.

"Nobody wanted to deal with what was the problem—only about the injuries." Stephen's water glass left circles of condensation on the table between us. "Nobody was willing to do anything to address the issue. When my locker was graffittied, the dean came out, rolled up his sleeves and cleaned it off right away but no one wanted to deal with **why** my locker was vandalized."

I nodded. We'd seen that among the drop-in center kids. It was so difficult to get acknowledgment that a bullying problem existed and/or kids who brought incidents of being battered or harassed to their principals or deans were so often blamed for bringing that treatment down on their own heads. The gender police are still alive and well. "Did you know any of them?" I asked.

Stephen tipped his head back and forth. "Two guys who really liked to torment me…I knew them from AP classes. I later saw one of them when he skated up to me wearing an Altoid speedo at the Pride parade saying, 'Oh my god, hey!'"

That's also not unusual. Some of the kids who are the worst bullies are themselves LGBT, and bullying other LGBT kids creates distance, allowing them to maintain their façade of heterosexuality. I suddenly wondered about the table of girls in the cafeteria during my 7th grade public school sting. Were any of them struggling to defend their questionable heterosexuality? Hmmm…

"Was being beaten up that day the reason you left school?"

The corner of Stephen's mouth twitched. "It wasn't the deciding factor. There were two people in the school among the adults that gave a shit about me and the rest seemed to actively dislike me. I was about to flunk out. Nothing challenged me. I was bored. And the structure was antithetical to learning."

Of course he was bored. He's brilliant.

"What do you mean by that?"

"When we worked on *The Scarlet Letter*, one guy was called on to read and he insisted he would change the pronouns so he didn't sound like a faggot and teacher said, 'Hey...come on now!' But if anyone said, 'Jesus Christ,' she would get angry and correct them aggressively. I called her a bigot. That's when she asked the dean to start the expulsion process. I worked with a counselor to be able to finish classes in the library."

Did you try hitting anyone in the face with a cap and gown? I bit my tongue on that and let Stephen continue.

"Adults think school is so awful because of 'that's so gay,' but it's really about the constant erosion of a person's fundamental value as a human being. How can schools provide an environment that reinforces someone's sense of value instead of eroding it? I was treated as a bad kid," he said, marking air quotes, "because I couldn't sit still and wasn't interested in the projects. Now with No Child [Left Behind], the structure is so rigid it doesn't allow for any creativity and curiosity. I used to get in trouble for reading—for reading! I would read ahead and get in trouble for not doing the projects in between because it felt too basic. Sometimes there were books we would read for school that I had already read at home and would get in trouble because I'd get excited in group discussions and they'd pull me out of class to lecture me. We don't value young people and the role they play in their own education. It's not just about heterosexism and homophobia."

"Was this before or after Youth Outlook?"

"During. I came to group after I got beat up. I regretted disclosing it in group because it felt like people were just experiencing their own reactions, not really tuned into my reaction. Would have appreciated some questions: 'What are you thinking about this? Is there anything we can do to be helpful?' I didn't think there was anything anyone could do for me but I didn't want to hear—'Oh my god, that's so terrible, how awful for you!' Stop calling it terrible, I have to go back there tomorrow! I needed resources, a phone number."

"So what did coming to Youth Outlook do for you?"

He laughed. "Got me out of my house! I got to meet other people. You came in. Speakers came in from the outside world. Even if they were boring as fuck there was a novelty in having adults there who wanted to talk to us. It was thirteen years ago. Want to hear my sign-in number?" he asked, laughing again as he rattled it off. "I didn't have access to library books, internet, cable TV. Group gave me a place to hang out with my friends.

"We'd go to Denny's after group and would always get kicked out. We could be as loud and raucous as we wanted, be really fucking obnoxious and spend a total of three dollars. It was like having a community. Youth Outlook provided that. I was never cool enough for Naperville, but Aurora was a bunch of poor kids. We were all freaks at the Aurora group. Everyone got invited to Denny's."

"How was it meeting the staff? Do any memories of any staff stand out more than others?"

"I connected with you when you came to group. Mark came to group to talk about being an old homo and talked about his relationship. He was the oldest, most married homo we'd ever met. Bravo movies didn't show us those kinds of relationships--how to be old and married, where you're together so long you're starting to ask questions like, 'Who replaced the Polygrip with the lube?'"

Gotta remember to ask Mark if he and Bob have ever made that mistake!

"What do you remember of getting more involved and taking on more responsibility?"

"I remember you came to talk up youth leadership and part of me was like, 'They get to have everything in Naperville.' I felt like I had grown out of group. Kids were rolling around on the floor. Not that I don't appreciate a good roll...I had also gotten into doing a lot of safer sex education. When we had guest speakers on safer sex, I started to think up games that I could do for programs. God bless Mickey for being there every week to deal with these obnoxious fucks...but I wanted to be the one who was leading programs."

"What do you remember of working as a youth leader?"

"It gave me the opportunity to develop my own skills as a leader. I got to make mistakes when I was seventeen that I see people at my job making now at twenty-five and thirty-five. They are still trying to figure those things out. I was pushed into a world where people listened to me and respected me."

I wondered how respected Stephen felt on those trips we took to Springfield to speak at a conference together when I prevented him from falling out the passenger window, as he tried to get the truckers to blow their horns. On one trip, I came very close to grabbing his belt, thinking he was about to splash headfirst onto the highway. Well, he **did** say he got bored easily. I refocused. He was still speaking.

"It built up my confidence, gave me something valuable to bring to the table to deal with classism even with the other youth leaders. Huge groups of adults would listen to me when I went out to speak. I found out I had some innate skills—before this I had always been alone, and now there was a recognition that I had some skills."

I hadn't refocused completely. "Do you remember the Springfield trips?"

Stephen had asked me before we left for the first Springfield trip where we were presenting at a conference if I objected to his getting a Mohawk. It being his hair, I told him he should feel free to do what he liked. That he also dyed it bright blue was a bit of a surprise, but oh well!

He chuckled. "I do, but I won't tell you what I remember because I don't want to embarrass you!"

On that same trip where I feared Stephen was about to become a hood ornament for the car behind us, I had what was probably the most awkward experience of my career. After we'd arrived at the hotel, I realized I needed to run out to the drug store for some personal supplies. I debated leaving Stephen and one of the volunteers at the hotel alone, but decided that was probably not my best choice. So I piled them both back in the car and trotted them to the closest drug store I could find.

Stephen waited for us outside to have a smoke. The volunteer and I went in, separated down different aisles and ended up meeting again. In the feminine hygiene section.

If there's one place a gender bending, butch social worker does not want to flex boundaries, it's in the arena of shopping for personal female supplies. And if there's one place where a trans masculine young adult does not want to share information about personal choice with his mentor, it's probably in the tampon section at the local drug store.

The volunteer's eyes bugged and started to rove everywhere but on the products in front of us. My ears burned and I could feel the blood rising into my face. *Ground, just open up and swallow me now...*

Quickly, I grabbed some product I'd never used before, in the wrong size, and bolted for the register. The volunteer waited a discreet amount of time before following me. If I was lucky, my uterus would just fall out in the car and we could go peacefully back to the hotel.

Shit! This is not happening!

I hit the front door like a battering ram and tripped over Stephen, who was now sitting on the ground outside the door. The volunteer barreled out behind me, looking a little wild-eyed, and I got very busy patting my pockets for my keys.

What the hell size are those anyway? Christ, I'm not going to be able to walk! They're frickin' tractor beam size! My head is gonna get sucked right down into my neck!

"What's wrong?" Stephen asked from the ground.

"Nothing!" The volunteer and I both snapped in unison as we rushed the car. I was sure we would both be in therapy over this one for a long time.

I pulled my attention back to Stephen.

"When we went the next year, it felt like I had to be more professional 'cause we had Ron with us."

That was another memorable trip to speak at the same conference, when the youth leader attending this year (who had the role Stephen had the year before) recounted his family's experience in a death camp during the Holocaust. Even Stephen sat silently as Ron described his grandfather getting off the train at the camp and being told to choose one of his family members to live—all the rest would be killed. He couldn't choose, so everyone was shot in front of him. Tears ran from my eyes as I listened to Ron's quiet voice. Sometimes, that's the only response.

"I was also worried about how to dress when we went out speaking. There were people in suits...I was wearing jeans, but people took me seriously anyway. After I dropped out and had left home, being able to be at a conference with you or on my own was a luxury. I had plumbing. I had food. It was a vacation."

"When you took your current job, you had the chance to make huge changes in kids' lives. What feels like the most important thing you've done so far?"

Stephen worked with youth in Chicago struggling to be heard, struggling to find acceptance and respect in their school systems, struggling to stay plugged in until they graduated. His pride was obvious. "There have been three youth leaders... watching them advocate for a project we'd all been working on was powerful. I just stood back, and all I could think was, 'These are my kids. Mine.'"

Oh, I am quite familiar with that!

"I thought another one of our kids was going to end up in jail, but he just graduated. He's lost almost every other adult in his life and has tried really hard not to lose me. He's the reason I have so much grey here before my thirtieth birthday. What if he hadn't found the people in his life? What if I had written him off?"

"You had a chance to form some unusual friendships—with me, with Carolyn—with folks who were significantly older than you. Now you have the chance to do that with your kids. How does that go for you?"

"It was pretty incredible to be able to be at your house after I started working for the agency. There was this place I could go that felt completely safe...safe in a different way. I love my mother. But people, especially my mother, wanted to know more about me than I wanted to disclose. I never felt like that at your house. There was this incredible dog that loved me—he loved everyone but I want to believe he loved me 'cause I was special..."

"He **did** love you." Zach was fourteen when Stephen would dog sit for him or come over for dinner or to work on a project with me. He adored Stephen, and I'd usually find them huddled together on the floor in a pile. In the days before Zach's death, Stephen came over and shot rolls of film of my giant orange buddy and me. He told me later he kept copies of a few of those photos because Zach was his giant orange buddy too.

"I was a big enough sucker to do anything for him," Stephen pointed out. "I'd even sleep on the floor with him when he whined in the night. I had this place to call home where things worked and there was food in the fridge. You had a tremendous amount of respect for me and never crossed any boundaries with me. We were always so careful to respect each other's boundaries...I always felt I was with this person who had this deep respect for me. You didn't need to take care of me, or social work me, or savior me...or do the I'm going to crack your shell and make you talk to me thing."

"I would never do that to you. People tried that with me—with disastrous results!"

He nodded. "It felt a little like paradise—full fridge, AC and heat, comfy couch. I remember sitting around in shorts, cranked up to sixty-eight—it was like summer. I found On Demand on HBO and panicked after I watched about four hours straight. It was like, oh my God, how much did I cost her? There was internet access. And there was Zach. Zach was one of my moments of stability.

"I remember once I had bronchitis and I felt awful and was taking drugs, and Zach just wanted to sit in my lap."

That would have been a sight. I'm sure Zach outweighed Stephen. I remembered that bout of bronchitis too, when I stopped at the food co-op and picked up echinacea tea and goldenrod capsules for him and left them on the counter without saying anything. They disappeared when Stephen left. We never spoke about it.

"I eventually lay down and he put his head on my chest, no matter how much I was coughing, and we just watched TV. It was almost as good as the time I brought over the laundry basket of kittens and kept them in the bathtub. Zach loved them."

"It really was fun having you around."

"Oh and then getting to hang out with Jedda after your wedding when I was supposed to be taking her to the airport and you left me your car keys. We couldn't figure out how to get your car into reverse, so we could only go places where we could pull straight in and pull straight out."

I laughed. "And she thought you were cuter than a speckled pup, as she put it. Or, as Kate G. put it, you were cuter than a rabid, speckled pup."

He laughed too. Then his voice became serious again. "It was like having a family. You included me in holiday celebrations and birthday celebrations—it was my first experience being included. I had stopped partying and was mostly sober...my social circle was very small. No matter what happened, no matter what time it was, I knew I could show up at your door and it would be okay."

No question about that.

"For the kids who are still experiencing violence, either at school or in their homes, what do you want them to know about surviving?"

"I would tell them the sense of isolation is real but there are places like Youth Outlook that will put you in a position to change your life. It doesn't mean that the violence will end, because it won't. But they have the chance to make some decisions to change their own lives. The agency makes sure of that. There is a movement that can impact change and they are a part of it. To say that they are victims takes away their power. Sometimes it doesn't get better. It gets better for upper middle class white guys. Sometimes our kids are faced with the choice to forget the people whom they love, or they can go back into that world of violence and try to make a difference for the people they left there. And if they choose to go back, all they have to do is call you, or call me, and we'll have their back."

When Stephen worked for Youth Outlook, he frequently told me that I was a good block to chip off from. We jokingly signed emails "Block" and "Chip". As with Max, the fact that he thinks I did anything to help him as a teenager is mind-bending to me. It is Stephen and Max, Ryan, Alex, Sydney, Tony and Michael and the thousands of youth who did not share their stories here who have given me room to grow, seeing the world through their eyes.

"…and all I could think was, 'These are my kids. Mine.'"

How the hell did THAT happen?

Acknowledgements

Writing Urban Tidepool was one of the most difficult things I've ever done. It wasn't originally intended to be a book; it started out with me writing a few memories and so that I could share more detail about these events at home with my most significant person. After a few events were written, it became clear that this was the skeleton of a book, and then the team formed around me.

Thank you to the beta readers who picked up every chapter as I poured them out, proofread them, edited them, and dealt with the technical aspects of writing. More importantly after those technical issues were addressed, this was the team who sat with me and helped me visit the violence, the loss, the addiction, the danger, the strength and the humor you'll find here. These were the friends who pointed out a missing comma and then sat with me to make sure I was holding up through the writing. They accompanied me into a story that had never been told from beginning to end. They listened to pieces they'd never known about me, no matter how long they'd known me. They bore witness to a story I had been so afraid to tell.

To my beta readers team, Sandra Hill, Lorrie Brenneman, Brooke Condon, Mary Shelden, Margie Cook, Melissa Thompson, Andrea Buford, Patti Krivo, Sara Belkov, Heather Bartmes, Carolyn Engle, Cindy Savage-King, Sarah Adkins, thank you for the time, the energy, the brunch meetings, the coffee, and the wine.

Thank you to the Youth Outlook staff, board and supporters, most especially Carolyn Wahlskog, Nancy Carlson, Sandra Conti, and Michael Gurley, who mined these chapters with me to address my concern that going public with my own story would open our agency for criticism or cause our supporters to rethink their support.

Thank you to Debbi Miller, THE Debbi Miller whose house became home in 1983, where the army cot with the air mattress became my refuge. Thank you for allowing me not just to share but to compare, to make sure I was relating 30 year old memories as accurately as possible. As high school BFFs go, I got the best.

Thank you to Pat Miller—Mom Miller-- who knew when I was 17 years old not to ask any questions about why this strange kid had just appeared in her house and welcomed me every time I walked through the door as if I really lived there. Thank you for taking the time to read Urban Tidepool and offering your thoughts, so much later, about how you and Jim navigated those days behind the scenes, with me unaware of your discussions: "We don't know what happened, but we know it was bad, and we have to help however we can. Let's not ask questions. She'll bolt." Your kindness and generosity can never be repaid.

Thank you to Kate Phillips, THE Kate who roomed with me in college, offered me a place to stay during semester breaks, who told me I'd never be homeless again as long as she was around, and who willingly sat awake many nights in college waiting for me to fall asleep first so that I could finally fall asleep safe in the worst months of post-trauma effects after I left Philadelphia.

Thank you to the former Youth Outlook "kids", now my colleagues and friends, who stepped up and shared more of their stories to give readers a view, in the supplemental chapters, of who I became as a professional and who I was to them. Thank you, Ryan, Tony, Max, Sydney, Alex, and Stephen for letting readers see so much through your eyes. Thank you to Junior just for being Junior.

Thank you to my beautiful friend, Denise Fairbanks, who allowed me to share Michael Fairbanks' story. We are bonded by an enormous gift and an enormous loss. I still think Oprah would have loved our boy.

Thank you to the Kickstarter supporters who helped make this dream a reality. We had 45 days to raise the funds for our first round of printing and met our goal in just 10 days. Thank you to the Purple Level donors who pledged to my dream: my dear friends, Karen Tornberg and Kathy Doud; my Youth Outlook board member friends, George Miller and Marie Grover; my longstanding family of choice, Kathy Lach and Pam Oettel (yes, THE Kathy at the end of the story who talked to me about potential and figuring out to how to carry such heavy baggage, often at her own risk, who just knew without being told that there was a massive story behind the sarcastic comments); my best guy friend, John Brenneman; Richard R. Weiss; and all who pledged within hours of the Kickstarter opening.

A most special thank you to Deb Miller, without whom this book would never have been started, and certainly never finished, who sat through the first reading of each chapter, who heard the horrors, who lived with both my nightmares and my sleepless nights, who hovered in doorways wanting to help as I cried through reliving the worst pieces. Thank you for creating the space in which I could finally tell the whole story. Thank you for hearing. Thank you for hovering. Thank you always.

Made in the USA
Monee, IL
08 December 2021